GREATNESS-CORED
LEADERSHIP

GREATNESS-CORED LEADERSHIP

KEYS TO BECOMING A GREAT HUMAN RESOURCES LEADER

TRI JUNARSO

iUniverse, Inc.
Bloomington

GREATNESS-CORED LEADERSHIP
KEYS TO BECOMING A GREAT HUMAN RESOURCES LEADER

iUniverse books may be ordered through booksellers or by contacting:

iUniverse
1663 Liberty Drive
Bloomington, IN 47403
www.iuniverse.com
1-800-Authors (1-800-288-4677)

Because of the dynamic nature of the Internet, any web addresses or links contained in this book may have changed since publication and may no longer be valid. The views expressed in this work are solely those of the author and do not necessarily reflect the views of the publisher, and the publisher hereby disclaims any responsibility for them.

Any people depicted in stock imagery provided by Thinkstock are models, and such images are being used for illustrative purposes only.
Certain stock imagery © Thinkstock.

ISBN: 978-1-4620-4708-6 (sc)
ISBN: 978-1-4620-4710-9 (hc)
ISBN: 978-1-4620-4709-3 (ebk)

Printed in the United States of America

iUniverse rev. date: 08/27/2011

CONTENTS

FOREWORD

Our beliefs form our inner rules in how we play our role in the organization. We have beliefs that our success, while most people have beliefs that keep them playing small. Since, *most people realize less than 10% of their potential.*

HR is recognized for the importance of its role in implementing organizational change, and Human Resources (HR) is viewed as critical to the success of the business. On other hand, HR function is still seen in contradictive views, i.e.:

1. Traditionally, its function consists of transactional activities, for instance, recruitment, payroll, training, recognition program, etc. It doesn't attract people to succeed their career through HR; they consider HR is a dead-end career path. The worst is that the best and brightest people don't go into HR; and 1.2% of B-school graduates went into HR.

    A study found that only 3.3 percent human resources executives were listed as one of the top five officers in their companies,

    The study suggested 66% of HR execs are not viewed as strategic partners by their executive team.

2. In today's environment, its duties i.e. finding new opportunities for top performers in the organizations, and integrate talent process, systems and data. Therefore, we are seeing HR right at the CEO's side at the time of strategic decisions.

    A research found 63% of companies of all sizes saying HR reports directly to the CEO.

> *They reported 75% of HR executives are advising Top Management on company's organizational structure change.*

> *The research indicated 75% of respondents said that HR effectiveness shown in its contribution to business result.*

When we are in HR, we are in HR all the way. In HR we are welcome.

One of the significant processes in Human Resources Management is leadership. Leadership is a decision.

It's too often HR leaders are put in a position of simply reacting to boardroom decisions. Whereas, strategic decisions made by organizations can have a significant impact on employees.

Greatness is the core of HR leadership. People see sense of greatness is the core of actions. The HR leaders inspire greatness in employees.

Sense of greatness makes people want to do more than what they are currently doing. Most often it stimulates them to think about doing things for other people, rather than directing toward self gratification.

Leaders act with sense of greatness. A HR leader should be a sense-maker; displays how makes sense of the circumstances, so he/she can act meaningfully in it.

Becoming clear, making sense, creating meaning, is the most powerful driver the leader has. He/she is working for us in leading people and organizations.

Leaders, as sense-makers, know that the way they view, review, reframe and build on past experiences—how they make sense of things—influences how successful they will be in setting positive, realistic expectations and successful outcomes. They are more rational during turmoil, inherently motivated, focused, effective and productive.

Greatness is scarce goods. *"The less people speak of their greatness, the more we think of it,"* Sir Francis Bacon, Renaissance author, said.

Greatness cored leadership is relevant for today's HR environment because:

1. Simple and humbleIt's represented by only five letters (G, R, E, A, T)

2. The values attributed by this leadership style are significant to individual, companies and any organizations' requirement (Growth, Responsibility, Entrepreneurship, Authenticity, Trust)

3. Be assertive and show gratitudeGreat!

HR leaders built reputation that distinguishes leadership in their company and generates economic advantage. Thus, leading in this new

reality will require the leaders to build on and reach beyond effectiveness. It needs greatness.

A successful HR leaders practice the attributes of Greatness Cored Leadership style. They focus their actions on growth, responsibility, entrepreneurship, authenticity, and trust.

Since GREAT attributes are the companies' requirement to achieve the topmost results, HR leaders should consider it in their daily life breath.

Author

ACKNOWLEDGEMENT

Writing this book is truly a challenging moment for me. While Greatness Cored Leadership Style was just introduced in 2009, through "Leadership Greatness" book, it brought me to a journey how to implement the new leadership style for not only common leaders, but also for Human Resources leaders.

This book title contains various insights of leadership, Human Resources philosophy, studies with different angle, and testimonies from great leaders.

Provided with comprehensive references, this book will be nice to read and to take the advantage of using it as a guide for leading the people, especially in Human Resources discipline. As we know, both HR leaders and Line Leaders have equal responsibility for HR function in the organizations.

I dedicate this book title to The Management of PT South Pacific Viscose, a group member of Lenzing, Austria. Its leaders' success has endlessly inspired me to deeply dig my talent in leadership capacity and put it on various new leadership books.

They have demonstrated their un-doubtful dedication to the organization and people. A few of them are Peter Untersperger, who is reappointed as Chairman and CEO; Guenther Krohn, The Global Manufacturing Director, who is successfully bringing the company out from global recession; Wolfram Kalt, the President Director, who has tough initiative to advance the local staff to the better position of the organization leadership; M.C. Bhurat, the Project Director for Asia Region, who has high perseverance in his work and career.

I would also like to thank the many people who have supported, and helped with this book, especially Diza; my children – Christian and Edward; my mom—Sumarti, my sister - Sri Hartini and my brothers - Budi Wardoyo, Sunaryo, Handoyo, Indro and Waluyo; and my colleagues, who have shared their empathy, i.e. Erlangga, Akhmad Basuki, Iwan Ruwiyadi, Krusdiharso, Sofyan Fatah, Adin Trisudono, Adarpen, Khanafin, Khaeri Heri, Indra Nurhanudin, Deden Rusfiandi, Rosa Belawan, Koswara, Anwar Winanto, Fathoni, A.M. Phatak, Anil Kumar, V.G. Vachhani, Johan Knoglinger, and many more that I can not mention one by one.

I understand there will be errors, misspellings, or omissions. For the time being, it might be the best I could do. If you find any error, please do not hesitate to let me know so that I can improve this book performance in future.

1st

Corporate Manifesto

Corporate manifesto is designed to bring everyone in the organization together. Corporate manifesto states the core intention of the company, the guiding principles of it, and the policies that guide organizations to effectively realize the stated intention. It describes:

a.   Who should benefit most from all the effort that is put into the corporate: Strengthen company's mission through personal commitment.

b.   Company's purpose into employees' feelings. It's mode of encouraging why an employee should do more than the minimum required.

        The manifesto must be something not only worth reading, but worth acting on.

c.   Who owns the corporate, how corporate behaves, importance of the corporate: Embed guiding principles in the day-to-day language of business.

Corporate manifesto is a declaration of what the company is really all about. It captures what employees stand for and strive to deliver. Corporate manifesto has characteristics as follows:

a.   Articulate credible, realistic attractive future for the company: To succeed in a business environment characterized by ongoing change, employees must never forget 'cause of company existence'—who we are. It is important to always keep in mind beliefs and values make the company unique.

      Acting in accordance with company's beliefs and values will keep employees on the right course, and will continually increase the strength of the company.

      Company's beliefs and values drive behaviors and enable achievement of company's mission.

b.   Stretch the company beyond its current capabilities. Companies' resources and capabilities is seen more critical to the strategic action than the external environment.

      Corporate strategy, in general, that is resource-based perspective, is based on the view of the company as a collection of capabilities.

      The resource-based perspective highlights the need for a fit between the external market context in which a company operates and its internal capabilities.

      "When I struck it, it just had to go in," says Andres Iniesta, who scored the latest-ever winning World Cup (2010) goal for Spain, sealing his team's 1-0 victory over the Netherlands.

c.   Be clear, focus on action and interface with the strategy of the company: Make sure the alignment of Human Resource Management with strategic company goals.

Global revolution is changing business, and business is changing the world. Technology and innovation makes old borders obsolete. No part of business is immune.

The structure of the company is changing; relationships between companies are changing; the nature of work is changing; the definition of success is changing.

We are in the business of change. Companies are looking for a new way to do something, a way to change the process, to reduce costs, improve revenue, etc. Change is something we want everyone in our company doing.

Company manifesto should be flexible, it would change whenever required to adopt the new environment.

Culture

Culture, vision, mission, value and goal will sharpen the trust, which needs to describe why the corporate exists. Culture describes 'how we do things around here'— it is created from the messages that are received about how people are expected to behave.

Cultures develop in any organization, which its people spend time together and who are bound together through shared goals, beliefs, routines, needs or values.

Corporate culture is like our personality. Since personality is made up of the values, beliefs, underlying assumptions, interests, experiences, upbringing, and habits that create our behavior.

Corporate culture is the 'glue' that holds organizations together by providing cohesiveness and coherence among the parts.

Corporate culture defines the behavior, habit, and rule which stakeholder uses to interact with each other or moral, social, and behavioral norms of a corporation based on the beliefs, attitudes, and priorities of stakeholders.

Culture is something that we cannot actually see, except through its physical manifestations in our workplace.

There are lots of companies out there that can attest to their success in building the right culture for their organization.

KFC is one of three highest-ranked large organizations in Britain's Top Employers 2010 in best HR practice.

KFC is the quick service restaurant operation famous for its 'finger lickin' good' chicken dishes. Its staff surveys generate high response rates (the last one was 93%) and consistently show that people find KFC's culture to be friendly, fun and challenging, yet supportive.

"The thing that I would single out KFC for more than anything else is a recognition culture," says Managing Director Martin Shuker. "This stems all the way down from our Chairman to team members working on the floor. It's something we do all the time."

A HR leader must be particularly strong in shaping and enhancing the company's values. Values are the cornerstone of a company's culture.

The shared values of the organization provide a common sense of direction for all of employees and basic guidelines for their day-to-day behavior.

The culture was created over time by the leaders, employees and the management they use.

The leader must assure that there is consistency between the company's stated values and all other aspects of their vision including the strategies, the people plans and the company's operational plans.

Organizations work well because of both the talents of the people and the actions that people take. There is a clear alignment between the core elements of the organization's strategy and the behaviors of people within the organization.

Cultures of successful organizations attract and retain people with desired talents, and encourage and reward desired performance.

Culture is, in fact, the result of what has been rewarded, what has been punished and how these consequences occurred. HR leaders understand this process, and know how to implement practices that create the desire culture, which include:

a.   Value, a belief, a mission, or a philosophy that is really meaningful to the company.

    Bank of America has increased lending to small and mid-sized businesses in 2010.

Since the economy collapsed into a deep recession in late 2007, one area that has resisted recovery has been credit for small and mid-sized businesses.

Consequently, any increase in lending to those sectors, which provide nearly three-quarters of all U.S. jobs, is seen as good news.

"Small and mid-sized businesses are the engine of job growth, so the extent to which creditworthy businesses are able to get credit is integral to economic recovery," said Greg McBride, of Bankrate.com.

The greatest potentials for the growth of company are generated by a commitment to corporate values.

b.   Behavior, the manner in which HR leaders and employees behave; how people, individuals, and groups act in organizations.

When Human Resources came around, employees weren't a costthey were an asset. They were an investment. They were a resource.

"People were looking to the leaders to act in a matter that demonstrated competence and professionalism," said Michael Alan Hamlin, author of "High Visibility."

When we treat people like resources, we dehumanize them. Employees are people, not merely resource. That doesn't mean that we can't demand great performance or that we should tolerate mediocrity.

When we think of employees as people, it changes the way we recruit, manage performance and focus on development. We may stop simply utilizing resources and start inspiring people to do amazing things.

Culture is the behavior that results when a group arrives at a set of—generally unspoken and unwritten—rules for working together which may need:

i.   Place emphasis on employees in changing organizations and on efforts to enhance the quality of the employees, as well as organizational effectiveness.

People are the most critical resource a business has, and effective utilization of employee capability is the focus of the HR leader.

ii.   Have emphasis on innovation and commitment: Develop organizational capability in innovation. Some of the best innovations come from applying new.

HR leaders foster a culture that promotes the values company wide. They encourage people for making productive mistakes. Innovation cannot happen without mistakes.

The mistakes may happen because someone dreams big and goes for it.

iii.   Non-discriminatory: Maintain a work environment that is free from discrimination or harassment.

HR leaders ensure adherence to a balanced approach to employment equity, equal employment opportunity and exercise appropriate oversight to ensure employees are treated equally and with consistency regarding employment, compensation, benefits, promotion, work rules, transfer, discipline and termination.

Good looks can kill a woman's chances of snaring jobs considered 'masculine,' according to a study.

Attractive women faced discrimination when they applied for jobs where appearance was not seen as important.

These positions included job titles like manager of research and development, director of finance, mechanical engineer and construction supervisor.

They were also overlooked for categories like director of security, hardware salesperson, prison guard and tow-truck driver.

> *"In these professions being attractive was highly detrimental to women," researcher Stefanie Johnson said, adding that attractive women tended to be sorted into positions like receptionist or secretary.*

iv. Committed to safety culture: Develop and maintain policies, practices and programs for demonstrating concern for employee safety, health and well—being.

Companies are to protect employees and will not tolerate labor violations.

v. Compete vigorously: Competition among companies grows to such an intense level that many firms were forced to re-examine their strategy, especially in terms of the tradeoffs among the competitive priorities, i.e. cost, quality, delivery/ service, and flexibility.

HR leaders encourage employees to compete on competencies.

They explore the potential of Human Resource Management to facilitate or inhibit the development and utilization of organizational competencies.

The HR leader focuses on the activities, functions, and processes that enhance or impede competency accumulation and exploitation, complements the behavioral perspective that potentially enhances the understanding of strategic Human Resource Management.

There is only one competence that can make us a winner in the organizations; and that is competitive competence.

The core competence is only useful as long as it is our competitive competence. Once the companies loose their competitiveness, they loose everything.

Therefore in today's business world where competitive landscape sizzles with innovation, the competitiveness must be robust enough to stand, and yet flexible enough to evolve as conditions demand.

Competitive-competence is at the heart of a company's ability to compete. It can be distinctive technological expertise, or skill set to provide better benefits to customers that rivals cannot match.

The creation and provision of customer value that other companies cannot compete is the essence of competitive-competence and is not limited to any particular industry.

The mantra today is to obsolete innovation and maintain our competitiveness.

Development of the key capabilities has strategic importance for organization, as it offers the benefits, i.e. lower operational costs, higher organizational effectiveness, higher market share, high customer retention, be faster and reduce cycle times, take new opportunities ahead of competitors. Competitiveness is characterized by:

1. Efforts to over-ride goal: Human Resource Management follows a set of guidelines with an objective of profitable business.

    Goal setting is a powerful process for thinking about organization future, and for motivating employees to turn vision of the future into reality.

    The setting of employee goals provides a useful means of measuring business success. It provides a direct means of feedback.

    Goal-setting is what successful people do. People perform much better, both professionally and personally, when they have a clearly defined and time-framed goal to focus on.

    By knowing precisely what we want to achieve, we know where we have to concentrate our efforts. We'll also quickly spot the distractions that would otherwise lure us from our course.

Properly-set goals can be incredibly motivating, and as we get into the habit of setting and achieving goals, we'll find that their self-confidence builds fast.

People get motivated to ride beyond the previous achievements. People will try to set aside them, and create new goals to aim overriding the old ones.

Understanding the person's personality preferences will add a new dimension to team interaction and with customers and prospects. Knowing what motivates individuals to action, how they prefer to communicate and how they make decisions brings teams to a new level.

2. Continuous and rapid improvement: Provide expertise, methodologies and tools that address the specific situation and this often leads us to additional areas where capabilities, improvements and change are needed.

3. Demonstration of competitive excellence: Excellence fosters quality, compliance to requirements and continuous improvement.

    Organizations direct all resources to meet the highest standards for satisfied customers, superior products and services, engaged employees, safe working environments and financial results.

    In today's interconnected, globally competitive world, organizations are realizing that strategic talent recruitment and human capital development are the new differentiators.

    Bringing HR function to Top Management is gaining currency. The wisdom to embrace strategic HR demonstrates not just that people are the central resource for the organization, but that its calculated, mission-driven development is at the center of competitive excellence.

c. Habit, a mental attitude of HR leader, employees and organization. It may require to:

i. Evaluate the needs of the organization, and find out people to fill those needs: Build capabilities, commitment, programs and tools that fit the needs of the organization.

ii. Provide an optimum environment conducive to high levels of motivation and performance. Organizational climate mediates the relationship between Human Resource practices and employees satisfaction.

World-class organizations fill open positions 31 percent faster than typical companies, and see 66 percent fewer voluntary terminations.

The lower turnover rate has benefits on two levels. It shrinks the direct cost of administering the employee life cycle processes, including hiring, orientation training, enrollment programs and termination processes, and also reduces the time and resources necessary to recruit and train new hires.

iii. Adhere to code of ethics and business conduct guidelines: The HR leaders can play an important part in role modeling, in the cultural initiatives the organization may choose to take on.

To influence in a credible fashion, HR functions must first and foremost be a model for the future culture of the company.

The companies in the top 50 layoff crowd cut 531,000 jobs between November 2008 and April 2010.

"CEOs are clearly not hurting," researchers say. "But they are causing others to needlessly hurt—by cutting jobs to feather their own already comfortable executive nests. The damage done by these champions of the cutback is enormous."

iv. Regularly consult with CEO as they develop their strategic workforce plans: HR leader is committed to have regular consultation with CEO and Top Executives in relation to change initiatives and in the development and/or review of Human Resources policy.

Where HR leader is considering a restructure of the workforce, introduction of new technology or changes to existing work practices which affect employees and company, he/she must take the opinion of CEO.

A successful HR leader demonstrates habit of management consultation more than six times; than poor leaders.

d. Rules—Guide for conduct or action which employees and organization use to interact with each other; i.e.:

i. Work without doing evil, i.e. Employee who exhibits inappropriate or disruptive workplace behavior that can be deemed threatening or potentially threatening may be subject to disciplinary action.

At least five Iranian companies in Afghanistan's capital are using their offices covertly to finance Taliban militants in provinces near Kabul.

The firms, set up in the past six months, provide cash for a network of district Taliban treasurers to pay battlefield expenses and bonuses for killing the enemy and destroying their vehicles.

Iran is paying bonuses of $1,000 for killing an American soldier and $6,000 for destroying a U.S. military vehicle.

ii. Satisfy the spirit of the law: HR leaders set up guidelines and modeling good behavior from the top down.

Employees are craving for the leaders of their companies to say and 'walk the talk.'

Women who wear short skirts that display a lot of leg may be overlooked for promotion and pay increases.

Unfortunately, men and women, whether consciously aware of it or not, who overt sexual behavior at work, can submarine their career.

11

A study finds that sexy dressing and sexual behavior negatively impacted the careers of women.

The women who never engaged in such sexual behavior had earned than women who had engaged in flirting and other overt sexual behavior.

e. Belief: The core of who we are, what we do, and the success that we acquire.

By controlling the factors like education and experience, women's earnings rise from 77 % to 81% of men's.

Factor in occupation, industry and whether they belong to a union; they jump to 91%. That's partly because women tend to cluster in lower-paying fields.

The most-educated swath of women, for example, gravitates toward the teaching and nursing fields. Men with comparable education become business executives, scientists, doctors and lawyers—jobs that pay significantly more.

Beliefs describe inward convictions, a feeling of certainty about what something means. These are what we hold dear and are rooted deeply within. A belief is both mental and emotional. It is imbedded in the mind and in the heart.

Anita Roddick—CEO, multi-billion dollar franchise, The Body Shop—is one of the world most outspoken, controversial, and successful entrepreneurs of the age.

Her passion for social and environmental causes the basis for every decision she makes reminds us that your decisions can create profits with principles and "you don't need to lose your soul to achieve success."

People develop personal values throughout life. When they join the company, they agree to live and act by a set of corporate beliefs that may include:

i. Paramount in company's drive to be the best: Continually strive to attract the most qualified people to work in team.

Toyota Motor Corp halted production at its main factory in China after a strike at a maker of plastic parts disrupted supply.

Work was suspended in the middle of the day shift at its Tianjin factory, near Beijing.

Companies that fail to develop effective recruitment, training and retention programs may risk diminished employee performance.

Company will judge its performance not based on the past performance. Every day might be a new challenge with a new goal.

ii.   Customer is the topmost value: Without customers, company would not exist. HR leaders and employees therefore respect each customer. They listen to customers and focus on the long term not just today.

iii.   Demonstrate an action with honesty and integrity in conducting the business and relationships while treating other with mutual respect and consideration. Be transparent and genuine to others.

HR leaders and employees understand that there are consequences for all of their actions. Therefore, company establishes clear expectations for employees. Everyone hold himself/herself responsible.

Employees who follow the corporate beliefs do what is right. They recognize that living the corporate values makes it easier for everyone to know and understand what is expected of them.

f.   Ethics: Written and unwritten codes of principles and values that govern decisions and actions within a company. The organization's culture sets standards for determining the difference between good and bad decision making and behavior.

IBM is a world leader in information technology and services. In a challenging year, IBM has remained at the top of its game, growing revenues and profitability due to a four-year transformation program focusing on clients, people, productivity, growth and reputation.

As the second highest-ranked large organizations in Britain's Top Employers 2010 in best HR practice, IBM has always attracted well-rounded people who value its ethical stance and relish an intellectual challenge.

Company provides ground rules that are necessary to ensure the key attributes of the company are preserved.

We humans are basically tribal animals, who are hardwired to fit in with our tribe. We read the signals about what it takes to fit in, and we adapt our behavior accordingly. This is a survival strategy.

If we absolutely cannot do this, we either leave the tribe, or the tribe ejects us. As we adapt to fit in with our new tribe, we in turn reinforce these tribal norms or accepted behaviors and thus reinforce the culture.

Ethics boils down to knowing the difference between right and wrong, and choosing to do what is right. The phrase 'business ethics' can be used to describe the actions of individuals within an organization, as well as the organization as a whole.

Company's ability to maintain an ethical corporate culture is the key to the attraction, retention, and productivity of employees.

HR leader makes his or her decisions and bases actions guided by business ethics.

Corporate culture and values are the foundation for superior product and service, which in turn reflects and is reflected by the caliber of HR leadership. This implies that personal commitment, involvement, and a sense of direction by Top Management are critical to the success of world-class company.

Every organization has its own unique culture or value set. Most organizations don't consciously try to create a certain culture.

The culture of the organization is typically created unconsciously, based on the values of the Top Management of the organization.

Corporate culture refers to both formal, written company policy concerning everything from dress code to employee relationships as well as the informal behavior.

Corporate culture matters for organization policy choices. Consistent with that, we find that the culture effects are long-term and stronger for internally grown business units.

Culture is the sum of the beliefs and values that shape norms of behavior and dictate the ways things get done.

Measuring and assessing the organization's culture at a given point in time is illuminating.

If the organization, has a desired culture in mind, and a picture of the current culture, then assessing the gaps and developing plans to close those gaps may not be difficult.

HR leaders have to take a stand for the values and behaviors that will underpin the culture of the future.

There is nothing more compelling and persuasive than a division that is walking its talk.

People follow leaders who do not compromise their values and standards for reasons of expediency, who keep their word, support the success of others, make and stick to clear decisions, look at themselves from the customer perspective, and are disciplined and are consistent.

The place to start if we are to become culture champions, and demonstrate the benefits culture can deliver, is in our own organization.

Vision

Vision is about what a company wants to become. The vision should resonate with all members of the organization.

Vision describes the desired future to which the company aspires. The vision should stretch the organization's capabilities and image of itself. It gives shape and direction to the organization's future, e.g.:

a.   Preferred choice product and service: Offer more advantage/ benefits to customers. Gain a reputation that leads customers using the product/service repeatedly—lead them to abandon their preferred 'supplier' lists in favor of the product/ service.

To become a preferred choice product/service, Human Resources leaders should offer their personal assurance to meet or to exceed customer's expectations.

They apply ethics that is reflected in everything the organization does, total commitment to excellence.

It will enable to synchronize people's achievements and accomplishments with the success of the companies.

The long term business represents the foundation of the organization and will be nurtured with competence, integrity and professionalism.

A new low-cost airline will begin serving mid-sized U.S. cities that it thinks larger carriers have left behind.

JetAmerica is targeting small and midsize cities like Lansing, which has seen the number of daily flights at its Capital Region International Airport fall from 35 to 12 the past five years. The decline is part of a national trend that has seen airfares increase at those airports as daily flights have decreased.

Prices will start at $9 a seat and top out at $199. The $9 price will apply to the first nine to 19 seats on each plane. Passengers will pay $15 to check a bag. Food, drinks and in-flight TV will also come at a cost.

b. Model of the desired environment: Strategy of an organization is the roadmap towards attainment of its long term goals and objectives.

Success of the organization depends on its ability to adapt and change over time. HR leaders and employees contribute to the organization's ability to adapt by monitoring the environment, interpreting events that occur, and making adjustment as needed.

Human Resource (HR) leaders plan the activities towards accomplishment of long term organizational goals.

According to a survey, Facebook holds the distinction of being the unrivaled leader for online divorce evidence with 66 percent citing it as the primary source.

Social networks don't destroy jobs and families, people do or they don't. It's their free will.

We must have self conscious about being an adult who checks our Facebook profile compulsively and/or post things we really shouldn't or not. It's our choice. (Helen A.S. Popkin, 2010)

HR leaders should be able to work in varied environment. They can only do their duties well, if they are updated with changing need of the employees.

They naturally have to keep themselves abreast with not only the environment in which the organization exists, but of the environment from which the employees are coming to work.

The term environment refers to factors that influence the organization and people.

Today's Human Resource Management and leadership is often considered a role model of strategic partner; those who work in the HR leader capacity often contribute to developing business plans across the organization as well as accomplishing objectives.

c.   Create value through innovation—Recognize that in a competitive and fast changing world, the values of products, services and companies are constantly changing. In order for things to have real value to the customer

d.   Exceeding the expectation of customer by embracing best practice: World-class companies instill within its organization and constantly reinforce the idea that all who are a part of the organization must know their customers and must seek to satisfy the wants and needs of not only the customers, but also all other stakeholders. They must be trusted by customers.

A survey found the indirect effects of HR practices on customer satisfaction were significant and relatively large while the direct effect was non-significant and near zero.

e.   Show as unique supplier model: Human Resources Management provides the proprietary information systems to save employees, customers' time and money throughout the processes.

f.   Deliver business value: HR leaders address the importance of Human Resources through models of management for organizational excellence.

The HR leaders provide faster and cheaper application development, higher quality applications, more predictable and consistent results, faster product development cycle times, faster time to market for commercial application development, reduced project costs, and reduced project risks—ensures that the focus is solving business problems.

g.   Cut development costs—Cutting development costs is the key benefit to provide Return on Investment (ROI) calculations that make investments easier to justify.

If we make good business decisions; communication is easy, even when the news is bad.

h.   Stop the spin: If we're doing something because it saves the organization money, tell people that.

i.   Fit to futureDemonstrate risk readiness, challenge, equality, critics and conflict readiness.

The worst is over and Dubai is looking for new opportunities for growth, according to Dubai's ruler, Sheikh Mohammed.

He says that he views the global recession as a challenge and that companies there are restructuring in response.

"I don't call it a recession, I call it challenge," said Sheikh Mohammed, who is also prime minister of the United Arab Emirates. "The companies are restructuring because it's a new world. You have to stop and restructure."

j.   Be recognized as the pioneer and leader in the development.

Increasingly, employers are demanding that HR leaders play the role of a business partner and a strategic enabler. In such an environment, Human Capital has assumed considerable significance.

Insightful HR leaders recognize that the greatest impediments to success are often related to people rather than to machine, technology, and systems. What is not quite clear to HR leaders is exactly how to develop and leverage this human capital in support of business needs.

The transformation of HR function from a back office support role to a strategic business partner requires new roles and competencies for HR leaders and professionals. Key challenges for HR leaders are to envision these roles and competencies and to develop and implement programs to translate the vision to reality.

Mission

Mission or purpose is a description of what an organization does. It should describe the business the organization is in. It is a definition of why the organization exists.

All world-class companies have an explicit and formal mission. Within the mission is the goal to become world class.

Mission articulates broadly the purpose, intent, and beneficiaries of the organization.

The mission statement identifies what the organization does, why and for whom it exists, and the nature and scope of its unique contribution. It provides the foundation for the organization's strategic plan. Beneficiaries are a subset of stakeholders.

While a mission statement is typically found at the macro level, the operational level should consider developing and periodically evaluating its own mission statement to assess and specify the purpose for its existence. Mission defines the reason for the corporation's existence, i.e.:

a.   Ensure customer satisfaction: Minimize complaint. HR leaders develop a culture in which employees learn to take pride and become passionate about the customers.

   Facebook company mission is to make the world more open and connected.

   Millions of Facebook addicts worldwide worry that someday soon they'll have to pay to use the site.

   The users understand that Facebook has never charged them for access.

b.   Provide the right service, at the right time, and be cost-effective

c.   Conduct the business in a fair, open, honest and professional manner

Six recruiters were accused of luring 400 laborers from Thailand to the United States and forcing them to work; where work conditions were the worst.

The recruiters lured the workers with false promises of lucrative jobs, then confiscated their passports, failed to honor their employment contracts and threatened to deport them.

d.   Bring positive relationships with employees, employers, and others affected by the employees' compensation system.

e.   Expect and recognize individual and organization achievements and contributions to the company.

HR leaders treat each employee as a valued customer while contributing positively to the bottom line of the company through comprehensive programming that displays a thorough understanding of all aspects of Human Resources.

They will continually develop employees' repertoire of skills and maintain a balance between their personal and professional lives.

The HR leaders committed to provide employees a stable work environment with equal opportunity for learning and personal growth.

Creativity and innovation are encouraged for improving the effectiveness of the company. Employees will be provided the same concern, respect, and caring attitude within the organization that they are expected to share externally with customers.

Goal

Leading HR programs generate financial successes through systematic people management processes, clearly defined goals and excellent leadership. (Chapel Hill, 2003)

Goals are general statements of purpose that establish the direction for a component of the mission. Goals may have multiple objectives.

Objectives are more detailed than goals, have shorter time frames, and are measurable, quantifiable, and achievable.

Objectives are clear targets for specific actions. An integral part of the planning process is to review the organization's goals, objectives, and strategies to maintain their alignment with the organization's mission.

If the goals, objectives, and strategies are not in alignment with the mission and the mission statement is still valid then the goals, objectives, and strategies must be adjusted. HR leaders should use best practices to accomplish their tasks:

a. Recruit and select excellent employees: Assist Top Management in locating top quality employees. Hire the wrong person can cause a company to lose customers. The quality of good hires is of paramount importance to HR.

    To be designated world-class, a company had to score in the top 25% in efficiency and effectiveness.

b. Define strategic direction for development programs: Evaluate development needs and align programs to fulfill the needs.

    World-class companies are much more closely aligned with its business goals, and are 67 percent more likely to have an explicit workforce strategy in place.

c. Develop an integrated leadership model to identify and understand key experiences associated with successful leaders.

d. Develop innovative reward, recognition and compensation systems to promote employee satisfaction: Assess, design and implement an integrated set of total reward programs that link people with the strategy of the organization.

Goal needs to be systematically rolled down up to the operation level, i.e.: Goal Roll Down (GRD); Key Performance Indicator (KPI); and Balanced Scorecards (BSC). Balanced Scorecard is a framework many organizations are using to translate strategy into operational terms by measuring a full range of perspectives: financial, customer, internal, and learning and growth. Evaluation is also required to track the progress, i.e.:

a. Set allowable variance and deviation: Related to the minimum requirements. It will cause dissatisfaction if it's not fulfilled, but do not cause satisfaction if it's met or exceeded.

b. Set standard: The set values cause satisfaction if the performance is high and dissatisfaction if the performance is low. HR leader should focus on recruiting and retaining quality employees.

    For each 1,000 employees, world-class companies employ about 10 HR staffers, compared with about 16 in average companies.

c. Set maximum, nominal, and expected level.

d. Provide control and inspection: Build an ethical climate in the organization characterized by transparency in organizational processes, control of human errors and encouraging responsible behavior.

e. Communicate the problem: People know how they are doing on a regular basis. They frequently receive and discuss 'real-time' feedback that indicates how they are doing.

    The process is more focused on 'fit' than feedback. This means that line leaders look for ways to utilize the unique abilities of the employees, and see performance problems as shared responsibilities.

World-class companies recognize the importance of measurement in defining the goals and performance expectations for their organization.

They routinely adopt or develop the appropriate performance measurements needed to interpret and quantitatively describe the criteria used to measure the effectiveness of their operational system and its interrelated components.

Strategy

Organization, that has the best strategy in the world; but a culture that won't allow it to make that strategy happens; is doomed from the outset.

Strategy is the key approach the company will use to accomplish its mission and drive toward the vision.

HR leaders at world-class organizations are 67 percent more likely to tie business strategy to people strategy and 84 percent more likely than their peers to have an articulated explicit workforce strategy in place.

Companies that are already at world class level, are able to quickly absorb other world-class company strategy.

The strategy to become competitive in the market includes:

a.   Economic rent: The cost of the capital employed in the business. It is the measure of the competitive advantage. Competitive advantage is the means by which companies in competitive markets can earn economic rent.

b.   Focus on the company's external competitive environment.

If the company want to be the first to market with the most innovative products, but live in an organization that is full of bureaucracy and afraid to take risks, it's the most the company will be the first one no where.

Strategies are the means for transforming inputs into outputs and outcomes and should allocate the use of budgetary, human, and other resources. Strategies are methods to achieve goals and objectives. All of these must be reflected in the business and operations strategy if world-class status is to be attained:

a. Customer satisfaction: The goal of satisfaction is pursued in regards to the product, order processing, delivery, quick response to changes, and service after the sale. To ensure these needs, company should focus their activities through:

i. Identify the needs of customers: World-class company integrates all elements of the operational system in such a way that the needs and wants of its customers are satisfied in an effective, timely manner.

ii. Communicate costumer needs to all relevant company functions:

1. Use competitive information to establish organizational goals and objectives, which they communicate to all members of the enterprise.

2. Encourage and motivate its suppliers and vendors to become co-equals with the other elements of the operational system.

3. Eliminate organizational barriers to communication and to organize the company in such a way that the core values needed to reach world-class status.

4. Set and review quality objectives based on the customer's requirements

iii. Plan, conduct, measure and control all activities: Assess and identify the measures the organization can use to focus the critical results and develop a high-impact process to use those metrics that drive desired results.

iv. Continually improve the performance of the company on all levels of operations: Regularly assess the appropriateness of the objectives to attaining and maintaining world-class status.

It may require expenditure of efforts and resources by all elements within the organization to ensure their proper integration.

HR leader needs to connect people priorities to business priorities.

b.   Competitiveness: Provide Human Resources Development that is the process of increasing the knowledge, the skills, and the capacities of all the people in a company.

Competitiveness is characterized by following remarks:

1.   Deliver superior product/service, includes:

i.   Produce ISO based-product/service

ii.   Implement the world-class tools—Such as just-in-time production (JIT), total quality management (TQM), manufacturing resource planning (MRP II) and total productive maintenance (TPM).

iii.   Identify key processes that are technology-based, or impacted by new or upgraded technology.

iv.   Identify facility and work environment; that should not deteriorate product and quality.

v.   Identify information flows within the organization which would influence process, technology selection, design, or implementation.

vi.   Define the parameters of and for change the customer in future: Use a data-driven framework to assist the decision-making process.

vii.   Operate in a safe, reliable and economical manner with minimum impact on the environment.

2.   Cost: Fulfill the needs of the customers in a structured and economical way

3.   Delivery: As long as we're given credit for delivering, we should focus solely on that. We knew there were people out there who didn't like our product, but as long as we delivered it quickly, that was good enough. We realized that there was simply no conflict between not only delivering quickly but in making a better product.

4.   Continual improvement and innovation: Produce added value. The objective of continuous improvement is to improve processes and add value to products and services in

such a way as to increase customer satisfaction and loyalty and ensure long-term profitability. Continuous improvement fosters:

i.   Give unwavering commitment to self-analysis and improvement: The results were supportive as a model of the impact of human resource practices on organizational outcomes.

If company wants to have the highest quality, lowest failure rate, but live in an organization where rules are lax and people make decisions quickly without much data, chances are they will be chasing initiative after initiative trying to make the goals happen, to no avail.

ii. Provide aggressive approach to technology that can turn visionary strategies into reality: Leverage technology to improve performance to world-class level.

IT application drives HR efficiencies—recruit employees and a knowledge system that lets non-HR staffers address personnel inquiries. It's freeing HR for more strategic matters.

World-class companies use IT more effectively for HR. They use technology to improve productivity.

HR leaders will do a dramatically better job of leveraging technology, even though they spend no more than their peers.

A well formulated business model needs an organization that can and does deliver the desired results. This means that execution of the company's strategy is in many ways more important than the specific details of the plans.

A strong organization can make necessary adjustments and grow more effective with increasing challenges. HR leaders know they are successful because of what people in their organization do.

Consequently, success depends on a combination of a well conceived strategy, an effective organization, people who are both capable and committed to the company's success and systems and practices that keep the organization going.

If we really want to make that strategy happen, we can't ignore organization's culture. And if that culture is not the right one to make the strategy happen, then that culture needs to change.

Changes in the company's strategic direction will often require cultural change.

Cultural change can often be very difficult and HR leader will have to commit significant time and attention to shepherding the change. There can be significant barriers. Many times hidden cultural barriers to change are overlooked.

2nd

Human Resources

Any company or organization desires world-class status.

The term world-class company is used to denote a standard of excellence: the best of the best company at the international level.

Each world-class company will be accompanied by 'a world-class taste' Human Resources.

Human Resource (HR) is a term used to describe the individuals who comprise the workforce of an organization.

Historically, the HR function has been an administrative function headed by HR leaders whose roles are largely focused on cost control and administrative activities.

It is also the name of the function within an organization charged with the overall responsibility for implementing strategies and policies relating to the management of individuals (i.e. the human resources). This function title is often abbreviated to the initials 'HR'.

Organizations consider the 'HR Department' as playing a major role in staffing, training and helping to manage people so that people and the organization are performing at maximum capability in a highly fulfilling manner.

Departments are the entities organizations form to organize employees, reporting relationships, and work in a way that best supports the accomplishment of the organization's goals.

The most common Human Resource jobs that are grouped in the Human Resource Department are the Human Resources Director, Human Resources Generalist, and Human Resources Assistant. Some organizations may have a Vice President of Human Resources.

"People management, retention, recruitment, manpower planning, skills development and trainingthese are indispensible for business survival. HR can and should be one of the essential business functions," says China Gorman, COO (Chief Operating Officer) of the Society for Human Resource Management (SHRM).

Large organizations look to the 'Personnel Department,' mostly to manage the paperwork around hiring and paying people.

Personnel Department is organizational unit or department having the functional responsibility of personnel administration. The personnel department must have sufficient power and authority to help ensure that personnel policies are implemented legally and proactively.

To become strategic partners, they should not perform the administrative function of an organization, such as handling employee benefits or recruiting, interviewing, and hiring new staff.

They have to move from behind-the-scenes staff work to leading the company in suggesting and changing policies. Increasingly, they should have more opportunities to consult with Top Management regarding strategic planning.

Top Management is the highest ranking executives (with titles such as chairman/chairwoman, chief executive officer, managing director, president, executive director, executive vice presidents, etc.) responsible for the entire enterprise.

On other hand, other organizations consider HR Department and Personnel Department has no difference. They have similarity, i.e. in the mission that the Personnel Department is to provide a full range of Human Resource Management services organizations and employees.

As a full service Human Resources department for the company, the department is involved in employee recruitment, salary plan administration, contract negotiation and administration, labor and employee relations, the maintenance of personnel records, and advisement on regulations and laws relating to employment.

Corporations are undergoing dramatic changes with significant implications for how human resources are managed and the HR function is best organized and managed. The forces driving change include the rapid deployment of information technology, globalization of the economy, and the increasingly competitive dynamic business environments.

Human Resources are every leader's job, both the line leaders and the Human Resource leaders.

Line leaders are people who have direct responsibility for the production of goods and services.

The HR leader's primary goal in any organization is to ensure that the business has the right talent and skills at the right time, in the right place and in the right role.

Human Resource Management

The most successful organizations are the ones that take people matters seriously and build Human Resource Management into an operational business process.

HR Management is the key strategic issue in most organizations, but HR leaders historically have not been taken as strategic partners.

HR leaders will analyze company's competitive situation, develop its strategic goals and mission, foresee its external opportunities and threats, and its internal strength and weaknesses to generate alternatives.

Human Resource Management is the function within an organization that focuses on recruitment, management, and the direction of the people in the organization. Human Resources management is also performed by line leaders.

Human Resources Management (HRM) function includes a variety of activities, and key among them is deciding what staffing needs they have and whether to use independent contractors (outsource) or hire employees to fill the needs, recruiting and training the best employees, ensuring they are high performers, dealing with performance issues, and ensuring the employees and management practices conform to various regulations.

Activities also include managing the approach to employee benefits and compensation, employee records and personnel policies.

It is important for organization to ensure that HR leaders employ the right people with the right organizations.

Human Resource Management is sometimes seen focusing on resource, rather than asset/capital. Base on this assumption, Human Resource is considered as 'hard perspective.'

They argue that people are organizational resources and should be managed like any other resource. They should be obtained as cheaply as used sparingly as possible; consistent with other requirements such as those for quality and efficiency; and they should be developed and exploited as fully and profitably as possible.

The word 'people' is used rather than 'employees' because techniques such as outsourcing, subcontracting and franchising would in certain circumstances be seen as entirely appropriate to a hard view of Human Resources Management. The approach tends to have a much closer relationship to corporate strategy.

A struggling worker told:" For the last thirty years, I changed jobs on average every two and a half years. Whenever I had an interview with a prospective employer, HR was always a roadblock, never an enabler.

If I couldn't get past the HR process to interview with the manager or supervisor, I would be working with or for, I simply discounted the opportunity. And with good reason, I did not once receive a call back from any organization that allowed me to interview only with HR. "

The role of Human Resources Management is to get the right organizational configuration; with the right people; in the right role and performing at the height of their capabilities.

HR leaders have to control and manage people. If they put their view of accounting, they will make people an expense and machines assets.

The main assets and primary drivers of economic prosperity in the Industrial Age are machines and capital-things. People are necessary but replaceable.

HR leaders can control and churn through manual workers with little consequence-supply exceeded demand. They get more able bodies that will comply with strict procedures. People are like things-they can be efficient with them.

Industrial Age educates leaders, people are put on expense; equipment is put on the balance sheet as an investment.

Human Resources Management was created for any organization to meet its strategic goals by selecting, developing, maintaining, and effectively managing the human capital.

The HR leaders need to therefore ensure that recruitment processes are fair and provide equality of opportunity thus encouraging a wide and diverse range of people to apply.

The organization must ensure that it develops the capability of employees. The leaders determine a plan of actions and deployment of resources to achieve the goals, include:

a. Ensure that the roles and responsibilities of all staffs are defined: HR leaders look at the roles and responsibilities of everyone in the organization.

    No matter what the position in an organization, if a person doesn't understand their role and responsibilities, the business will not be efficient.

    It is the responsibility of the line leaders to understand their own roles and responsibilities and to work with HR and staff to clarify the organization members' roles and responsibilities.

b. Ensure that all staff are trained and experienced: Many organizations where employees struggle to meet users' demands without fully understanding the logics and processes behind their actions.

Properly trained employees find it easier to cope with the demands placed on them in areas such as works that aimed to meet customer's expectations and maintain their satisfaction levels.

Training doesn't have to be a budget buster either and it can often be worked into daily routines at little or no extra cost.

"Nothing is more terrible than activity without insight," *observed Thomas Carlyle, essayist and historian.*

c. Ensure that employees have access to advice and resources in order to carry out their roles effectively: HR leaders make sure access to resources is made available to the employees to enable them to carry out their responsibilities.

The leaders understand how important it is to make the right decision when progressing in their goals. Employees will succeed in their work place, if HR leaders offer an environment where the focus is on personal development, quality and growth.

d. Ensure equal opportunity in the recruitment process: HR leaders give emphasis on equal opportunities and do not discriminate on any grounds other than ability to carry out the task.

An equal opportunities attitude helps to ensure that there is no unjustified discrimination.

Citigroup have a long-standing commitment to equal *employment practices.*

Their diversity work has been recognized by external organizations like Working Mother magazine, which names Citi as one of the 100 best companies for working mothers 19 times, and Diversity Inc. magazine, which recognizes Citi as its top 25 noteworthy companies for diversity.

In many opportunities, it deals with issues related to people such as compensation, hiring, performance management, organization development, safety, wellness, benefits, employee motivation, communication, administration, and training.

Human Resource Management also seeks to ensure that the individual employee is satisfied with both the working environment and the compensation and benefits that he or she receives.

Human Resources Development is a framework for the expansion of human capital within the organization.

People might include Human Resources Management in Human Resources Development, explaining that Human Resources Development includes the broader range of activities to develop personnel inside of organizations, e.g., career development, training, organization development, etc.

Human Resource Management is based in the efficient utilization of employees in achieving company goals, i.e. effectively make use of the talents and abilities of employees to achieve the operational objectives that are the ultimate aim of the organization.

Human Capital Management

Company's performance lies on the hands of employees.

For companies, important people are element of intangible value. Intangible value is constantly increasing in importance as the very existence of most of the organizations depends on the ability to innovate, to capture the support of customers, to establish the brand and to respond to an ever-changing marketplace.

All of this depends on employees and getting the best from employees depends on understanding what motives them to perform, to give outstanding service to customers, to run that extra mile when it counts.

Without this information, HR leaders have to make decisions largely in ignorance of the impact these decisions might have on the performance of employees.

Top Management is increasingly looking to HR for human capital strategies to help accomplish business goals.

Human Resource leaders and line leaders are struggling to strategically position and manage Human Resource initiatives to optimize their workforce potential.

By adopting Human Capital Management, HR leaders can get better at providing the information that will help them understand just what it is that their employees contribute.

This in turn will improve management decision making and help them move towards developing strategic measures to help identify the drivers in the business.

Additional for the above assumptions, Human Capital Management is seen as the 'soft perspective' of Human Resources Management.

The use of quality employee data is the key to good Human Capital Management. Analyze and link this data with business performance metrics (i.e. sales, customer service and financial performance) and we begin to get deep organizational insight into how effective employee strategy is and its impact on business performance and bottom line.

Human Capital Management is a journey. Where HR leaders start will largely depend on the information available. Where they go will depend on what they do with the information and how they are able to grow and communicate it.

Effective Human Capital is critical to an organization's success and therefore the HR function's focus must be more strategic. Human capital and innovative Human Resource Management techniques are the driving forces behind most business productivity gains.

Research found a clear correlation between growth in market capitalization and growth in profits per employee. Talent is the ultimate generator of wealth creation in this new digital age, requiring a very different focus in maximizing returns on people, not capital.

When all HR leaders want is a person's body and they

don't really want their mind, heart, or spirit (all inhibitors to the free-flowing process of the machine age), they have reduced a person to a thing.

When we treat people like things, it insults and alienates them,

depersonalizes work, and creates low-trust, unionized, litigious cultures.

A survey found 97% of CEO's stated retention of top talent is a key to sustaining business advantage for the long term.

Human Capital is the most important differentiator that sets apart winning organizations from average ones. Settling for ordinary leaders with less than ideal people development skills or interest will seldom lead to extraordinary business results.

Human Capital is often represented as both a challenge and an opportunity. A challenge to identify relevant measures and provide meaningful information which can be acted on, and an opportunity to both evaluate and maximize the value of people.

Companies realize that their employees' talents and skills drive their business success.

A study found that talent identification and development initiatives are lacking, with 91% of organizations challenged to identify high potentials early in their careers.

Developing talent often receives minimal attention in people development programs.

One of the major problems faced by many companies in today's fast paced market is how to grasp and retain employee that is of the best caliber.

In the highly competitive business environment, the best talent quickly gets swept up by employers eager to strengthen the quality and efficacy of their workers.

Organizations put tremendous effort into attracting employees to their company, but spend little time into retaining and developing talent.

That's why it is important for a company to stay on track by utilizing the best Talent Management.

Talent Management is being used to refer the activities to attract, develop and retain employees. Some people and organizations use the phrase to refer especially to talented and/or high-potential employees.

Talent Management is distinct from Human Resources Management, in part, because it is the responsibility of leaders across the organization rather than a discipline that can or should reside in just HR leader.

The phrase often is used interchangeable with the field of Human Resource Management.

Talent Management is also known as HCM (Human Capital Management), HRIS (Human Resource Information System) or HRMS (Human Resource Management System), and Human Resource Module.

A study found 54% of CEO's acknowledge that senior management spends insufficient time on talent management.

It cannot be left solely to the Human Resources Department to attract and retain employees, but rather must be practiced at all levels of the organization.

The business strategy must include responsibilities for line managers to develop the skills of their immediate subordinates.

HR leaders are be able provide HR solutions to help the organization avoid problems and maximize returns on human capital investments.

Human Capital Management concentrates upon the 'human' side of Human Resources Management. It argues that employees are a resource unlike any other.

For most organizations it's far more costly than other resources. But for all organizations, Human Resource becomes the one resource which can create value from the other resources.

This is the resource whose creativity, commitment and skill can generate real competitive advantage. This is the most precious resource, therefore careful selection, extensive nurturing and development, proper rewards and integration into the organization.

Human Capital Management (HCM) activities should be more related to *corporate* strategy. Companies that focus on developing employees' talent integrate plans and processes, include:

a.   Sourcing, attracting, recruiting and on-boarding qualified candidates: Corporations often hire people to do jobs that don't really need doing. Sometimes it's because CEO is building an empire. Sometimes it's the result of random corporate confusion.

Some are execs that are both highly-paid and exist in almost every large firm—even though they're not really accomplishing anything.

Despite that fact that Microsoft, Oracle and IBM work closely with the IT groups inside thousands of corporations, none of those three companies lists a Chief Information Officer (CIO) as a key player in their own firm.

The length of time spent on sourcing potential candidates can vary greatly depending upon the level and complexity of the position.

A survey found the majority of hiring managers (93.3%) start the screening process on potential candidates within a month's time.

b. Managing competitive salaries: When HR leaders to hire new people as employees, they definitely will be interested in setting competitive salaries instead of offering the already lowest salary.

Competitive salaries will help to attract qualified and competent candidates who will be interested in working for the company. They should set competitive salaries to help encourage employees to stick with the company

Every organization wants to attract, motivate, and retain the most qualified employees and match them to jobs for which they are best suited.

A competitive salary should not mean the HR leaders have not yet decided what they want to pay. They prefer to see what the candidates expect and then negotiate down from there.

Or they want to take advantage of the candidate. They are hiding the fact that their salary is below average. It competes, but on the loosing end.

c. Training and development: It is not enough that HR programs are efficient, effective, and competitively priced; employer wants to see a return on these investments.

Through their persistent efforts, they have greatly expanded their capacities, i.e. mentalvision, possible in employees and organization to fit needs and possibilities; physicaldiscipline, show commitments; emotionalpassion, demonstrate compassion in personal relationship and organization; spiritualconscience, show moral sense of what is right and wrong, the drive toward meaning and contribution.

d.	Performance management: HR leaders evaluate employee performance by measuring performance and reinforcing positive behavior and growth.

It incorporates a range of different tools and activities used to drive improvement.

The leaders take action in response to actual performances by creating a development plan to increase employee productivity.

e.	Retention programs: Many leaders are assuming they know what an employee wants. However, not all employees will think like a leader.

Failure to take the time to do the research could mean costly programs that do not have an impact.

Hiring and training new employees is costly and time consuming.

Company should have a system of retention strategies in place to keep employee turnover rates down.

HR leaders should be able to achieve the organization's objectives through increased productivity, decreased turnover, and bottom-line improvements.

Employee retention programs should improve employee morale and inspire employees to reach their full potential.

Retaining qualified and experienced employee is an important part of managing human resources. Turnover due to low job satisfaction is not only expensive, it can stagnate business growth. It is not always easy to replace employees with key skills and knowledge.

Each employee is motivated by different things. Everyone has different goals and needs. Some focus on money, others thrive on recognition. The first step to determining what employee retention programs will work best is to find out what is important to the employees.

Once Management understands what is valued by the employees they can select programs that will fit the needs of the group. The best approach to developing a retention program is to have a variety of tools to address job satisfaction.

f.   Promotion: In general, promotion is the advancement of an employee from one position to another position that has a higher salary range.

Promotion can result in a higher level title and higher level job responsibilities. Decision making authority may follow to rise.

Indeed, promotion comes from both sides HR leader and employee. A successful worker can create their own path to promotion; they don't rely on luck.

It happens because the employee has successfully created an opportunity to demonstrate his/her value to the organization.

HR leaders provide an environment where people feel appreciated, recognized, challenged, and appropriately compensated.

A successful HR leader is a know-how leader who can make the human capital takes part in the formulation and implementation of the Human Resource policies which stem from and influence the workplace environment.

HR leaders should seek not only to hire the most qualified and valuable employees but also to put a strong emphasis on retention, and more importantly to place the individual in a position where his/her skills are being extensively utilized.

The executive leading the HR function is a strategic change agent, a savvy business person, a proven leader, a global authority, and a credible and trusted member of the executive team.

Today's HR leader leads a mission-critical corporate function, requiring a broad and deep level of expertise and leadership skills. He or she plays a role in driving growth and innovation. That's why he/she should not be merely effective but demonstrating great HR leadership.

Great HR leadership requires a style that guides the HR leader to achieve his/her topmost perspective, as a leadership brand setter. His/her achievement as a great leader will also improve employer brand. And automatically, it brings the company to become the most desired organization.

3rd

Value and Capacity

HR leaders build more engaged, high performance cultures by energizing their employees. They focus on helping employees meet each of these needs, recognizing that it helps them to perform better and more sustainably.

Only few leaders take the time to figure out what they truly stand for, beyond the bottom line, and why employees should feel excited to work for them.

The leaders clearly define how success to be achieved. The job of leaders is not to do the work of those they lead.

They have the capacity to recognize all that they perceive. The leaders also recognize that the best way to get the highest value is to give the highest value.

Value

Values form the foundation for the organization. Values permeate the workplace. We naturally hire people who share our values. Whatever we value, will largely govern the actions of our workforce.

Leading companies are learning how to measure their intangible assets—employees that truly 'live' the company's values.

HR leaders create value through leadership. The leaders must have a rock-solid value system which is congruent with organization and employees' values.

They need Value Management that provides a well-established methodology for defining and maximizing organization's value.

It is a framework that allows needs, problems or opportunities to be defined.

Therefore, it enables a review of whether the organization objective can be improved to determine the optimal approach and solution. Value Management encourages innovative thinking, business problem solving and performance improvement.

HR leader must uphold the corporate values so that employees will become committed to the organization. Corporate value is defined as activities, those are most important to the company that include but not limited to:

a.   Partnerships: Working collaboratively. It needs to align HR with the business of the organization, and ensure Human Resource policies are aimed to congruence the individual goals with the organizational goals.

As HR leaders, we have to remember that if the main activity of the organization does not exist, then Human Resources department would not exist.

Working collaboratively with employees, we do not only increase their skills, we often accelerate the level of desired change. To be successful in the collaborative environment, it requires:

i.   Work together in partnerships, both internally and externally, to achieve shared goals: By imposing togetherness and teamwork across divisional boundaries companies risk losing the people whose tacit knowledge actually drives growth.

Early in the troubled relationship between Barack Obama and Benjamin 'Bibi' Netanyahu, Israeli ambassador Michael

Oren told his American counterparts that what was lacking between the two leaders was 'intimacy.'

"What we're looking for is a sense of intimacy, where the trust

HR leader ensures and oversees an effective and fair collective bargaining process with unions representing employees, and fosters positive labor relations designed to achieve company's objectives.

ii. Encourage teamwork: Build teamwork and mutual support by encouraging cooperation and collaboration among the employees.

Leaders expect people, in teamwork, people demonstrate interest in performing as a team and take joy in team results instead of individual accomplishments.

A flight attendant who stepped in for a sick co-pilot and helped land and American Airlines flight in Chicago is brushing off praise, saying she 'was just trying to be part of a team.'

Patti DeLuna, 61, obtained her pilot's license in 1970. It came in handy, when the first officer of a flight from San Francisco to O'Hare International was struck with serious flu symptoms.

DeLuna, who has worked as a flight attendant for more than three decades, stepped up after the flight's pilot asked if any passengers were licensed to fly.

iii. Excellent service—Values release tremendous potential for success and accomplishment. Provide customers with excellent service and products. World-class company should be able to compete effectively in a global market.

Even though, Human Resources Department is not the centre of activity for any organization, it must contribute to the main activities of the organization.

The Human Resources function is structured and organized to meet employee and organizational needs.

Deb Levine started her online sex education company because she was bored putting condoms on bananas as a way to teach students about safe sex.

What began as a simple Internet sexual Q&A column nearly 20 years ago—Go Ask Alice!—has grown into a nonprofit corporation that disseminates sexual health information via electronic tools such as text messaging and social media.

"What it showed me was this incredible power of the Internet to reach large numbers of people with sensitive information," said Levine, who was included among PopTech's 2009 Social Innovation Fellows, a class of roughly 20 cutting-edge thought leaders.

iv.   Achievement: Fulfill commitments and achieve desired results. Understand its business model, vision and strategy, as well as, its critical success factors.

HR leaders encourage employees to be more responsible and act and think like owners.

b.   Respect: Most organizations operate with a diversity of cultures. Therefore, leaders should:

i.   Treat employees with dignity and interpersonal sensitivity: One culture can evolve, two or more, however, will not.

Merging two or more cultures well is supreme challenge that needs to be actively shaped and carefully managed. HR leaders should have sensitivity in dealing with the concerns and problems of employees.

The Vatican issued a revised set of rules to respond to clerical sex abuse.

The new rules represent the first major Vatican document since the scandal erupted, with hundreds of new cases coming to light of priests who allegedly molested children.

"It recognizes that the adults who are handicapped or mentally impaired—any kind of abuse against them—will be considered as abuse against a minor," said Vatican observer, Robert Mickens.

ii. Share information with staff, customers, and partners: Companies have known for attracting employees, who will subscribe to the organization's belief system and the consistent application of the principles, are communicating values that give them a competitive edge.

As HR leaders, we may want to influence our organization to identify its core values, and make them the foundation for its interactions with employees, customers, and partners.

When corporate values are published, followed, and consistent with their own, employees feel that the climate that is fair, inclusive, and ethical. This increases cohesion, promotes creativity, and improves overall productivity.

iii. Act with integrity: Understand the leadership philosophy and desired culture. Interact among leaders and with employees honestly. Build relationships based on trust.

Hewlett-Packard found that Mark Hurd, chairman and CEO, submitted inaccurate expense reports that concealed his personal relationship with Jodie Fisher. These expenses totaled about $20,000.

The $20,000 in expenses that Hurd allegedly fudged is spare change for a $115 billion company like HP. Plus, he has promised to pay that money back. But for a CEO, sometimes the severity of the mistake doesn't matter.

"The error in judgment may not seem very significant," says Paul Hodgson, from Corporate.

"But those errors can now potentially spill into other areas of a CEO's daily life. Once that happens, you've lost that trust, and it's extremely difficult to get back."

Hurd's indiscretion could also magnify within a company like HP, which possesses a strong corporate culture. The company, founded in 1939, has long espoused the guiding principle known as 'the HP Way.'

"We work together to create a culture of inclusion built on trust, respect and dignity for all."

iv. Listen and respond to the needs of customers: Anticipate, understand, and respond in timely and effective manner to the needs of our customers. Both leaders and employees must welcome customer feedback.

U.S. Trade Representative Ron Kirk outlined actions President Barack Obama's administration has taken to enforce U.S. rights under global trade rules and various bilateral agreements.

He touted Obama's decision to slap duties on Chinese-made tires in response to a plea from union workers who said a surge in imports threatened their jobs.

"No other U.S. president has ever used the United States' authority to hold China accountable for flooding our country with cheap products that undercut American goods and put our workers out of work," Kirk said.

c.   Learning and growth: Grow the business with great opportunities to learn. Values are the most powerful way to release and harness the company's latent, unutilized energies for growth.

Culture can be developed and maintained through extensive training of leaders and employees. Growth should evolve:

i.   Demonstrate continuous employee and company improvement: Identify and fulfill personal and organizational needs, and planning for future needs.

ii. Provide the best services and products: HR leader is to provide higher levels of efficiency and effectiveness at a lower cost.

Although directors devote more time to strategy (37%), they still spend the majority of their time on day-to-day concerns.

The HR leader should be able to ensure timely recruitment, selection and placement of highly qualified employees.

iii. Promote high individual performance and employee development: Bring together workers and employers to address training, and career development.

iv. Passion for customers, for partners, and for technology: HR leaders follow the dictates of good management.

They listened closely to their customers. They carefully studied market trends. They allocated capital to the innovations that promised the largest returns.

And in the process, line leader missed disruptive innovations that opened up new customers and markets for lower-margin blockbuster products.

v. Be adaptable to change: One thing is certain, that everything is changing. Many enterprises are anticipating, and indeed pre-empting change, by taking greater control over their own destiny through i.e. business process re-engineering.

"You have to be willing to change when it makes sense," Jeffrey R. Immelt, the chairman and CEO of General Electric, says.

In general, corporations are bureaucracies and leaders are bureaucrats. Their fundamental tendency is toward self-perpetuation. They are, almost by definition, resistant to change. They were designed and tasked, not with reinforcing market forces, but with supplanting and even resisting the market.

Successful organizations are becoming more adaptable, resilient, quick to change direction, and customer-centered.

They do not achieve a change by accident. They achieve it with a defined strategy for high involvement and a measurable action plan.

A study found 41% of change projects fail and of the 59% that 'succeed' only half meet the expectations of senior management.

The only way to change corporate culture is to alter the way we treat employees, not to hire a culture consultant.

d. Dignity: Human dignity is a regulator to human attitude and behavior. Company upholds the right of employees to be treated with dignity. It is committed to fostering healthy environment in workplace. Dignity signifies that a being has an innate right to:

i. Treat with respect and consideration: Maintain respect for employees. Treat people the same no matter their race, religion, gender, size, age, or country of origin.

HR leaders who respect the one's dignity means to respect his/her life and integrity. HR leaders should also understand his/her autonomy, especially related to his/her free choice.

If employees are always treated with respect, they do more for the organization.

HR leaders spend time with employees and to communicate with them in a variety of ways.

They bring people to feel fulfilled and to be happy. They radiate the demeanor that they are proud of the employees. They are interested in employees as individuals, including the good and bad things that happen to them.

Bastoy island, 46 miles (74 km) south of Oslo (Norwey), isn't an exclusive resort: it's a prison.

Arne Kvernvik Nilsen, Bastoy's governor describes it as the world's first human-ecological prison—a place where inmates learn to take responsibility for their actions by caring for the environment.

Prisoners grow their own organic vegetables, turn their garbage into compost and tend to chickens, cows, horses and sheep.

Norwegians see the island as the embodiment of their country's long-standing penal philosophy: that traditional, repressive prisons do not work, and that treating prisoners humanely boosts their chances of reintegrating into society.

ii.   Demonstration of effective communication is the foundation of personal and business relationships.

Leaders communicate in a truthful manner about how the company is run. They actively seek to understand the perspectives of others by listening with an open mind and communicating honestly, with appropriate discretion.

e.   Fairness: Treat employees equally and without prejudice or bias.

In support of the commitment in fairness, no form of harassment or bullying will be tolerated within the company, i.e. race, creed, color, nationality, ethnic origin, age, language, religion or similar belief, political or other opinion, affiliation, gender, gender reassignment, sexual orientation, marital status, disability, national or social origin, birth or other status, or membership or non membership of a union.

Google Inc., which runs the world's most popular Internet search engine, was ordered to defend itself against a lawsuit by a former manager who said he was fired for being too old, clearing the way for a trial.

The California Supreme Court unanimously agreed that a trial court erred in dismissing a complaint by Brian Reid, who was hired in 2002 as a director of operations and engineering, and fired less than two years later at age 54 after being told he was not a good 'cultural fit.'

i.   Work for employee and company interests: HR leaders helping employees maintain work-life balance. It isn't something the leaders do just for them; it can be vital to the health of the company.

Ron Wayne, 76, one of the founders of Apple Computer, living off his Social Security and does a modest trade in collectors' stamps and coins.

He used to come to the Nugget Hotel & Casino in Nevada, a couple of days a week to try his luck on the video poker machine.

Wayne's tenure at Apple began on April 1, 1976. His name is signed on the legal document that established Apple—next to those of Steve Jobs and Steve Wozniak, the Silicon Valley giants most people associate with the popular tech company, which makes the iPhone and iPad.

Eleven days after Apple was formed, Wayne removed himself from the company charter. He eventually was given $800 for his stake in Apple.

"Obviously he didn't have the foresight to know what Apple would become," said Ben Bajarin, from Creative Strategies.

ii.   Be the voice of the employee and interpret and enforce company policy: Listen to the needs, desires, and wants of the employee and customize a benefit to meet that employee's needs.

HR leaders help to translate company goals into employee actions, and assure they receive meaningful feedback, coaching and assistance to make them successful.

iii.   Advocate employees and assist Top Management: The role of a HR leader, instead of serving as an advocate for the employees, he or she is an advocate for the business. He or she understands market trends and the company's capability to capitalize on them for future growth.

The HR leader knows that an organization must continue to adapt to ever-changing market conditions, and takes the leadership role to affect organizational change.

The AFL-CIO labor federation and six Guatemalan unions filed a complaint in April 2008, accusing the Guatemala government of failing to effectively enforce laws guaranteeing workers the right to organize and bargain collectively as well as the right of association and acceptable conditions of work.

Other Guatemalans "have tragically lost their lives in their quest to exercise their human rights as workers, while their government refused to act," AFL-CIO President Richard Trumka said. "We want to see the government of Guatemala take specific and effective action—including, if appropriate, legislative reforms—to improve systemic failures in enforcement of Guatemalan labor laws."

iv. Educate and regulate: Regulate best practices in the organization and educate employees to understand company regulations and policies. Treat equally all the employees before the law.

v. Foster employee and organization development: Employee development will mean the difference between retaining good employees and losing them.

Studies said sixty four percent of new executives hired from the outside won't make it in their current jobs. Forty percent will fail within the first 18 months.

vi. Bring to competitive employee compensation and competitive employee's capability: HR leaders develop and administer a job evaluation and compensation system that attracts, retains and motivates employees to accomplish company's objectives.

HR leaders seek to provide the highest quality benefit packages possible given by the current financial position of the company.

Human capital resources include the skills, judgment, and intelligence of the firm's employees can provide competitive advantages.

Competitive employee is distinguished from the level of performance in relation to the performance of other employees.

Worker productivity dropped this spring for the first time in more than a year, a sign that companies may need to step up hiring if they hope to grow.

Productivity declined at an annual rate of 0.9 percent in the April-to-June quarter. Unit labor costs edged up 0.2 percent in the second quarter.

Experts believe companies need to stop slashing their work forces and start rehiring laid off workers.

It could be a signal that employers can no longer squeeze extra output out of leaner staffs. "This could be a turning point as far as hiring goes," said Joel Naroff, president of Naroff Economic Advisors.

Companies cut their payrolls during the recession and relied on fewer workers. For all of 2009, productivity shot up 3.5 percent, the best performance in six years.

vii. Focus on relationships and task: Clarify and integrate the roles, accountabilities and desired working relationships of the organization so people function as an effective team to achieved superior performance.

Diversity in culture, attitude and experience can mean that what is perceived by one person as harassment may be perceived by others as normal social exchange.

viii. Encourage training for the job and doing the job: Training will improve employees' performance and it develops the competence of workers that enhances organizational competitiveness.

Trained employees can deliver what customers want, and provide them the kind of support that will bring the customers satisfaction.

ix.   Put on high platform for employee satisfaction and customer satisfaction: HR leader must be committed to providing the highest quality product and service, and work environment where all are welcomed respected and treated in a consistent and non-discrimination manner.

Debrahlee Lorenzana, 33-year-old single mother received rave reviews, awards and citations from companies like the Municipal Credit Union, Metropolitan Hospital in Queens and Bank of America.

She did her job well, and brought in a lot of new business; but before long, she was told that, "as a result of the shape of her figure, such clothes were purportedly 'too distracting' for her male colleagues and supervisors to bear," according to her lawsuit.

Lorenzana attempted to comply—she tried to 'dress down,' coming to work without makeup, not straightening her hair and wearing flat shoes. But that drew flack as well, and she was instructed not to do that. It seems she just couldn't win.

So she complained to Human Resources, and when she got no response from that department, she complained to their superiors.

Finally she was given a transfer, to the Rockefeller Center Branch, where she was put to work in telephone sales, something she wasn't familiar with, and was eventually fired for 'disciplinary problems and poor performance.'

f.   Honesty: Human Resources leaders face business ethics choices and their consequences daily.

With all the business scandals from Enron to Bernie Madoff, honesty in business seems sometimes to be in short supply.

Dishonesty can lead to a loss of customers.

The IMF needs Asia on its side. As the fastest-growing part of the world economy, the region will wield more clout at global institutions like the IMF and provide more of their funding.

The problem, to put it bluntly, is that Asia does not need the IMF or like the IMF, whose invasive policy prescriptions are blamed in the region for having exacerbated the 1997/98 meltdown.

"Let me be candid: we have made some mistakes," Dominique Strauss-Kahn, IMF managing director, said. "We have learned the importance of focusing on essential policies, and of protecting the most vulnerable, when tackling a crisis."

Honesty will help a person to excel in their career to the best of their ability and solve problems in the workplace. Honesty fosters:

i.   Treat employees truthfully: Company's performance lies in the hands of its people. Investing in human resources development allows a company to continuously drive productivity and profits.

ii.   Honest communication throughout the company: The behavior rules and boundaries should be made clear and communicated often.

iii. Practice open—Be transparent and maintain a high degree of disclosure levels.

g.   Be accountable: A norm of accountability will help make the organization successful. Tolerating poor performance or exhibiting a lack of discipline to maintain established processes and systems will impede our success. Accountability emphasizes:

i.   Decisions and actions are clear, reasonable and open to examination: HR leaders clarify decision accountability. They assign clear roles for the decisions that most affect the company's performance. Decisions that routinely stall inside the organization, hurting the entire company's performance.

Gunmen who killed 17 people at a party in northern Mexico were let out of prison to carry out the attack, state prosecutors say.

Guards at a prison in Durango State are accused of lending the inmates weapons and vehicles to commit the murders in neighbouring Coahuila state before returning them to their cells.

The prisoners were acting as contract killers for a drugs gang, and were thought to have carried out two other mass killings in Torreon using the same weapons.

"They were allowed out of prison to kill using the weapons of the guards and travelling in official vehicles," an official said.

ii.   Be committed: Have HR programs that generate financial successes through systematic people management processes, clearly defined goals and good leadership.

HR leaders are committed to a supportive work environment, where employees have the opportunity to reach their fullest potential.

iii. Accountability to customers, shareholders, partners, and employees for results, and quality: Take right talent at the right time at the right cost, contributing to the achievement of key strategies and objectives of the company.

The reputation as a company that customers can trust is everyone's most valuable result.

Companies should consider the needs and interests of multiple stakeholders, not just those with a direct financial stake in the organization's profits and losses.

Organizations that approach business ethics from a stakeholder perspective consider how decisions impact those inside and outside the organization.

Stakeholders are individuals and groups who affect or who are affected by a company's actions and decisions.

Shareholders are definitely stakeholders, but they are not the only ones who fall under the definition of stakeholder.

Stakeholders include: employees, suppliers, customers, competitors, government agencies, the news media, community residents and others.

The idea behind stakeholder based ethical decision making is to make sound business decisions that work for the good of all affected parties.

iv. Serve and protect the interests of the company: HR leaders are always faced with the task of finding a resolution that protects the interests of the company, but at the same time provides and acceptable level of satisfaction to the employee.

A conflict of interest exists when a person's private interest interferes in any way with the interests of the company.

A conflict situation can arise when employee or HR leader takes actions or has interests that may make it difficult to perform company work objectively and effectively.

v. Challenge: Achieving HR leader's task is a challenge that requires the expertise and involvement of all key players in the relevant institutions for the desired results.

In today's driven competitive business world, accountability is becoming a more critical issue for HR leaders and employees.

According to the report, a quarter (24%) of employers looks for candidates who have experienced failure and bounced back from difficult challenges, when looking for the next generation of leaders.

If we start with the type of person we want to hire, presumably we can build a work force that is prepared for the culture we desire.

vi. Continuous improvement: HR leaders use in reviewing and enhancing current human resource management structures, systems and processes.

Continuous improvement involves a mind-set and a range of techniques to review and evaluate work processes. As a mind-set, it is a way of approaching work so that a culture of innovation and creativity is encouraged.

As a range of techniques, continuous improvement includes approaches such as Benchmarking, Re-engineering, Quality Management, Organizational Reviews, Performance Management etc.

h. Personal integrity: HR leaders must be on top of things. The leader must be an expert in the details of how the vision is being implemented. This does not mean that they should micro manage. Personal integrity is demonstrated by following attributes:

i. Constructive: We are now entering a new era in which people are the drivers of success and which places HR in 'hot seats.'

For top-performing companies, CEOs want workforce strategies that align the company with corporate goals and objectives.

They want human capital and talent management professionals who can lead teams of highly skilled individuals focused on developing the workforcethe engine of growth.

The majority of HR leaders (53%) believe HR will become more integrated with the business.

ii. Self-criticism: World-class companies are always examining their business processes and continuously seeking solutions to improve in key areas, such as lead time reduction, cost cutting, exceeding customer expectations, streamlining processes, shortening time to market for new products, and managing the global operation.

90% of HR directors interviewed say they are close enough to the business to help the organisation achieve its goals.

iii. Self-improvement and personal excellence: Encourage employee empowerment, growth and development of employees by realizing their potential, and encourage innovative ideas and fair distribution of rewards.

Training can be extremely boring for many employees, if not done appropriately. Many of them in organizations view training as some opportunity to socialize with colleagues and develop interpersonal relationships. They 'somehow' manage to complete it and go back to their work places.

iv. Proactive: Anticipate needs or problems and attempts prevent them.

v. Responsibility: Focus on outcomes and results that enhance organizational competitiveness.

The top priority for business is cost-effectiveness, change management, restructuring, and growth. HR leaders should always find themselves positioned to help organisations to achieve these strategic goals.

World-class HR executives are over four times more likely than their peers to own one or more strategic initiatives.

i. Professional—Deliver professional services in accordance with relevant technical and professional standards.

Astronauts keep it professional in space. When veteran NASA space flier Alan Poindexter was asked during a visit to Tokyo what would happen if astronauts had sex in space, he emphasized that he and his colleagues were 'a group of professionals.'

"We treat each other with respect and we have a great working relationship," Poindexter, who commanded a space shuttle mission to the station, said: "Personal relationships are not an issue. We don't have them, and we won't."

HR leaders should look for attitudes that are positive and for people who can lend themselves to causes.

j.   Motivation: Every organization wants to attract, retain and motivate employees. Many think that these are the primary objectives of compensation and reward programs. In today's environment, to increase employees' satisfaction with their jobs and working conditions, HR leaders should consider:

i.   Autonomy: Demonstrate self-direction. Employees are humans. Human nature is to direct their own lives and to resist control. The really good people want autonomy—if we let them do it, and they will do it successfully.

Most great pieces of art, most great pieces of music, many great architectural triumphs, and many great technological innovations are resulted because people want to do it.

ii.   Mastery: The desire to get better at things. Biggest motivator at work is making progress.

The days, that people feel most engaged, most motivated, are the days when they've made some progress in their work. Therefore, one of a HR leader's biggest roles is to help employees see their progress, and to recognize and celebrate it.

iii. Purpose: Do what we do in service of something larger than ourselves. Employees tend to work better when they know what they're doing matters in some way.

Value management framework focuses on customer requirements. It is action oriented rather than compliance based. It focuses on optimizing customer value. Therefore, HR leader must:

1.   Stimulate effectiveness by enabling employees to reach both their personal potential and their organizational potential:

Build a high performance culture in the organization that affords opportunity to employee to realize his or her full potential.

2.   Take a role in developing, expressing, and defending values.

3.   Nurture new leaders and ensure the continuation of the corporate culture.

Companies which rated their implementation of key corporate values the highest also reported the highest levels of revenue growth and profitability.

When leaders values align with corporate values, this helps employees commit and fully participate in pursuing corporate goals.

The most successful organizations have a set of values that everyone must follow. These values include, but not limited to:

- Ability
- Acceptance
- Acknowledgement
- Activity
- Achievement
- Accomplishment
- Accountability
- Action
- Accuracy
- Advance
- Adventure
- Advantage
- Agreement
- Alertness
- Ambition
- Appearance
- Appreciation
- Appropriation
- Approach
- Approval
- Art
- Attentiveness
- Attractiveness
- Audit
- Authority
- Autonomy
- Availability
- Award
- Awareness
- Balance
- Beauty
- Belonging
- Benefit
- Boldness
- Bottom line
- Boundary
- Brand
- Braveness
- Brotherhood
- Calm
- Capability
- Capacity
- Career
- Caring
- Cautiousness
- Celebration
- Certificate
- Challenge
- Championship
- Character

- Cheerfulness
- Cleanliness
- Competitiveness
- Creation
- Credibility
- Championship
- Chance
- Change
- Charisma
- Charity
- Chastity
- Children
- Choice
- Citizenship
- Clarity
- Collaboration
- Colorfulness
- Commitment
- Communication
- Community
- Compassion
- Competence
- Competency
- Competition
- Completeness
- Compliance
- Confidentiality
- Conscientious
- Consistency
- Contentment
- Content Over Form
- Contribution
- Concept
- Conclusion
- Conformity
- Content
- Continuity
- Control
- Cooperation
- Coordination
- Courage
- Culture
- Customs
- Creativity
- Criteria
- Crystallization
- Decision
- Decisiveness
- Dedication
- Definition
- Degree
- Democracy
- Desire
- Detail
- Determination
- Development

- Dignity
- Diversity
- Dignity
- Diligence
- Discernment
- Discipline
- Discovery
- Discretion
- Distance
- Dream
- Dress code
- Dynamic
- Economical
- Efficiency
- Effectiveness
- Eligibility
- Empathy
- Empowerment
- Encouragement
- Endurance
- Enlighten
- Enthusiasm
- Enjoyment
- Evolution
- Environment
- Equality
- Excellence
- Excitement
- Existence
- Expectation
- Experience
- Expertise
- Fairness
- Faith
- Fame
- Family
- Family Feeling
- Famousness
- Fearlessness
- Fertility
- Figure
- Flair
- Flexibility
- Forecast
- Forgiveness
- Form
- Foundation
- Frank
- Freedom
- Friends
- Friendliness
- Fruitfulness
- Fulfillment
- Fun
- Function
- Fundamental

- Future
- Generosity
- Gentleness
- Global
- Globalization
- Glory
- Goal
- Good will
- Goodness
- Governance
- Gracefulness
- Gratification
- Gratitude
- Gratefulness
- Greatness
- Growth
- Guaranty
- Happiness
- Hard work
- Harmony
- Health
- Help
- Heritage
- Hero
- History
- Holiness
- Holistic
- Home

- Honesty
- Honor
- Hope
- Hospitality
- Humanity
- Humility
- Idealism
- Idol
- Image
- Impartiality
- Impression
- Improvement
- Inclusiveness
- Income
- Independence
- Individuality
- Influence
- Information
- Initiative
- Inner peace
- Innovation
- Input
- Inspection
- Inspiration
- Integrity
- Intellectuality
- Intelligence
- Intention

- Involvement
- Job
- Joy
- Justice
- Justification
- Kindness
- Knowledge
- Label
- Law
- Leadership
- Learning
- Legality
- Lesson
- Level
- Life
- Listening
- Literacy
- Luck
- Love
- Loyalty
- Luxury
- Management
- Marriage
- Market
- Maturity
- Meaning
- Media
- Mediation

- Meekness
- Meeting
- Memory
- Merit
- Mindfulness
- Mission
- Moderation
- Modern
- Money
- Morality
- Motivation
- Name
- Neatness
- News
- Negotiation
- Neighborhood
- Network
- Nature
- Neutrality
- Nobleness
- Nurture
- Obedience
- Objectives
- Objectivity
- Openness
- Opportunity
- Orderliness
- Organization

- Originality
- Other
- Outcome
- Ownership
- Paradigm
- Partnership
- Passion
- Patience
- Peace
- People
- Perception
- Perfection
- Performance
- Perseverance
- Persistency
- Personality
- Persuasiveness
- Philosophy
- Picture
- Planning
- Pleasure
- Popularity
- Population
- Position
- Power
- Profit
- Practicality
- Practice

- Predictability
- Preference
- Preservation
- Principle
- Priority
- Privacy
- Privilege
- Prize
- Productivity
- Professional
- Progress
- Progressiveness
- Promotion
- Properness
- Prospect
- Prosperity
- Protection
- Punctuality
- Purpose
- Qualification
- Quality
- Quantity
- Question
- Quietude
- Record
- Recognition
- Reconciliation
- Relationship

- Registration
- Regularity
- Relaxation
- Relevance
- Reliability
- Reliance
- Religiosity
- Report
- Representative
- Reputation
- Respectfulness
- Responsibility
- Responsiveness
- Result
- Reverence
- Reverential
- Reward
- Rights
- Role
- Romance
- Rule
- Sacrifice
- Safety
- Satisfaction
- Save
- Secularism
- Security
- Selection
- Self-esteem
- Sensitiveness
- Sense
- Serenity
- Sensuality
- Seriousness
- Service
- Sexuality
- Share
- Signature
- Simplicity
- Sincerity
- Situation
- Size
- Skill
- Society
- Solution
- Soul
- Soundness
- Space
- Specialization
- Speed
- Spirit
- Spirituality
- Sportiveness
- Stability
- Standard
- Star

- Statement
- Statistic
- Status
- Stewardship
- Strength
- Structure
- Success
- Suggestion
- Supervision
- Support
- Survey
- Survival
- Sympathy
- System
- Systemization
- Target
- Teamwork
- Technology
- Thoroughness
- Thriftiness
- Thought
- Tidiness
- Time
- Timeliness
- Togetherness
- Tolerance
- Top
- Toughness

- Tradition
- Tranquility
- Trust
- Truth
- Universe
- Union
- Unity
- Understanding
- Uniformity
- Up to date
- Utilization
- Validity
- Value
- Variety
- Verification
- Victory
- View
- Virtue
- Vision
- Vocation
- Vote
- Warranty
- Wealth
- Welfare
- Willingness
- Wisdom
- Witness
- Work

Value Management is undertaken by confirming a consensus about the organization objectives and how these will be achieved by people.

Value Management provides structured approach to defining what value means to the organization.

A successful Value Management will be able to increase company's value. Company valuation or market value has two parts: tangible valuevalue that is clearly grasped by the mind; substantial rather than imaginary, like cash flow and earnings, and intangible value.

A company's value depends less on tangible assets and more on intangible ones.

Intangible value of a company is based on the market's perception of whether the company is likely to keep its promises about future growth. The goodwill or brand value of a business is an intangible value.

High valuation reflects employers have more confidence in the future of the companies than others.

Today's HR leaders are under increasing scrutiny, not only from their current employees, but also from prospective employees and employers.

HR leaders must deliver value. HR leaders know what they value. They will require implementing strategies that create value by delivering business results in efficient and effective ways. The value management strategy involves:

a. Have continuous awareness of value for the organization, establishing measures or estimates of value, monitoring and controlling them.

b. Focus on organization objectives and targets, and seek solution to achieve it.

    Most CEO's are satisfied with HR leader's strategies. Many are less satisfied with their performance.

c. Show organization purpose and provide the key to maximize innovation and outcomes

Leadership that can only produce gains for some at the expense of others is of no interest to the organization as a whole.

a. HR leaders have ability of identifying and investing in organizational and individual actions that create value. They deliver both intangible and tangible values, i.e.:

i. Intangible value: HR leaders demonstrate business performance for the organization. It includes:

Deliver consistent and predictable results: A leader's value is based on their individual productivity, the productivity of their direct reports, and their ability to retain those direct reports. HR leaders demonstrate their value by incurring fewer costs while simultaneously increasing profit.

LG Electronics Inc ousted its chief executive, replacing him with a founding family member in a bid to turn around its loss-making mobile phone business, the world's third largest.

Koo Bon-joon, the head of trading firm LG International will take over from Nam Yong, who resigned from the top job to take responsibility for poor management.

ii. Envision the corporate future: HR leaders who envision corporate future build enthusism among employees.

Globalization, regulation and technology have changed the meaning of how people development strategies impact larger business goals. Symbolic of this change is the fact that many corporations have tapped business executives to take on HR.

At the heart of every company there is business concept, mission, vision, and strategy. All organizations strive for excellent execution of their strategy hoping thereby to satisfy their customer base and show increasing profits.

iii.   Demonstrate effectiveness: Put resources where their strategy is. HR leaders help deliver and evolve employee experience that finds, motivates and retains the best and brightest.

According to a study the head count at the average HR department fell from 13 in 2007 to nine in 2008.

HR leaders focus on boosting productivity by helping employees better understand what's expected of them and by showing line leaders how to be more effective.

iv.   Improve organization capabilities: Build value through people and organization. Organization capabilities are the ways an organization applies people and processes to the tasks of competition.

23 percent employers say break-even investment returns can be considered an achievement. And around 40 percent of them say they are seeking lower risk in their investment.

b.   Tangible value: Leaders have ability to elevate organization's value and create competitive advantage. They demonstrate the invested dollar delivering a healthy payback.

In today's organization, HR leaders have significant roles. For most organizations, a new service delivery model is needed that simultaneously improve customer service, provides strategic consulting to the line leaders and reduces the cost of HR administration.

A study found 25% of HR leaders take hold of the job and proactively show Top Management how they can add tangible value. They will restructure their organization, if necessary, to meet changing circumstances.

Unfortunately, 50 percent of HR leaders in the world do not come near to fulfilling their potential.

The best way to build broad endorsement—and gain financial approval—for new investments in HR solutions is to build a comprehensive business case that pinpoints all costs, potential benefits, and even project risks.

It will act as a management tool to ensure that the project stays on course.

A successful HR leader's value is based on his/her individual productivity, the productivity of his/her direct reports, and his/her ability to retain those direct reports.

The leaders demonstrate their value by incurring fewer costs while simultaneously increasing profit. HR leader tangible value factors include:

1. Deliver higher return than his/her salary: HR leaders must return more than what they are paid, thus producing profit.

   "If employers are going to invest a billion (dollars) plus. They will have to make sure that investment generates sufficient returns to make it worthwhile," said Mirko Bibic, Bell's senior vice president.

   Experience seems to be the driver of the higher salary ranges for HR leaders who have demonstrated success in various projects and a proven knowledge of information technology, business processes, and quality control.

2. Ability to manage more number of direct reports: The more direct reports a HR leader has, the greater their impact on the organization.

   Direct report is subordinate in corporate hierarchy who reports to the HR leader.

   In a large corporation, the D*irector of Human Resources* may supervise several HR departments, each headed by a HR leader who most likely specializes in one human resources activity, such as employment and placement, compensation and benefits, training and development, or labor relations. The director may report to a top human resources executive.

Span of control measures the number of direct reports for each manager. Span of control is used to assess the organizational structure and optimize the number of direct reports by level of management and functional area.

Too many direct reports given to a HR leader could complicate communication and lengthen response time for critical decisions; it could also indicate that the company is under-managed. Too few direct reports could indicate that the HR leader is top-heavy.

The HR leader must demonstrate the building people capability competency and foster long term learning and development among his/her *direct reports*.

3. Provide higher salary for direct reports: Company values employees based on their salary. Employee's salary reflects a little more about the qualities and achievements which distinguished him/her from the competition.

    Jack Welch, Chairman and CEO of General Electric between 1981 and 2001, skillfully uses rewards to drive behavior.

    Although GE set an overall 4% salary increase as a target, base salaries can rise by as much as 25% in a year without a promotion.

    Cash bonuses can increase as much as 150% in a year, to between 20% and 70% of base pay. Stock options, once reserved for the most senior officers at GE, have been broadly expanded under Welch.

    Some 27,000 employees get them, nearly a third of GE's professional employees. More than 1,200 employees, including over 800 below the level of senior management, have received options that are worth over $1 million.

    Awareness of salary improves organizational productivity.

4.   Gain higher productivity of direct report: A direct report who is contributing to the company objectives is a liability the organization cannot afford.

A successful HR leader gets at least 10 percent more productivity out of his/her direct reports than an average leader; poor leaders get 10 percent less.

HR leaders switch from a role of personal achievement to a role where they achieve results through others. Part of achieving results through others means that the leaders who are supporting the productivity of direct reports take precedence over personal productivity.

This includes time spent monitoring and tracking progress, communicating strategies and goals, and providing feedback and coaching.

5.   Maintain low turnover level of direct reports: Turnover is a costly expense especially in lower paying job roles, for which the employee turnover rate might be the highest.

Employee turnover is a ratio comparison of the number of employees a company must replace in a given time period to the average number of total employees.

Companies take a deep interest in their employee turnover rate because it is a costly part of doing business. When a company must replace an employee, the company incurs direct and indirect expenses.

These expenses include the cost of advertising, headhunting fees, human resource costs, loss of productivity, new hire training, and customer retention—all of which can add up to anywhere from 30 to 200 percent of a single employee's annual wages or salary, depending on the industry and the job role being filled.

Poor HR leaders have 25 percent more turnover than average leaders; good HR leaders have 25 percent less.

Wages, company benefits, work ethics, and job performance are all factors that play a significant role in employee turnover.

6. Number of days a direct report position is left open before being filled: When a position is left vacant, it has the impact of lost productivity. This lost productivity and stress equates to increased costs.

    Vacancies may cause overworked employees (because they have to fill in), which may cause tire and frustration. It will lower the productivity.

    In fact, the length of many vacancies often exceeds 100 days. Key leadership positions may cost as much as a hundred thousand dollars or more per day.

    If the vacancies are a result of a slow recruiting process, it is important to realize that a failure to fill vacancies rapidly, or at lease in a timely manner, will probably also mean that all of the top candidates will be gone by the time we make a hiring decision. This result in further delay or we may refill the vacancies with lower quality hires.

    Vacancies in a single team can have an impact on many other teams (because of interdependencies), which can cascade throughout the entire company.

7. Cost to replace a direct report: If there is a vacant job in a revenue-generating position, that revenue will be lost if no one is in that position. Furthermore, if we don't have employee in the job every day, they cannot produce the value reflected in the budget allocated to them.

    The cost of a vacant position can be significant. It will show the dollar impact of voluntary turnover and involuntary turnover, or the impact of a slow recruiting process that's incapable of meeting the organizations growing talent needs.

Poor HR leaders will have more turnover and greater vacancy rates, thus producing more costs.

If the vacant position is replaced by a temporary employee, we have to determine the lower productivity of a temp compared to having a regular employee in the same position.

The higher error rates and lower productivity that any fill-in is likely to generate and add the extra costs of overtime pay.

Excessive vacancies may cause management to panic and to quickly hire some poor performers. Once the team is saddled with a large number of poor performers, we may never be able to hire any new top performers.

Organizations are unlikely to place the requisite emphasis on addressing recruitment issues if they are unaware of the negative impact such vacancies may be generating. Spending the time to avoid vacancies may have a huge Return on Investment (ROI).

A HR leader must continually create value for employees and company and it doesn't have to cost a penny. He/she may compete against his/her potential every time. Look for ways to add that which will create value for others by adding the good stuff and subtracting the bad stuff.

HR leaders build value by building employee confidence in the future.

A leader's value is based on their individual productivity, the productivity of their direct reports, and their ability to retain those direct reports. They demonstrate their value by incurring fewer costs while simultaneously increasing profit.

HR leaders must take responsibility for creating value within their organization.

They must figure out what they can and should do to create intangible value, and to make intangibles tangible.

A value is a belief, a mission, or a philosophy that is really meaningful to the company. The beliefs and moral principles lie behind a company's culture. HR believes, i.e.:

a. Believe employees must be treated with dignity: Employees are entitled to be treated with dignity and respect; they will be valued and honored as individuals. Unacceptable behaviors, i.e. unwelcome attention, intimidation, humiliation, ridicule, offence or loss of privacy would be considered seriously.

The earning power of young single women has surpassed that of their male peers in metropolitan areas around the U.S., a shift that is being driven by the growing ranks of women who attend college and move on to high-earning jobs.

In 2008, single, childless women between ages 22 and 30 were earning more than their male counterparts in most U.S. cities, with incomes that were 8% greater on average.

These women have gotten a leg up for several reasons. They are more likely than men to attend college, raising their earning potential.

Between 2006 and 2008, 32.7% of women between 25 and 34 had a bachelor's degree or higher, compared with 25.8% of men, according to the census.

And men have been disproportionately hit by heavy job losses in blue-collar industries.

HR leaders optimize the use of high performance work practices include comprehensive employee recruitment and selection procedures, incentive compensation and performance management system, and extensive employee involvement and training.

These practices can improve the knowledge, skill and ability of employees, increase their motivation, reduce shrinking and enhance retention of potential employee, while encourage non-performers to leave the company.

b.   Believe communication should be open, honest, timely, and defined: HR leaders make sure to have mastered communication framework before embarking on the journey to becoming business partner with line leaders.

The best way to improve communication and bridge gaps is through a shared set of beliefs.

c.   Believe employees should have fair and equitable compensation in the fair assessment. HR leader provides environment that demonstrates equal opportunity and brings life time employment.

When asked to name fair compensation for their work, a majority of women listed a salary that was lower than men for the same type of work, a survey found.

The study found that equally qualified women earn about 20 percent less than their male competitors, giving Germany one of the highest wage gaps between genders in the European Union.

"Many Germans, including women themselves, still see men as the main breadwinners," Juergen Schupp, a researcher, says.

d.   Believe continued growth is impossible without the trust of all of the stakeholders.

e.   Believe Human Resources are the key to the success and growth of the company: Provide the organization with well-trained and well-motivated employees who will employ their skills and abilities effectively to enable the company achieves its goals and promote a sense of belongingness and harness retention of employees.

This policy is accomplished by creating an environment that: Applauds learning, welcomes new ideas, capitalizes on differences of opinions, understands and deal with risks.

When Larry Montgomery stepped down as chief executive at Kohl's department stores to assume the Human Resources function, some thought he was being punished for poor performance.

But to the retailer and other observers, the change made sense and was in keeping with Kohl's reputation as a talent management leader.

Beliefs can be very empowering, but they can be equally disempowering. Many times our beliefs are negative, or pessimistic about a person, situation, even ourselves, and they limit us and sabotage our results.

It is important to contemplate and take time to analyze our beliefs. We have to consider whether our beliefs are helping or hindering; move us forward or hold us back.

HR leaders need to be unshaken in their belief that what they are doing is the right thing to do. This requires a certain degree of mental toughness.

Being tough is standing true to our beliefs regardless of challenges and setbacks or when others doubt us or our ability to succeed. This type of toughness is called commitment and good leaders must have it. True toughness is going over the hill without knowing what is on the other side.

Capacity

Leadership capacity can be seen whenever HR leaders have the right skills and capabilities to pull the strategy off. They must be able to take CEO where they need to go to next, with no fear.

HR leaders possess the capacity to recognize all that they perceive.

Capacity describes their ability to achieve objectives, solve problems and perform in which they function.

About 20 percent HR leaders are becoming critical members of the executive team, and 16% of them play a key role in promoting organizational growth in their companies.

HR leader capacity relates to soundness of mind and to an understanding and perception of their actions.

Capacity is personal competence, which is influenced by values, i.e. cultural, knowledge, etc. Capacity can be recognized from the ability of HR leader to make a decision and count consequences of each option (i.e. risks, burdens, and benefits).

HR leaders embody great human relations skills. They use these skills to maintain leadership effectiveness with their key stakeholders.

Competency is a requirement for HR leaders to properly perform a specific task. It encompasses a combination of knowledge, skills and behavior utilized to improve performance.

A report said one-fourth of Fortune 1,000 companies have selected their HR heads from other units (instead of its successor).

Competencies should be consistent with the organization's strategic objectives; so that HR leaders are able to successfully perform the task.

Good leadership drives sustainable performance. Companies with positive reputations for leadership tend to outperform their peers.

HR leaders are capable to position themselves as strategic partners within their respective organizations.

Most problems that occur in organizations are characterized by lack of adequate ownership and leadership.

Leaders create conditions under which all the employees can perform independently and effectively toward a common objective. Success in leadership comes when the leadership style meets with the characteristics of the employees. Leadership demonstrates:

a.   Behaviors: The process of directing the behavior of employees toward the accomplishment of common objectives. HR leaders attempt to change the culture of the organizations to fit their own personality preferences.

HR leaders know how to make ethical decisions and establish standards.

Good HR practices will help the HR leaders demonstrating the best results, whereas they must be a role model of ethical behavior themselves.

b. Actions: Direct, supervise, encourage, inspire, and coordinate.

Human Resource leaders have a vital role to play in accelerating their organizations' innovation efforts.

The purpose of HR leaders is not only to develop the plan for action but also to lead, stimulate, and challenge the discussion at the management table; to test best practices; and to define the change tools that connect the workforce into the corporate objectives.

The US and its allies accuse Tehran of seeking to develop nuclear weapons.

The UN Security Council approved a fourth round of sanctions against Iran over its nuclear programme.

There are new restrictions on foreign trade, financial services and the oil and gas sectors—the backbone of Iran's economy.

The new EU measures are banning the export to Iran of key equipment and technology for refining and for the exploration and production of natural gas.

New European investment in major sectors of the Iranian economy will also be banned. There will be restrictions on sales to Iran of any goods which could potentially have military applications.

Ships will be inspected if they are suspected of carrying illegal material.

There is expected to be tight scrutiny of Iranian banks operating in the EU.

HR leaders need to be passionate and willing to courageously stand up to the tough business, ethical, and moral issues and to be successful, need to surround with people who do the same.

c.   Inspiration: Leaders articulate their vision and ideals to employees, convincing them of the value of their ideas.

Facebook will never charge visitor to be a member and use the site.

Larry Yu, Facebook spokesman, says: "We have absolutely no plans to charge for the basic service of using Facebook."

Facebook makes its money bringing together as big of an audience as possible and then selling that audience's attention to advertisers.

If Facebook started charging users, its membership would start shrinking fast—and so would its revenues.

Everybody knows there's no such thing as a free lunch.

The fact that people keep coming back to Facebook makes it easier for Facebook to sell more ads—and make more money.

Our lunch isn't free, it's sponsored.

d.   Self-images and moral codes: HR leaders engage emotional contents, norms and values. Their behavior and self concept or self image is congruent each other.

Edward Sweeney, senior VP of National Semiconductor Corp emphasizes that the person who chooses HR as a career path to be a nurturer rather than a business person has the wrong mindset.

Self-image is crucial. It would directly or indirectly affect the outcome, i.e. decisions, actions, behavior and values.

We all have a mental picture of who we are, how we look, what we're good at, and what our weaknesses might be.

Self-image is the term used to refer to a person's mental picture of himself or herself, and is based on interactions with other people and personal life experiences.

A career is an extension of an employee's self-image, as well as a molder of it. People follow careers they can see themselves in and avoid those that do not fit with their perceptions of their talents, motives, and values.

Barack Obama has backed a controversial project to build a mosque close to the site of the former World Trade Centre in New York.

The US President said: "Muslims have the same right to practice their religion as anyone else in America."

"That includes the right to build a place of worship and a community centre on private property in lower Manhattan, in accordance with local laws and ordinances," he said.

"This is America and our commitment to religious freedom must be unshakable."

About 2,750 people were killed till September 11, 2001, when al Qaeda hijackers crashed two passenger planes into the twin towers of the World Trade Centre.

Families of the victims have campaigned to stop the mosque being built, saying it would be a betrayal of their memory.

"Al Qaeda's cause is not Islam—it is a gross distortion of Islam," he said.

"These are not religious leaders—these are terrorists who murder innocent men, women and children."

When HR leader's self-image is aligned with his or her business role, great things can happen. They are more energized and genuine; they reach out to employees more to learn and seek feedback; they build support faster and they act with a greater sense of purpose and impact.

e.   Ethics: Know what he/she ought to do when no one is watching. HR leader will showcase their ethics and values.

British troops wounded in Afghanistan have to share wards with Taliban fighters.

The troops, who have arrived at the advanced medical facility at Camp Bastion in Helmand province, found themselves lying alongside their enemies.

Injured Taliban are routinely treated at the Camp Bastion Field Hospital in line with the Geneva Convention.

"A lot of people are getting injured out there, and the last thing they want to see when they come round is the Taliban on the same ward. It's just not right."

Another said they were 'appalled' by the practice, adding: "I know we have to treat them under the Geneva Convention, but no one should have to wake up in the same place as someone who may have injured them or their mates."

The Ministry of Defense said the same level of care was provided for all patients at the Camp Bastion Field Hospital.

"This does sometimes include local nationals and enemy forces," a spokesman said.

f.   Not an authority, technical skill, nor one's I.Q: People trust and respect leader, not for the skills he/she possesses.

A skill is different from knowledge. Skill can be defined as the proficiency to apply the knowledge in practical situations and produce desired results. Acquiring skills typically require a basis of conceptual knowledge and specific practical experience.

In many cases, whenever line leaders are asked to fill in the performance appraisal forms of their subordinates, they don't show any interest. They throw it into desk and respond only when the HR leader pressurizes.

Leaders must stay current with issues, research, trends, and opportunities bearing on the fields of human resources and organizational and leadership development.

Building leadership capacity has emerged as one of the most pressing business issues of our time.

Leader And Manager

A leader is the person who is able to take the line forward in an orderly fashion by setting the example for others; provides the vision for how the line fits into the larger scheme of things, and engages the line-followers in a respectful manner.

Leadership unleashes energy, sets the vision so we do the right thing. Leaders developed through a never ending process of self-study, education, training, and experience.

But on other hand, the skills of a manager facilitate the work of an organization because they ensure that what is done is in accord with the organization's rules and regulations.

Leadership as a kind of stewardship, stresses the importance of building relationships, initiates ideas, and creates a lasting value system within the organization.

A manager is the person that designs the construct of a line, sets the expectations for the line to form, thinks through how the line might be best composed and prioritized, and ensures that the queue is executed per spec.

Management is the activity that allocates and uses resources to achieve organizational goals. Managers are more interested in efficiency, current issues and doing things right.

Management controls, arranges, does things right. Manager needs to make the best use of all resources to achieve an existing direction.

Leadership occurs any time one attempts to influence the behavior of an individual or group, regardless of the reason; while management is a kind of leadership in which the achievement of organizational goals is paramount.

More distinction between leader and manager are, but not limited to:

Leader	Manager
Seek influence - Use personal power to influence the thoughts and actions of others.	Seek control - Direct energy toward: goals, resources, organization structure, determining the problems to be solved
Leader derives his/her power from the influence s/he might have on his/her followers.	Manager has a legal power derived from his/her professional status
Attract employees - Direct energy toward guiding people toward practical solutions.	Pull, prod, push employees
Emphasize what is invisible - Intuitive, mystical understanding of what needs to be done.	Emphasize what is visible - Rationally analyze a situation, developing systematic selection of goals and purposes (what is to be done).
Focus on becoming - See themselves as a constantly evolving human being, focusing more inwardly than outwardly	Focus on doing - Doesn't insure imagination, creativity, or ethical behavior
Concerned about the spiritual	Concerned about the physical - See the world as relatively impersonal and static (black and white).
Show originality - Finds self-esteem through self-reliance and personal expression	Copy other
Mission oriented - Works best when things are somewhat disorderly or chaotic.	Goal oriented - Issues orders
Reflect on personal values to make difficult choices	Make decisions based on organization standards and practices

Focus on the whole - Work to develop harmonious interpersonal relationships.	Focus on the parts - View work as something that must be done or tolerated.
Provide meaning - See the organization as full of color, and constantly blending into new colors and shapes.	Provide form and structure - Influence people through the use of logic, facts and reason.
Play with the boundaries - View work as something challenging and exciting.	Stay within the boundaries - Innovate by 'tinkering' with existing processes
Promote instability	Preserve stability - Become anxious when there is relative disorder.
Do the right things - Focus on the decision to be made	Do things right - Focus attention on procedure
Values-led	Needs-driven - Find harmony in living up to society's, company's and family's expectations
Long-term perspective - View work as developing fresh approaches to old problems, or finding new options for old issues.	Short-term perspective - View work as an enabling process, involving a combination of ideas, skills, timing and people.
Create what does not yet exist - Innovates through flashes of insight or intuition	Administer what already exists
Steward resources	Administer resources
Train for self development	Train for skill development
Influence through love and caring, i.e. ask the right questions	Influence through power and authority

91

Seek to serve followers - "How can I serve you?"	Expect employees to serve
Show where we are going	Tell employees how they are going to get there - Use their accumulation of collective experience to get where they are going.
Deal with the interpersonal aspects of a manager's job	Plan, organize, and control - Know all the answers
Seize opportunities	Avert threats - Perpetuate group conflicts.
Interpersonal influence directed toward the achievement of goals.	Given formal authority to direct the activity of others in fulfilling organization goals.
Establish direction - Develop a vision of the future and determine the strategies for producing the desired change.	Establish the steps needed to achieve specific results, create a timeline for completing those steps, and obtain the resources necessary for goal accomplishment.
Align people - Communicate the vision to those whose cooperation is needed and form coalitions to support the change.	Establish the structure needed to implement the plan and then organize and staff - Acquire and assign the needed personnel.
Motivate and inspire - Energize people to overcome barriers to change.	Control and problem solve - Monitor results and take action to correct deviations from the plan.
Amplify strengths - Develop themselves through personal mastery, struggling for psychological and social change.	Reduce weaknesses

Deal with change, inspiration, motivation, and influence.	Deal more with carrying out the organization's goals and maintaining equilibrium.
Not possess the formal power to reward or sanction performance	Have to rely on formal authority to get employees to accomplish goals.
Produce change - Disrupt the status quo and encourage creativity and innovation.	Produce order - Establish stability, predictability, and consistency.
Deal with getting people to do what needs to be done	Task and process oriented - Communicate through 'messages' heightening the emotional response
Cope with change - Able to tolerate aggressive interchanges, encouraging emotional involvement with others	Cope with complexity
Execute the win with passion - Coach and mentors others	Set up the win with perfection for his/her team
Harness the power inherent in human motivation.	Rely on authority to make things happen
Leading people - Act as role model	Managing work - "Here's what we're going to do!"
Authority is represented in his/her capacity to make his/her followers want to achieve given goals.	Use authority to boss people.
Have followers	Have subordinates
Facilitate decision - Empowers	Make decision
Power comes from personal charisma	Power comes from formal authority

Appeal to heart - Take in emotional signals from others, making them mean something in the relationship with an individual; often passionate about their work.	Appeal to head
His/her energy is passion	His/her energy is control - Communicate with subordinates indirectly, using 'signals'
Proactive - Values creativity	Reactive - Feel threatened by open challenges to their ideas, are troubled by aggressiveness
Establish clear vision, direction, goals, efficacy, purpose, and the trust-inspiration of the followers.	Concerned with short-term achievement by controlling the workers' performance.
Motivator - Persuade by selling	Drill Sergeant - Persuade by telling
Leadership style: Transformational	Leadership style: Transactional
Excitement for work - Influence people through altering moods, evoking images and expectation.	Money for work
Preference – striving, invite speaking out	Preference – Focus on how things need to be done.
Voluntary membership	Demand unquestioning obedience
Want achievement - Focus on what needs to be done, leaving decisions to people involved	Want results - Relate to people by the role they play in a sequence or in a decision making process.

Take risk - Risks are necessary to make changes happen	Minimize risk - Have an instinct for survival; seek to minimize risks and tolerate the mundane.
Break rules - Often jump to conclusions, without a logical progression of thoughts or facts	Make rules - Impose discipline, Keeping people on their toes
Use conflict - Use of conflict will impact on relationship quality	Avoid conflict - Develop themselves through socialization, seeking to maintain the balance of social relations.
Show new direction - search for opportunities for change.	Use existing direction - See themselves as an integral part of their social structure and social standard
Seek truth - Reach out	Establish truth — Emphasize information availability
His/her concern - What is right, teaching archetype	His/her concern - Being right
Give credit — Reward, pay for performance. People learn to perform certain behaviors through either the rewards or negative consequences that follow their behavior.	Take credit - Demand respect
Take blame: Leaders learn from mistakes. Within those failures are the seeds for improvement. Look at them as opportunities for constructive growth.	Blame others - Have a low level of emotional involvement in their work.
Create future - Leaders will not just see the future, they will make it	Maintain present - Limit and define

Plan from imagination	Plan from memory
Motivate people - Relate to people in intuitive and empathic ways.	Manage things - See themselves as conservators and regulators of an existing order of affairs; belong to the organization; believe in duty and responsibility to their organization.
Process driven - Do not take things for granted.	Product driven - Take things for granted.
Value anchored - Stay grounded in their core values	Technically anchored - Lead toward the technical side
Opportunity driven - Sometimes react to the mundane and routine as an affliction.	Crisis driven - Focus on the past, tend to be abusive
Forms intensive one-on-one relationships, which may be of short duration; often have mentors	Form moderate and widely distributed personal attachments with others
Advance recognition - Excel at creating opportunities to provide rewards, recognition and thanks	Use punishment - Learn that punishment is more effective
Network - Endeavor connectivity	Hierarchy - Information control
Connection: Employees learn culture by interacting with other employees.	Rank - Reach up/down
Flexible – Have ability to flex, alter and adapt their style according to the situation, context and circumstances.	Rigid - Military archetype, Not interested in new answers

Consult - Counsel and coach	Performance review - Automatic annual raises. The primary role of management within an organization is to align the employees' performance with the organization's strategic objectives.
Wholistic – Consider matters from all point of view	Mechanistic – Not see things interrelated
Systemic – Approach from different perspectives	Compartmental – Approach from divided and small thought
Facilitating - Nourishing environment for growth	Commanding - Order giving
Inspire in its overall vision regardless the reasons or goals behind it	Anchor on the realization of a concrete plan in a specific time frame
Innovate - Expect members to be innovative if they do not know the direction	Administer – Prioritize procedures
Have a wider vision of the horizon with a focus on people	Focus on systems and structure of the organization.

Good managers do not necessarily make good leaders and good leaders do not necessarily make good managers. Each has a distinct role.

Managers need to be leaders; their workers need vision and guidance. Leaders also need to be good managers of the resources entrusted to them.

Leadership process seems to be synonymous with management practices in the sense that both managers and leaders hold the same responsibility towards their organization, and have a direct authority over the latter's employees; thus, leadership style can be also applied to management style. HR leader must be able to:

a. Be grounded about themselves: Leaders need a deep understanding of corporate culture, and powerful tools for rallying executives to work effectively with variables.

b. Communicate effectively with others: While HR leaders are aware of their companies' cultures, they might be unsure about how it is maintained, transmitted, or influenced.

c. Hold individuals accountable for their actions: Since HR leaders are making themselves accountable for achieving a specific goal, i.e. telling exactly what steps they are taking each day to achieve that goal, it will motivate employees take responsibility on the consequences of their actions.

d. Facilitate team needs, wants, and performance: HR leaders assist company in understanding their corporation's identities more clearly and managing them more effectively.

   There are no problem people, only problem processes. Brainstorms, clearer descriptions of processes and expectations, and kindly suggestions and hints will cure all misunderstandings.

   Well-meaning and intelligent people at all levels in the company will put professional behavior and team goals ahead of personal agendas.

e.	Understand how those actions fit into the bigger picture of the organization and what steps need to taken, when, with whom, and how.

It's not instinctive to spend personal or conscious effort to find and groom people we really believe can replace us. We have to think about time when our mortality may come, and we are not really rewarded by the business.

Business environment is increasingly complex. With innovation in technology, emerging markets, cultural and demographic shifts, tomorrow's leaders will have to be faster, smarter and well-rounded.

Most poor leaders have in common is they're not consciously aware that they're poor leaders.

And if they are aware of it on some level, they're probably not willing to admit it to anyone, least of all themselves. That's because *nobody* wants to believe *they're* the problem. Good HR leaders maximize the productivity and potential of employees, including, i.e.:

a.	Utilize and develop employee's talents rather than their weaknesses. HR leaders build sufficient human resource capacity.

They will offer solution what to do with the mobilisation of the excess human resource capacity for export.

b.	Spend more time with their best employees, not with their least productive employees.

Some people are excellent at performing a job, but cannot get to the next level of managing people. Part of HR leader's job can be to mentor them and provide them with a goal that they can perhaps apply to another position in the future.

HR leaders sometimes assume too much of importance in the organizational matters when their job is to support productivity of the line leaders. It may waste of resourcetime, energy and money.

Every organization wants to attract, motivate, and retain the most qualified employees and match them to jobs for which they are best suited.

c.   Don not treat everyone the same—Treat each employee as the employee would like to be treated. He/she has to get to know the employees well.

Google Inc., which runs the world's most popular Internet search engine, was ordered to defend itself against a lawsuit by a former manager who said he was fired for being too old, clearing the way for a trial.

The California Supreme Court unanimously agreed that a trial court erred in dismissing a complaint by Brian Reid, who was hired in 2002 as a director of operations and engineering, and fired less than two years later at age 54 after being told he was not a good 'cultural fit.'

Radical transformation of HR functions has been instigated by forces: Pressures to reduce costs, higher expectations of customers, the constant drive to meet global competitive challenges, and opportunities offered by advancements in information technology. HR leaders accelerate the transformation of the HR function. A successful HR leader results admired organizations, that characterized by:

1.   Satisfy with the quality of leadership at both line leaders and Top Management levels: HR leaders assist the CEO set the company's strategy and its long-term goals and objectives.

The CEO's actions and reputation have a major impact on inside and outside views of the organization and affect the organization's ability to attract resources from its environment.

"In the long run, the best thing we can do to delight customers is to delight our own employees," says James Goodnight, a CEO.

"If we have really happy, dedicated employees who love their jobs and love to come to work every day, they will take care of our customers."

2. Less tolerant of inappropriate leadership behavior: HR leaders need to understand their approach to the leadership role. Employees who come from different cultures may have different approaches and different views of what is appropriate or inappropriate leadership behavior.

   The combined perspectives of several cultures can lead to even greater success than viewing the world and its opportunities through only one lens.

3. Place more value on leadership development: Leadership capability development is increasingly a vital business priority.

   Adding leadership capability is never a short-term endeavor; hiring from the outside takes time, and the incidence of new executive derailment in major corporations is frightening.

   A few years ago, American Airlines was a success story because they used a lot of complex technologies and heavyweight algorithms to do scheduling, profitability and pricing.

   Southwest is later making American's life really miserable with a very simplified model and pricing schedule.

   Application of IT to American Airlines' business model may not be delighting many people anymore.

4. Put more emphasis on efforts that are linked to strategic business goals and supported by reward programs.

   For HR to be strategic, it must be in tune with overall business goals and have a key role in shaping them.

   When a behavior is rewarded, it is repeated and the association eventually becomes part of the culture. A simple thank you from an executive for work performed in a particular manner, molds the culture.

A study found 27% of HR leaders do not perceive themselves to be close enough to the core business.

5. Use competency models and a wide variety of developmental programs in selecting and advancing their leaders: HR leader succession can be risky for organization, if it's not planned correctly.

No longer can CEO let management run HR leader succession planning without tight oversight, including setting specific standards and requirements, taking responsibility for results, and exercising maturity of the candidates.

6. Demonstrate more emotional intelligence: Emotional Intelligence, or EQ as it is referred to, is what we used to call 'people skills' and is about how aware we are of others, and how we interact with other people.

A study found 94% employees believe their leaders do not have the necessary leadership qualities and therefore need to develop these vital characteristics.

The most important leadership qualities are emotional intelligence (36%) and the ability to motivate staff (34%).

Emotional Intelligence is increasingly relevant to organizational development and developing people, because it provides a new way to understand and assess people's behaviors, management styles, attitudes, interpersonal skills, and potential.

One of the most effective tools to promote successful change is organization development.

With the strategic link between organization development and HR, organization development fosters the development of a healthy and productive workforce.

HR leaders should put their focus on building organizational learning, skills and workforce productivity, the effective use of organization development to help achieve company business goals.

HR leaders need the conceptual ability to see the organization and its environment, present and future, and formulate strategies for continued success and growth of the organization. In today's business environment, the HR function has been engaged in nothing less than a process of reinventing itself in many companies as evidenced by:

a.   HR functions becoming both centralized and decentralized: HR responsibilities, once tasked to HR staff, slowly are being delegated to managers.

Many organizations have already begun outsourcing key HR services on a temporary, recurring or permanent basis. Others have restructured their HR delivery systems in an attempt to save money, improve effectiveness and/or ward off threats of outsourcing.

For example, the U.S. Department of Defense (DoD) has undertaken HR regionalization on a grand scale.

In 1994, DoD made the decision to regionalize its HR delivery system. A primary purpose of regionalization was to address existing HR structural deficiencies that prevented greater efficiency in service delivery.

The DoD service ratio was then 1 HR professional for 61 employees (1:61). DoD plans ultimately to increase this ratio to 1:100 through regionalization that includes the full implementation of technological enhancements.

Annually, approximately $150M dollars of personnel savings and avoided costs are expected.

To be a strategic partner, HR leader must become players in the business operations, playing prospective roles rather than being passive admonishers.

Unfortunately, they are still reacting to the requirements of the organization and not participating in its design.

b.   Roles and responsibilities of line leaders and Human Resource leaders are being redefined: No one can influence business strategy if it doesn't know how the business works.

The HR leader needs to tap into Top Management networks and ensure that HR has a voice in the decision-making process. Otherwise, HR will only ever implement strategy, rather than shape it.

c.   Business needs receiving higher priority in the delivery of HR services.

Top performing companies successfully leverage their organization more effectively than rivals and derive over 64% more profit per employee than next-tier performers.

d.   Many of transactional activities of HR functions being automated streamlined and reengineered, thus freeing HR leaders for strategic and managerial challenges.

It's the HR leader's responsibility to make sure technology is being deployed in a way that allows employees to have better access the company's service.

e.   Ratio of HR staffs to employees decreases: The change is likely due to layoffs and reductions-in-force that have not been accompanied by proportional adjustments in HR staff levels.

HR employees have been kept on board to deal with the fallout from job eliminations, hiring freezes, etc.

The median ratio of HR staff per 100 employees is around 1.0.

A study shows after some dips to 0.9, the 2003 HR staff ratio climbed back up to the 1.0.

There is no ideal HR staff ratio because of a number of factors—how much employee we have in HR functions, economies of scale, and the extent to which outsource HR can have impact.

HR staff ratio—the number of HR staff relative to total number of employees—is an important metric for budget planning purposes because it measures the efficiency of HR department operations.

Since a HR leader has the key to success, it will be used to differentiate their skills from others.

HR leaders will influence organization to identify its core values, and make them the foundation for its interactions.

They have clear expression of a value, and values are visible through the actions people take, not their talk.

The leaders manifest values in daily decision making, and the norms or relationship guidelines which informally define how people interact with each other.

More than one-third (34%) of HR managers and other HR staff feel they are not close enough to the business.

Yet two-thirds (65%) of HR departments describe themselves as primarily administrative, and only 35% as strategic.

4th

Greatness Cored Leadership

One of the significant processes in Human Resources Management is leadership.

Leadership in Human Resources Management reflects an individual's abilities to efficiently direct employees toward achieving pre-set goals given by organization or company.

Leadership styles in Human Resources Management is mainly defined by the culture of the company as well as the leader's values, skills, and the given situation that might favor a certain style over others. The leadership style includes, but not limited to:

a.   Laissez-Faire Leadership: This style can be effective in situations where employees are highly qualified in an area of expertise.

b.   Democratic Leadership: HR leaders will share decision making and problem solving responsibilities with employees.

c.   Situational Leadership: It is utilized to fit character of employees and organization and situations appear.

d.   Bureaucratic Leadership: HR leaders ensure that their employees follow procedures exactly. This is a very appropriate style for work involving serious safety risks or large sums of money.

e.   Autocratic Leadership: The leaders retain as much power and decision-making authority as possible.

f.   People-Oriented or Relations-Oriented Leadership: Focus on organizing, supporting and developing the people in the team. It tends to lead to good teamwork and creative collaboration.

g.   Task-Oriented Leadership: The HR leader will actively define the work and roles required, put structures in place, plan, organize and monitor.

h.   Transactional Leadership: The employees agree to obey the HR leader totally when they take a job on. The organization pays the employees, in return for their effort and compliance.

i.   Servant Leadership: Servant leaders as individuals with a natural inclination to serve. Such people make a conscious choice to lead to serve rather than lead to gain power or acquire material possessions.

The core perspective of servant leadership is that supervising has less to do with directing other people and more to do with serving them. This style stresses 'service to others' is the most efficient and effective way to lead.

They try to serve their organizations through characteristic such as listening, empathy, healing relationships, awareness, persuasion, conceptualization, foresight, stewardship, commitment to human resource development, and commitment to building community.

j.   Transformational Leadership: Inspire the employees with a shared vision of the future. The HR leaders don't necessarily lead from the front, as they tend to delegate responsibility amongst their teams.

A successful leader is skilled at several styles and instinctively understanding when to use them. The more leadership styles that he/she is able to master, the better he/she will become.

Success in leadership comes when the leadership style is matched with the characteristics of the organization and employees.

The people within the organization and those we bring in who are the indispensable asset, who figure out the best path to greatness.

The purpose of leadership is to realize the maximum value of human potential. Leadership has never been an easy proposition. Throughout history observers have wondered if there were enough capable leaders to manage the challenges facing all types of organizations.

Today, business or organization faces something of a 'perfect storm' of problems that have profound implications for current and future leaders.

Jim Collins, an author said: "Good is the enemy of great. And that is one of the key reasons why we have so little that becomes great."

We are all born with the potential for greatness. HR leaders inspire greatness in employees.

Greatness is the core of HR leadership. For a world class organization, sense of greatness is the core of actions.

Great achievers are people who have had the greatest influence

on others, those who have made significant contributions, those who have simply made things happen.

HR leaders make greatness happens. They use their talents to make the company, more hopeful workplace.

Leadership skills and behaviors are necessary and the role of leaders must change in order to accommodate the evolving organizational mindset. Greatness-cored leadership is the answer, since this leadership style demonstrates a set of sense of greatness that makes up a successful HR leader.

Greatness-cored leadership is a leadership style that implies HR leaders, employees and the company to truly act with sense of greatness. It consists of at least five attributes, i.e. growth, responsibility, entrepreneurship, authenticity, and trust.

To be successful, company must grow. HR leaders' strategic role in company growth includes:

i.   Show high quality of development: Provide framework for the expansion of human capital within the organization.

Companies need Human Resource Development taht is aimed to help employees develop their personal and organizational skills, knowledge, and abilities. Human Resource Development includes such opportunities as employee training, employee career development, performance management and development, coaching, succession planning, key employee identification, and organization development.

HR leaders develop and translate the mission, vision, values and competitive strategy of the organization into an integrated deployment strategy, and provide the necessary guide to focus and utilize the talents of the organization.

Everyone wants to grow and develop their skills. The vast majority of employees don't just want a job to pay the bills, but rather a career that makes use of their strengths while helping them develop their weaknesses.

We have to start early and think way ahead. It takes three to five years from the time we start to impose the exposure, training and techniques before we begin to get returns. And if we are not thinking about the competitive business demands that will dominate in the next 20 years, we can't prepare people for them.

Development is a combination of training and education that ensures the continual improvement and growth of both the individual and the organization. HR leader should drive the process between training and learning.

The leader focuses on developing the most superior workforce so that the organization and employees can accomplish their work goals.

A successful development program fosters competency sharing based development, self-learning based development, company contribution based development, 3rd party sponsorship based development, and employee participation.

ii.   Advance empowerment: The process of enabling or authorizing an employee to think, behave, take action, and control work and decision making in autonomous ways.

HR can provide a crucial supporting role to leaders who are focused on growth.

Empowerment is the state of feeling self-empowered to take control of one's own destiny.

Empowerment evolves challenge, delegation, etc.

iii.   Show the purpose: HR leaders provide programs and processes that govern employee treatment, communications, support systems and services which promote employment conditions conducive to high levels of employee satisfaction, motivation and productivity.

Purpose demonstrates success, accomplishment, etc.

The common thread among great business achievers is that success is not their ultimate goal. They build causes; not businesses. They are crusaders, propelled by a vision to make the world a much better place, with conviction and perseverance to make it happen.

iv.   Visioning: Attain organizational excellence by developing and inspiring the true potential of company's human capital and providing opportunities for growth.

"I was worth about over a million dollars when I was twenty-three; over ten million dollars when I was twenty-four;

over a hundred million dollars when I was twenty-five and it wasn't that important because I never did it for the money." Steve Jobs, CEO, Apple.

Visioning includes giving hope, passion, inspiration, etc.

A HR leader is not only expected to have a clear vision on the future of the organization but also required to communicate this vision with the employees and make them active participants in its realization, by providing them with both directions and motivation.

The heart of leadership is the willingness to assume responsibility. A responsible leader must recognize that he/she is responsible for the decisions made by him/her and therefore he/she should analyze the structure of how decisions are made within the organization.

This attitude will attract individual responsibility of the employees for making sound and ethical decision. Take responsibility for their actions.

HR leader is one of the most important key to open a lock hanging on the door of success in the organization. If the HR leaders are efficient enough to handle and to take out best from their employees and the organization, they can achieve more from their target goals.

HR leader plays a very important role in hierarchy, and also in between the higher management and low level employees. Stated below are traits that foster the responsibilities of HR leader:

i.   Accountability: Responsibility is developed through accountability.

Leadership is not possible without a strong sense of accountability.

While the organization as a whole is accountable for results, within the organization the issue of accountability is directly linked to a person, an individual who is charged with and accepts responsibility for the success or failure of strategies. Accountability is a personal attribute.

ii.   Courage: A HR leader will take a courageous decision; when other not. The key to courageous and conscious action is how one responds to what arises on the path

    Leaders with courage take risk, consider the right time to make decisions, see consequences as a challenge, demonstrate sense of hero, etc.

    Greatness is establishing the habit of risk taking.

    HR leaders accept responsibility for their decisions and actions. They are also advocates for the profession by engaging in activities that enhance its credibility and value.

iii.   Confidence: An employee holds a responsible position in the organization; it's because he/she makes the organization exists. He/she can make or break an organization hence on his/her shoulders lye responsibility.

    Whether challenged with taking on a startup, turning a business around, or inheriting a high-performing unit, a leader's success or failure is determined within the first 90 days on the job.

iv.   Focus: Human Resource focus addresses key human resource practices—those directed toward creating and maintaining a high performance workplace and toward developing employees to enable them and the organization to adapt to change.

    It requires Human Resource Development and management that work in an integrated way, i.e. align with organization's strategic objectives and action plans.

    Human Resource focus includes work environment and employee support climate.

As business becomes increasingly competitive, the marketplace is calling out a new brand of *HR* which requires a more *entrepreneurial* approach to.

HR leaders create a compelling vision of where the organization is headed. They also continuously communicate how to proceed, and energetically guide the development of the organization to advance the vision.

Sense of entrepreneurship shows the ability to define importance, and urgency. The changing nature of Human Resource Management fosters the development of entrepreneurial activities, which include:

i.   Standard: Standard is now at the very core of what makes business competes worldwide.

Standard is aimed to support efficiency, as well as an ability to adapt to changing conditions.

Standards maintain uniformity that eliminates barriers to trade, fosters the realization of scale benefits, and prevents races to the bottom.

The standards allow diversity that tailors the values to particular requirements.

The evolving role of standards puts focus on Human Resources Development. Standards have allowed companies to expand the markets for their products and services worldwide and to gain greater benefits.

Standard is one of the most developed and useful tools in supporting companies in Human Resource leader efforts.

Standard that provides a guide to the good Human Resource disciplines within the organization includes:

a.   Quality: HR leaders aspire to consistently achieve the highest level of quality in all products and services and to be premier in the chosen business. They aim for greatness.

Quality is the outcome of the sum of all of the features and characteristics of a program, process, or service that impact their ability to meet or surpass the needs and requirements of a customer.

Quality is a measure of excellence; quality defines desirable characteristics of a product, a process, or a service.

HR practices normally deal with people, performance, information, and organization because they create an infrastructure that affects employees, customers, line managers, and employers.

Quality refers also to the character traits of an individual. One of the qualities of a leader is his or her ability to share the mission and vision in such a way that employee wants to follow and accomplish the goals.

When HR practices align with strategies, goals are met and sustained.

b. Ethics—Standard that builds ethical accomplishments. Adherence to the standard for HR leader's work-related conduct requires a commitment to the lifelong effort to act ethically; to encourage ethical behavior of employees, and to consult with others concerning ethical problems.

HR leaders are expected to exhibit individual leadership as a role model for maintaining the highest standards of ethical conduct. They set the standard and become an example for others.

c. Principle—Standard that clarifies both the general principles and the decision rules that cover most situations encountered by HR leaders.

d. Value—Standard that identifies a common set of values upon which HR leaders build their professional work

e. Excellence: Organizations that desire to become the standard of excellence should be reflected in the outstanding results, show continuously as engine for success and catalyst for positive change.

A research found seventy percent of the people in the world are average, ten percent are winners, and twenty percent fall into the bottom third, with fifteen percent of them suffering the indignity of being born into a circumstance that they can't get out of, and five percent, who could but won't (the worst kind).

Companies have to streamline the business systems to stay competitive and excel.

f.   Security: Standard that has as primary goal the welfare and protection of the employees and organizations;

g.   Procedure: A system requires documentation of both management and technical activities.

Procedure provides a standard working tool that can be used to document routine quality system management and technical activities.

Procedures are intended to be specific to the organization or facility whose activities are described and assist that organization to maintain their quality control and quality assurance processes and ensure compliance with governmental regulations.

A research found 75% of organizations struggle with paperwork and compliance.

If not written correctly, the procedures are of limited value. The best written procedures will fail if they are not followed.

Therefore, the use of procedure needs to be reviewed and re-enforced by HR leaders, preferably the line leaders.

Procedures also need to be readily accessible for reference in the work areas of those individuals actually performing the activity, either in hard copy or electronic format, otherwise procedures serve little purpose.

h.   Service: HR leaders are responsible for adding value to the organizations they serve and contributing to the success of the organizations.

They create and sustain an environment that encourages employees and the organization to reach their fullest potential in positive and productive manner.

The most important thing of customer care is to make it easy for the customer to complain. And make sure the leaders respond to any customer complaints personally and promptly.

Service emphasizes urgency, response, communication, etc.

ii.   Spirituality: Many HR leaders are still applying the Industrial Age control model to knowledge employees.

Industrial Age was a period of great change. New industries developed rapidly as a result of a number of new inventions and the way in which things were produced, and the way in which people lived and worked, changed rapidly as a result of these developments.

Because many in positions of authority do not see the true worth and potential of their people and do not possess a complete, accurate understanding of human nature, they manage people as they do things.

This lack of understanding also prevents them from tapping into the highest motivations, talents, and genius of people.

Spirituality demonstrates state of transcendence that focuses on honesty, beauty, goodness, unity, etc.

iii.   Competence: Understanding of humor calls for a specific competence. Competence in humor can be considered as competence in communication.

It involves knowledge of communication strategies, social norms, etc.

HR leaders have a positive and constructive sense of humor. They can laugh at themselves and with others. If it's appropriately funny and they can use humor to ease tension.

iv. Connectivity: If HR leaders manage employees like things, they stop believing that leadership can become a choice. Most people think of leadership as a position and therefore don't see themselves as leaders.

Connectivity builds good team work, partnership, community, followership, etc.

To be successful, HR leaders should display authenticity in their character.

Authenticity in HR is about telling the truth. And that truth has to be grounded in something more than the flavor of the mouth. It has to be based on true experience. HR leaders can't expect people to believe them if they change their mind with the prevailing winds.

If they want others to listen, participate, and follow them, then they need to be honest and authentic: 'walk the walk and talk the talk.'

Being authentic is central to trust. Leadership requires authentic and effective interpersonal communication that can realize the full potential of individual and organization.

Being an authentic leader is about being true to themselves and thei values—not presenting a false corporate image or trying to emulate the leadership style or characteristics of others.

The leaders are honest, and able to speak out to right wrongs, admit to personal weaknesses and own up to their mistakes. HR leaders authenticity can be seen though:

i. Integrity: This word is important in all professions, particularly management positions and Human Resources.

Human Resources leaders have important role in the company; they should be the conscience of organization to ensure that all the actions that are taken are fair and within the restrictions of the law.

Human Resources leaders should be objective and balance the needs of employees and organization, and ultimately the HR leaders need to do what is best for the company.

HR leaders who have good personal integrity show honesty, transparencyopen for examination, etc.

ii.   Wisdom: Being a HR leader means learning how to wear many different 'hats.'

Multitasking may create more problems of efficiency than increasing productivity.

It is to maximize productivity with minimum employees, and multitasking seems to do just that.

Though it may have captured the attention of employers, it hasn't won over employees. While it stretches employees, it also helps them in becoming more efficient and skilled.

HR leaders will advance win-win attitude, show wisdom in their daily actions, etc.

The employee-employer relationship is such that there is mutual benefit. The employer meets all the required expectations while the employee attacks the key results areas so as to deliver results befitting of the benefits accruing to their name.

When there is a gap between expectations and delivery on either side, friction is inevitable resulting usually in the ending of the relationship prematurely.

The longer we keep our employees, the better it is for us as we do not have to keep training new people ourselves but existing employees who carry the business genetics keep passing them forward.

iii.   Maturity: Organizations no longer compete in terms of financial capital only, but increasingly also in human capital. Mature Human Capital Management is increasingly regarded as a significant factor in sustaining competitive advantage in high performing organizations.

The relationship between human capital investments and a company's business performance should be measured by Return on Investments (ROI).

Dynamic market conditions require companies to have competitive workforce and processes, practices that are consistently aligned to business strategy.

HR leaders should ensure the systemic integration of practices, processes and data, and meaningful reporting that enables exceptional, cost-effective Human Capital Management.

Matured HR Management refers to the proactive management of highly co-dependant core practices that when integrated, have greater value than they do individually.

HR function maturity implies organizational discipline and rigorous methodology with regard to doing business and uncompromising HR data integrity and information management that allow critical business decisions to be made about people.

Maturity is attribute that fosters consistency, humility, self-worth, belonging, expectation, responsibility, accountability, equality, etc.

iv. Excellence: Organizations that have innovative and competitive management strategies and consistent with the fast-pace changing marketplace where only the most adaptable, resilient, and customer-centered organizations will survive.

Most people are average, and that's because they only do what they like to do. Excellent HR leaders are separated from the rank. It's because they are in the right circumstance, and they have established the habit of discipline.

v. Identity: While HR leaders learn from their past, they do not let the past define them. Nor do they let their current circumstances dictate their future. Persinal identity is their constant quest to reinvent themselves, their lives and their businesses that catapult them above the rest.

"Credit goes to the man in the arena whose face is marred by dust and sweat and blood: who strives valiantly—who knows the great enthusiasms, the great devotions, who spends him/herself in a worthy cause, who at the best knows in the end the triumph of high achievement, and who at the worst, if he fails, he fails while daring greatly, so that his place shall never be with those cold and timid souls who have never known victory nor defeat," said Teddy Roosevelt

Identity describes one's acceptance, character, etc.

vi.   Control: Most of the employees do not realize their aspect of the job and just work on what they are asked to without understanding the head and tail. It is the employee's duty to apprehend why they are performing a particular task and what should be the end result.

Control needs understanding of discipline, awareness, direction, etc.

vii.   Commitment: HR leaders must strive to meet the highest standards of competence and commit to strengthen their competencies on a continuous basis.

They should expand their knowledge of Human Resource Management to further their understanding of how the organizations function. And advance their understanding of how organizations work.

Commitment to leadership development is not supported at the executive level, a study indicated.

Only 32% said executives demonstrate strong commitment to leadership development and are willing to finance that commitment, while 81% are challenged to persuade managers to release high potentials for development assignments.

Therefore, lack of leadership is becoming a threat to business growth.

HR leaders with high commitment on their duties demonstrate actions, presence, etc.

Today's competitive marketplace requires Human Resource leaders to have an expanded role in the organization due to increasing importance of relationship capital.

Trust is the essential ingredient for a healthy organizational relationship between the employees and the HR leader.

Trust breeds confidence and conviction.

A HR leader must be trustworthy. The leader must examine his/her motives and intent, and know him/herself to be trustworthy, that emphasizes:

i. Credibility: A successful HR business requires two important words to keep in mind: credibility and trust. Customers must be able to trust us and our organization. Credibility comes before trust and is part of how trust is created.

    HR leaders know that trust and credibility must be created and earned. One of the best ways to create credibility is to be endorsed by others. Leaders credibility reflects:

a. Honesty: Honest behavior also enhances reputation. Honesty is the prerequisite of trust and credibility. Dishonesty will bring credibility gap, which increases costs and ultimately deters development.

b. Competence: HR leaders' challenge today is to gain and use influence to become a better strategic partner, to determine where the organization is headed, and to get out in front and use the Human Resources function to help lead the way.

    Competency demonstrates the existence of intellect, knowledge, thought, learning, etc

Commit to continuous learning, skills development and application of new knowledge related to both Human Resource Management and the organizations they serve.

Competent leaders are consistent. Change and improvements are the keys to organizational survival and success. Consistent means that they are reliable, predictable, and use judgment as often, i.e. as consistently as possible. In this sense, HR leaders should be fair and rational.

ii.   Fairness: HR leaders are responsible for promoting and fostering fairness for all employees and the organizations.

Honesty is the central point of the sharing of information. An opinion is necessarily sharp, biting and ruthless, because it is honest. There is no such thing as an unbiased view. Hence it is important to have a plurality of views.

Fairness will work if HR leaders emphasize openness.

iii.   Sincerity: Recognition provides the motivation that can sustain employee performance and engagement across the organization's value

Trustworthy leaders display loyalty to employees, and organization. The leaders will produce loyal employees. They demonstrate a willingness to go out of their way to help others save face, to avoid embarrassing situations, or avoid presenting substandard work.

People trust a leader who brings his/her sincerity in the form of recognition, hard work, loyalty, duty, devotion, seriousness, care, empathy, example, listening, counsel, protecting, simplicity, giving, forgiveness, encouragement, harmony, balance, ownership, etc.

iv.   Respect: Treat people with dignity, respect and compassion to foster a trusting work environment free of harassment, intimidation, and unlawful discrimination.

Hr leaders ensure employees have the opportunity to develop their skills and competencies. They assure an environment of inclusiveness and a commitment to diversity in the organizations.

They believe that a healthy work environment will provide a workplace with no discrimination, no domination by individual employee on others, and accept plurality.

v. Courage: The greater the change and more difficult the challenges, the more relevant they become.

Courageous trait indicates the willingness to seek opportunity for change, creativity, flexibility, adaptability, etc.

Company performance and productivity is an indicator of the satisfaction level of its employees.

The above set of attributes that successful leaders possess, articulate them in ways that could be transferred across all leaders, and create leadership development experiences to ensure that future leaders possess these attributes.

5th

GROWTH

Companies are not only scrambling for the talent they need to keep growing, they tend to have a strong focus on issues such as meeting customer needs, delivering quality products and staying innovative. A lot of HR leaders don't have much expertise in these areas. It requires a different kind of strategic HR to drive growth.

"It can be hard for HR leaders to keep up in high-growth companies," said Jay Jamrog, i4cp's Senior Vice President.

The HR leader's job today is tougher than ever before. It has become the growth engine for business. Because of developments such as competitive cost pressure, HR leader should strengthen the understanding of the labor market, accelerate organizational adjustment, improve competitiveness of products/service to enhance the company profit margins and ease upward pressure on costs.

HR leaders who envision growth build enthusiasm among employees.

"You can't grow long-term if you can't eat short-term. Anybody can manage short, they can also manage long. Balancing those two things is what management is," Jack Welch of GE said.

Everyone in the organization wants good people. Therefore, sometimes, the negotiating power is shifting to the employees from the employer.

Most organizations will be presented with the challenge of developing the necessary skills and areas of expertise to enable them to cope with the demands on them, master technological opportunities at their disposal, learn how to exploit modern management concepts and optimize value to all the stakeholders they intend to serve.

A study found that HR leader is not reacting fast enough to the strategic challenges related to organizational growth. They indicate the emphasis on growth in their organizations is changing the meaning of strategic HR.

Most great business leaders have had growth mindset. They build an appropriate organizational climate and culture for the growth and development of the employees and encourage organizational citizenship among the employees.

Facebook founder Mark Zuckerberg announced his social networking behemoth passed 500 million active users today (July 21, 2010).

Facebook's growth continues at a prodigious rate. The site passed 250 million users nearly a year ago to date, announcing that milestone on July 13, 2009.

The job of enhancing the value of people in organizations is everyone's job, not the job of Human Resource leaders or the human resource department.

Human Resources leaders are expected to come to the table with highly developed strategic, financial, analytical, and technical skills.

They are separate and distinct from conventional growth challenges and are addressed through leadership development.

To compete in the global arena, employers demand dramatic improvement in efficiencies. To approach it HR leaders demonstrate their capacity to:

a.　　Build an organization that makes significant profits: Train employees to behave and think as business people.

World class organizations demonstrate 13% lower HR costs per employee and 15% fewer HR staff.

In today's challenging business environment, it may seem like we are facing insurmountable obstacles to growth. We've had to shift our focus somewhat from increasing business to retaining business and minimizing loss.

A survey suggests that business growth is changing the HR function and HR is struggling to adapt.

People are the most important asset of most companies.

At the same time, human resources represents the single most costly asset, consuming up to 40% of total operating costs for most organizations.

It is becoming increasingly difficult to hire, cultivate and retain a workforce.

In companies that managed their human resources very well, there was a 64% total return to shareholders over a 5-year period. In contrast, for companies not managing their human resources well, they experienced only a 21% return during the same time frame

Growth attracts talent, creates the capital to grow faster, and can transform the market valuation of a company.

Employers didn't expect, or want, payouts. With growth slowing, shareholders need better rewards for the company's risks.

Cash can be more easily hoarded when big opportunities for more profit exist.

Amazon's return on invested capital has averaged around 50 percent a year over the past several years. So it makes sense to plow money into the business.

Employers will prefer companies that offer better rewards.

This leverage plays a key role in helping HR leaders generate significant return on investment in the form of decreased costs, less staff, and a wide range of other efficiency and effectiveness benefits.

b. Develop high level of trust and cooperation. The most important requirement for the creation of higher levels of trust for any organization is to discover the purpose of the organization.

The arrival of Mohamed ElBaradei on Egypt's political scene has electrified a country where autocracy is as old as the pyramids.

Nobel Peace Prize winner, one of Egypt's most prominent figures on the world stage, ElBaradei has emerged as a possible contender for the presidential elections scheduled for the autumn of 2011.

Many Egyptians look to the distinguished former head of the International Atomic Energy Agency (IAEA) as the man who will shift the Arab world's biggest nation into a new era of democracy, after nearly three decades of Hosni Mubarak's authoritarian rule.

"I didn't tell them I am coming to lead," he said. "I'm coming to lend a hand."

Great organizations have great purposes. HR leader has courage to do what is right to change and improve the organization.

Organizations that place these higher purposes at the very core of their business model tend to inspire trust from all of their major stakeholders: customers, employees, investors, suppliers, and the larger communities that they exist in.

c. Encourage prompt organizational learning: HR leaders encourage high-potential employees to have willingness to take the risk of jumping into an area that may be unfamiliar to them and in which, despite that un-familiarity; they are expected to produce measurable results and real innovation.

d.   Protect the organization against corporate predators: We need to take 'control fraud' seriously if we want to stop the corporate predators. Control fraud is what happens when the person who controls a large company is a criminal.

He/she can use the corporation's resources to shape the environment in which he/she operate.

Predation is an action that involves tense, violent, kill-or-be-killed scenarios. Predator describes individual or group that victimizes, plunders, or destroys, especially for their own gain.

Predation may include corporate and white-collar crimes such as pollution, procurement fraud, financial fraud, corruption and occupational homicide, while it does document murder, robbery, assault, burglary, street crimes, etc.

For instance, a corporate predator unethically acquiring business rivals; or corrupt corporate executive who is often in league with high ranking political figures denying ethics in corporate culture by acting something that limits profits.

Predatory attitude rules, i.e. 'If you're not making more profit than this month a year ago, or last quarter, then you're failing.' More, grab more, take more, and gain more.

Enron was the most conspicuous example of a pervasive phenomenon in corporate behavior, a white-collar criminologist. Enron's failure was followed by so many other shoes dropping.

International stock markets have been pummeled by the resultant loss of investor trust. The market destroyed this bad company.

Six city police officers were arrested in connection with the killing of a mayor in northern Mexico as the country's escalating drug violence targets more public officials.

The suspects included the officer who guarded the house where Santiago Mayor Edelmiro Cavazos was seized recently. The officer was kidnapped with the mayor but was later freed unharmed.

The officers confessed to being involved in the Cavazos' killing. One of them took part directly in the kidnapping, while the others kept watch on roads surrounding the mayor's home.

The predatory people are psychopathic about grabbing excessive profits and power. They have no conscience for how their decisions harm others.

They are arrogantly manipulative. And they mask themselves and their vicious behavior with lies and pretentions that make them appear normal and respectable.

HR leaders protect organization against corporate predators. They should discourage predator employers from exploiting any more already cheapest labor.

HR leaders teach, coach, ask others for their ideas, explain themselves, accept responsibility, and are accountable.

Success

HR leadership success can be seen as the process of influencing the activities of organized groups in the corporate towards goal achievement. Successful HR leaders are indicated by three components, include:

a.   Leadership brand: Leadership branding in organization can be seen from the personal perspectives and organizational perspectives.

In personal perspective, the leaders maintain their relationship and employee or employees in the group, whereas from organizational perspectives, it involves a relationship between the leaders and customer.

Chris Perry was just named head of marketing for Hyundai a few months ago, but he's already leaving to join General Motors and lead marketing for Chevrolet.

At Hyundai, Perry replaced Joel Ewanick who left the head marketing job there in March to go to Nissan. But within weeks Ewanick jumped to GM.

Ewanick and Perry were credited with creating effective marketing programs that helped the South Korea-based automaker weather last year's brutal downturn in auto sales.

Perry will be the third head of marketing for the Chevrolet brand in less than a year.

Leadership brand represents an intangible value and shared identity among organizational leaders, which differentiates what an organization can do compared to the competition.

The lack of attention to leadership brand is a missed opportunity for companies, and HR leaders have the perfect platform to address it and to accelerate economic value through helping their organizations recognize and optimize their leadership brand.

HR leadership in a company is branded when the unique attributes and specific business results are integrated for all leaders within the company.

To improve leadership brand, HR leaders must increase their efficacy of attaining results while CEO advertises these results.

Leaders who develop only common attributes of leadership do not establish leadership brand. When the attributes the leaders demonstrate are linked to desired results, distinctive branding follows.

b.   Achieve a profit of minimum 30 percent.

A study found, companies whose employees understand the mission and goals enjoy a 29 percent greater return than other firms.

Say, there is about 40 percent deviation in performance for a given role to HR leader. With average performance, HR leader might be worth $200,000 per year; good HR leader worth $280,000 (+ 40%), and poor HR leader worth $120,000 (—40%).

CNOOC (China's oil producer) agreed to fund 75 percent of Chesapeake's share of drilling (equal to $1.08 billion).

The purchase of a 33 percent stake in the Eagle Ford shale (one of Chesapeake project) is seen to be attractive.

The deal is believed able to help CNOOC gain exposure to the complicated shale-gas extraction technology that it still lacks.

At the end, CNOOC shares had climbed 4.4 percent, their highest since October 30, 2007.

c.   Ability to develop future leaders in their organization and company hierarchy: Developing leaders is key to become a successful HR leader.

HR leaders represent the array of organizational leaders' credibility, capabilities, and the capacity to foster and sustain future leaders.

Investing in leadership training and development should enhance the competencies and capabilities of existing leaders, ensure the leaders have the ability to effectively resolve competitive and economic challenges, and help the leaders inspire and engage the organization and its management team to enhance overall business performance.

Both employees and organizations need to establish a strategic framework for significant success.

Therefore, companies need to create opportunities for their employees to share in the success.

A winning business attitude comes from the top. People lower in a business cannot overcome pessimism, incompetence, negativism and lack of leadership from the top.

Leadership success in today's competitive environment requires the combination of leadership traits, skills and behavior, and the understanding of how these elements interact in the leader's role.

Successful HR leaders aren't becoming allergy to deadlines. A deadline is a commitment. The leaders who cannot set, and stick to deadlines, cannot honor commitments. A failure to set and meet deadlines also means that he/she can't ever feel a true sense of achievement.

Visioning

HR leaders are more likely to have a far better understanding of what long-term investments are required for building critical capabilities. They will be more adaptive at balancing long-term goals with short-term needs.

The leader must align HR vision with the overall corporate vision.

Visioning evolves the projection of reducing the traditional HR function; by transferring of many HR functions to the line, outside vendors, and high-efficiency processing centers; and an almost exclusive focus on business consulting and the management of the organization's core competencies.

Toyota Motor America CIO Barbra Cooper says she wants to develop leaders who can deliver value for the next 20 years.

Traditionally, organizations have always had vision statementsthose declarations of what they want to be long-term. HR leaders encourage people to develop personal vision statements, think about their contributions as an individual, etc.

A vision should stretch the organization's capabilities and image of itself. It gives shape and direction to the organization's future.

"If Alibaba cannot become a Microsoft or Walmart, I will regret it for the rest of my life," Jack Ma is already a billionaire and one of China's most spectacularly successful Internet entrepreneurs said.

A HR leader brings in his/her deep experience that related to HR business processes required to align his/her HR vision with the organizational goals.

HR leaders identify the most critical HR capability that contributes strategic assessment, organizational design, development and learning, strategic staffing, and envisioning the organization of the future.

Development

Companies are required to develop corporate activities that balance the needs of the employees and profit.

If we treat employees like children, they will behave that way—which means trouble. If we treat them like professionals, they may just respond likewise.

Leaders are able to perform multi tasks. A HR leader, who has just one competency, i.e. coaching, will not succeed. He/she may results complaints, i.e. doesn't understand compensation, bad manager, doesn't understand technology, etc.

Development is essential for HR leaders to find ways to grow the fullest potential of employees. Poor HR leader used to:

a.   Have no time or interest in dealing with people development: Successful HR leaders ensure HR Development becoming the training and education resource of choice for all employees by offering one-stop access.

b.   Focus on tactical, not strategic: Very few matters in business must remain confidential and good leaders can identify those easily. Secrets make companies political, anxious and full of distrust.

Strategic Human Resource designates the practice of human resources as a key function of the business objectives. A HR leader, who is focusing on strategy, will make sure human capital is managed in the best way necessary to achieve short term and long term results.

HR leader position is in general becoming more strategic, and CEO's (Chief Executive Officers) and CFO's (Chief Finance Officers) of the companies are increasingly recognizing that they need HR leader at the table with them.

c.   Delegate development of his/her employees to other people in the team.

HR leaders who are getting involved in development training and proving their participation in the programs will increase enthusiasm and greater confidence delivering stronger workplaces.

d.   Expect to develop people by sending them to a workshop or consultant rather than doing it by his/her own hand.

Addiction to consultants is a common sense but expensive. The way is to put off making decisions which hires consultants who can recommend several alternatives.

e.   Prefer to hire only experienced people, instead of people with potential who may need additional development.

A HR leader is to eliminate poor performers; hiring from several choices of excellent candidates, develop succession planning; and increase training and cross-training opportunities.

Development is framework that can help employees develop their personal and organizational skills, knowledge, and abilities.

World-class company recognizes that employee involvement and empowerment are critical to achieving continuous improvement in all elements of the system.

The continuity of organizational development and renewal comes primarily through the involvement of the employee. World-class companies invest comparatively more in their relationships with their workers, providing significantly more training than their competitors.

Leaders are learners and in the same time are teachers. HR leader focuses on his/her growth through work. He/she spend most of his/her waking hours at work.

HR leaders also demonstrate the bottom-line impact of human resources initiatives and differentiate themselves by acquiring advanced degrees and certification demonstrating his/her competency.

The important twist, however, is to allow employees to determine the areas in which they want education and training. These ideas will help organization increases employee motivation by providing opportunities for development, which includes:

a.   Competency sharing-based development: Developing employees is a key management competency, yet it is also one of the most overlooked responsibilities, especially when dealing with conflicting work priorities.

HR leaders put their efforts to maximize participation of people in sharing their skill, knowledge, and experience (attitude/behavior) in their own department, i.e. training, presentation, etc.

This development strategy allows employees to connect with each other and share their knowledge and experiences in a way that offers tangible and practical solutions.

HR leader provide cross-training opportunities that enable employees to learn all of the jobs in their work areas.

Employee participation can help companies to achieve world-class status.

Salman Khan, an ebullient, articulate Harvard MBA and former hedge fund manager, produces online lessons on math, science and a range of other subjects; that have made him a web sensation.

Khan Academy, with Khan as the only teacher is the most popular educational site on the web.

Khan's playlist of 1,630 tutorials (at last count) are now seen an average of 70,000 times a day—nearly double the student body at Harvard and Stanford combined.

Since he began his tutorials in late 2006, Khan Academy has received 18 million page views worldwide.

Employees, who share their knowledge, earn trust and a solid reputation, which increases their value in the organization.

Those who participate in sharing-based development are eligible for bonus or incentive for achieving company objectives.

b. Self learning-based development: HR leaders encourage employees to maximize their capacity of self learning and participate in developing others, i.e. write article/journal, book, research, etc.

Textbook publisher Houghton Mifflin Harcourt said it had launched a $100 million ideas fund as the next step in bringing the digital age to the classroom.

The Boston-based Houghton Mifflin said the fund would invest in ideas on future education tools, switching the focus away from traditional textbook publishing and e-books to online and interactive learning.

CEO Barry O'Callaghan said:" The fund was providing the capital to identify and incubate the next generation of innovation in education and was open to submissions from students, teachers and technology companies around the world."

"Simply transferring traditional physical books to read-only format e-books was an outdated way to look to the future," O'Callaghan said.

The leader creates a highly spirited learning environment. The key to leadership success lies in creating a learning environment, a new kind of business architecture that promotes a culture in which employees can learn, solve problems, challenge one another's perspectives, and go beyond their present knowledge, skills, and attitudes.

A learning environment promotes honesty, direct communication, safety to speak one's opinion without negative consequences, and the ability to recreate ideas and solutions in one's own context.

The environment emboldens employees to play with new skills and test new attitudes in a safe setting with co-workers.

If employees are committed to personal quality, innovation and continuous improvement, they are more likely to contribute their maximum potential to company objectives.

HR leader values continual learning; has the ability to grasp the essence of new information, masters new technical and knowledge, recognizes own strengths and weaknesses and pursues self-development.

He/she demonstrate personal growth that leads to a superior level of self-awareness, self-insight, and objective awareness of and insight into people.

In performance reviews leaders ask employees what new opportunities they're interested in pursuing. Self-learning based development emphasis:

i.   Internet-based self learning: Maximize utilization of internet as self learning media. Internet teaches many-people-in-a-leveraged-way category. Bill Gates, CEO of Microsoft and the world's first-richest, is a voracious consumer of online education. *"I've been using with my kids,"* he says.

Beginning in 2002, the Ugandan government introduced zero taxes on imported computers. This, in turn, increased the number of available computers, lowering their cost and enabling increased access.

Soon after, the government formed the Rural Communication Development Fund, which installed 76 internet access points across the country, reaching the majority of the population. It also put up 60 wireless communication masts, enabling telephone access to villages, thus uniting the country via cell phones.

In 2006, Ugandans created the Ministry of Information and Computer Technology to officially promote and largest undertaking began the next year, with the installation of fiber optic cable and the National Data Transmission Backbone, to, among other things, interconnect 28 districts for information sharing.

Now, as each district develops information portals on administration, education, agriculture, business and health for its own people, other districts can also access them.

World-class companies have a different attitude toward technology than the average company. *"They understand it better and work hard to ensure that they derive as much value from it as they can,"* Stephen Joyce from Hackett Group, says.

ii.   Self pay based education: Employee may take initiative to continue education. Continuing education can help an organization meet or enhance its quality, increase overall communications, and improve productivity.

Employees who are initiating to be lifelong learners will strive to attain the highest degree of expertise and professionalism.

A college degree is the key to employment. In U.S., over 3 million jobs will go unfilled because of a lack of qualified graduates, according to a report.

The report has found that not enough Americans are completing college to qualify for available jobs.

Nothing will have greater impact on their success in life than education.

A better-educated work force will help companies compete globally.

Continuing education is a highly effective way to 'sharpen the saw' while waiting for the next career opportunity to come.

Sharpen the saw, the seventh habit, is what Covey, the author, says when he means that the most effective among us make a habit of engaging in personal renewal.

Education is a kind of training the people to do a different job. Unlike training, which can be fully evaluated immediately upon the learners returning to work, education can only be completely evaluated when the learners move on to their future jobs. It will be used to increase performance in a different job.

Smart employees invest in education itself. They may not be waiting for the company to invest in them. They invest in their knowledge and education. They know, the number one product in the sale of U.S. companies today is knowledge.

Few would argue with investment advice from Warren Buffett, one of the world's wealthiest people, who has often wisely said the most important investment anyone or a company can make is education.

Working women under age 30 have opened up an eight percent income lead over men in the same age group.

The gains are driven by higher graduation among women from college and graduate schools, according to James Chung of Reach Advisors, who notes that women are collecting bachelors and advanced degrees at 1.5 times the rate of men.

HR leaders should not take otherwise, as it happens very rarely, that there's a list of successful Americans who never completed a college degree, including Microsoft co-founder Bill Gates, Apple co-founder Steve Jobs, Facebook co-founder Mark Zuckerberg and Oracle founder Larry Ellison.

c.   Company contribution-based development: The Corporate Social Responsibility (CSR) mandates corporate contributions in people development, internally and externally, that includes education, training, etc.

In seeking to provide product and services of the highest quality, companies rely heavily upon contributions from the employees.

People development is undoubtedly a time-consuming, albeit a worthwhile, proposition. Often, it can also be a challenging and frustrating undertaking, depending on each particular case and the amount of work involved.

Assessing unskilled employees and helping them improve their skills as people developers is therefore a critical task for organizations in general and Human Resources leaders in particular.

Shell pays a share of its profits into an education fund for the rehabilitation, restoration and consolidation of education in

Nigeria. In 2009 the company paid about $45 million into the fund, bringing the total investment in the past nine years to over $232 million.

Therefore, to be successful in people development, HR leaders may need to:

i. Give time to learn and train employees. Spending time for people development is crucial. The most important thing is to show a willingness to invest time in growing others. HR leaders need to set aside development or coaching time.

Quality of time contributed by the HR leader depends on each individual and the level of their skills versus job requirements. Typically, each direct report will require at least 1 hour of direct coaching per month. For a team of 5-6 direct reports, that means at least 5-6 hours should be dedicated to coaching every month.

A study found that HR leaders are struggling to play a key role in their organizations' growth strategies. Thirty-three percent of them were 'on the sideline,' contributing instead in spot roles such as talent acquisition and integration. Another 10% said HR leaders weren't involved at all in growth strategy, and 22% said HR's overall role is 'below the executive-team level.'

ii. Help employees to help themselves: By encouraging self-learning and competency sharing, HR leader should be able to minimize contribution given by the company for people development.

Company which supports employees' desire to educate themselves will increase its knowledge base.

Rwanda has just finished a pilot OLPC program and plans to buy and distribute another 100,000 computers—at $181 each—to children. It also wants to distribute laptops to half of Rwanda's 2.5 million schoolchildren.

OLPC wants to transform education in poor countries by giving children laptops that will spark collaborative, joyful, self-empowered learning.

The results of the deployment in Rwanda will be a proving ground for OLPC's premise, that distributing laptops to the world's poorest children will make their lives better.

Company may consider paying for classes, conferences, books, and other learning opportunities for all employees.

HR leaders provide proven methods of management assessment, in which they can determine who has the greatest potential for future leadership and understand what employees would bring to organization as well as how the employees might benefit from time spent in the function.

iii.   The practice company has in building competency within the outside organizations bore fruit within the company, i.e. training, seminar, work shop, visits, etc.

HR leaders pursue seminars, professional growth or other similar skills for employees.

BP committed to oil and gas exploration and intends to make absolutely sure all the lessons against accident on 20 April 2010; the Deepwater Horizon oil rig in the Gulf of Mexico exploded and oil began spewing out of ruptured pipes; which killed 11 workers.

A source says offshore inspection records showed BP did not comply with rules about regular training for offshore operators on how to respond to an oil spill.

BP's head of safety, Mark Bly said: "It is true a handful of people had not undergone all the training."

HR leader offers a full range of training including needs assessment, development program, and evaluation. He/she can provide a training development staffs whose capacity to build a custom program designed specifically for employees and the organization. Development program can be implemented through:

1) Coaching: Offer regular, active assistance to enable employees to carry out their plans. If we need a coach, who is not readily available in the organization, then perhaps we need to go outside and find someone who has been through a high growth cycle with another organization.

2) Training: The acquisition of knowledge, skill or technology which permits employees to perform their present job to standards. It improves their performance on the job the member is presently doing or is being hired to do.

Cross-fertilization: Interchange program between different cultures or different ways of thinking that is mutually productive and beneficial; i.e. 'plant visit' will benefit the organization in the long run. Ask employees to regularly visit customers or vendors to learn more about their needs from the organization.

Or send company's top people to companies worldwide, with or without similarity of disciplines. It increases exposure to the world beyond the organization.

Analysts say al Qaeda is inept. Or they might be becoming incompetent now.

Today's generation of al Qaeda recruits are bumblers. They hardly seem capable of a September 11-style attack, i.e. they couldn't get themselves to explode, or ran away from their truck before it exploded.

U.S. success in wiping out the group's leaders has exposed the incompetence of its grassroots.

The difference between then and now is not that the quality of the operatives has declined, but that the quality of al Qaeda's management has significantly reduced.

U.S. Vice President Joe Biden said that al Qaeda is 'on the run.'

With the destruction and disruption of al Qaeda's management cadre and central command, it's no longer able to provide long-term training in 'operational security.'

The loss of training is having a major effect, i.e. lack coding skills, and violate orders, etc.

The government of Quebec, Canada, introduces a program which obligating companies to contribute in people development based on its total payroll.

Contribution to the Workforce Skills Development subjects to if the companies' total payroll exceeds $1 million for the year, they must participate, for that year, in the development of worker training by allotting at least 1% of their total payroll to qualified training expenditures.

If the companies fail to do so, they must pay to the WSDRF (Workforce Skills Development and Recognition Fund) a contribution equal to the difference between 1% of companies' total payroll and the amount of their eligible training expenditures.

iii.   Company contribution based education: Kind of education opportunities funded by employers. Since the rising cost of tuition is a huge and growing concern, company should offer tuition reimbursement.

It may be un-returnable investment. But each penny earns higher capacity of the employees.

Many jobs now require degrees that some people are unable or unwilling to obtain. This is especially hard on an employee who may have started the job years before, when all that was expected was that applicants have a certain skill set.

It would be hoped that employers gave the employees the courtesy of an explanation if this was the only obstacle to their obtaining the position.

But some people, who feel they cannot get that degree at this point in their lives, will still be bitter. HR leaders encourage employees to take advantage of any tuition reimbursement programs the company offers.

Americans owe some $829.8 billion in student loans (both federal and private), and they're finding those loans harder to pay back.

President Barack Obama said that the United States must boost educational achievement if it is to thrive economically and compete on the world stage.

He said the United States cannot afford to ignore troubling trends in higher education.

The president added that a brighter economic future will only be possible with a well-educated workforce, and that today's students carry the nation's hopes for a more prosperous tomorrow.

When measuring the rate of return an employee brings to the organization, education always adds value. Company sponsored education can foster stronger bonds with employees. Most employees will not forget that the company paid for their education.

Development is also seen as training people to acquire new horizons, technologies, or viewpoints. It enables leaders to guide their organizations onto new expectations by being proactive rather than reactive.

It enables employees to create better products, faster services, and more competitive organizations. It is learning for growth of the individual, but not related to a specific present or future job.

d. 3rd party sponsorship-based development: As a courtesy to the employees, companies should provide willingness that allows third-party sponsors for education tuition and fees (including books and supplies).

Qualified sponsors include corporations, government agencies etc. In case, payment is not received from the sponsoring agency by the due date of the invoice, the companies should charge the outstanding tuition and fees to the employee's account and payment will be due immediately.

e. Maximize employee participation: High performance organizations usually require significant employee participation, innovation and teamwork.

Companies may form HR related-committees: i.e. Management Development, Centers of Excellence, System Thinking, etc.

Imoveyou.com is a social network designed to persuade people to exercise more often by engaging them in quick 'if/ then' challenges with friends.

A user might type a challenge like this into the site: "I will walk the dog for 20 minutes if you will ride a unicycle around the block."

The person who has been challenged is notified by Facebook, Twitter or e-mail, and can accept or reject the challenge. The idea is likely to be persuasive because it encourages people to act as soon as possible, and it notifies them about the challenges wherever they are.

It may engage people in a bit of competition.

Unlike training and education, which can be completely evaluated, development cannot always be fully evaluated. It will be used to acquire a new viewpoint so that the organization can become more competitive.

Development occurs to enhance the organization's value, not solely for individual improvement. Individual education and development is a tool and a means to an end.

Empowerment

People who have power usually do not give it up voluntarily. Since, power means control.

HR leader has the responsibility to create a work environment which helps to foster the ability and desire of employees to act in empowered ways. The organization has the responsibility to remove barriers that limit the ability of staff to act in empowered ways.

Empowerment exists when employees have the authority to make decisions and take appropriate actions.

Empowerment allows the employees to act quickly, improving satisfaction and boosting morale. The important principles for managing people in a way that reinforces employee empowerment, i.e.:

a.   Share vision: Make sure employees know and have access to the organization's overall mission, vision, and strategic plans.

HR leaders engage the workers in an ongoing honest discussion of the quality of work that is needed for the program to be successful. HR leaders not only listen, but also encourage workers to give them any input that will improve quality.

Tired of Islamic terror camps grabbing headlines, a Pakistani Muslim cleric is fighting back by holding his own 'anti-terror camp.'

Islamic cleric Shaykh Muhammad Tahir ul-Qadri is the man behind "Al-Hidayah," an Islamic retreat, an Islamic learning program, especially for a younger generation, at the University of Warwick, in the UK.

147

He preaches peace and love and tolerance.

He issued the fatwa on terrorism in March 2010—a 600-page religious edict that denounces terror attacks. It condemns suicide attackers to hell and disowns them from Islam.

HR leaders re-think the process and fundamentally change its orientation—to make it either a highly engaging, value creating function or simplify its features and maximize its efficiency.

There is no single right approach, best form or system that eliminates the need to involve leaders and employees. The best process creates value and is viewed as worth the effort by both leaders and employees.

b.   Trust people: Allow employees to do the right thing, take the right decision, and make choices.

Britain's advertising watchdog banned an anti-terrorism commercial that asked people to watch out for suspicious behavior by their neighbors, including keeping curtains closed and paying for things in cash.

The Advertising Standards Authority said the radio ad could cause serious offense to law-abiding citizens.

The watchdog said innocent listeners who identified with the behavior described could be offended by the implication that it was suspicious.

"We also considered that some listeners might be offended by the suggestion that they report members of their community for acting in the way described," it said, ruling that the ad should not run again.

c.   Provide information: Employees should have access to all of the information they need to make thoughtful decisions.

Google Inc. launched a website for users who want to sift through news, comments and other information on the Internet in real time.

Google's effort underscores the importance of real-time data on social media, in an increasingly competitive Internet search arena which it dominates. Microsoft also announced partnerships with Twitter and Facebook to provide real-time search results.

d.   Delegate authority: It should be accountable for results. HR leader has to be duly empowered through clear delegation of authority in all areas. It empowers employees to participate in decisions affecting the organization.

The primary objective of delegation of authority is to foster a more efficient use of resources and facilitate the emergence of more agile and responsive organizations, thus enhancing overall performance.

Performance improves when the people who are closest to the work have authority and responsibility delegated directly to them.

Company ensures that internal processes provide the people with the authority and flexibility they need to contribute to the organization's objectives.

The British government's plan to drastically reshape the socialized health care system would put local physicians in control of much of the national health budget. It would be the most radical reorganization of the National Health Service.

The plan would also shrink the bureaucratic apparatus, in keeping with the government's goal to effect $30 billion in 'efficiency savings' in the health budget and to reduce administrative costs by 45 percent.

The government admitted that Liberating the N.H.S., and putting power in the hands of patients and clinicians, means we will be able to effect a radical simplification, and remove layers of management.

It will put more power in the hands of patients.

"One of the great attractions of this is that it will be able to focus on what local people need," said Prof. Steve Field, chairman of the Royal College of General Practitioners.

e.   Solve problem: HR leader should demonstrates him/herself as a problem solver. They are people, who innovative and proactive and lead by example—seeking out and solving—problems in the organization. Simply, leaders lead; others wait to be told what to do.

i.   If there's a way to do our job more efficiently, do it first, then bring that solution to our superior.

ii.   Highlight results: Emphasize how we've increased productivity, saved the company time or money, or improved morale.

HR leaders focus more on outcomes than on activities.

Guatemalan police arrested Alejandro Giammattei, the former head of the national prison system, accusing him of orchestrating the executions of seven prisoners during a 2006 government raid on an infamous jail.

The jail had ostensibly been controlled by prisoners for a decade with guards only patrolling the perimeter while allowing inmates to build private houses, restaurants, video arcades and even hard-drug laboratories on the inside.

The raid, carried out by thousands of police and soldiers backed up by helicopters. They said the prisoners were heavily armed.

Authorities bulldozed the part of the prison farm with churches, pool halls and telephone banks where prisoners extorted people on the outside.

f.   Provide feed back: Develop the performance planning, feedback and management process that strengthens the ability of the organization to realize its strategy.

Expect a mistake. Continuous improvement cannot be achieved without measurement.

In 2009, Smart sales plummeted to 14,600 units from 24,600 the previous year. And so far in 2010 sales are off another 60 percent from 2009's dismal rate.

Now the company is aiming to restart stalled sales with a reinvigorated marketing effort that puts Smart, a family car manufacturer, in front of the kinds of consumers who are apt to be interested.

They are recognizing the need for Smart to start selling its cars, rather than just taking orders from consumers, to boost its marketing effort.

"We measure the effectiveness of our marketing not only by how many people we attract but what they do after we attract them," vice president of marketing, Kim McGill noted.

g.   Celebrate results: Acknowledge employees for their successes, achievements, and results. Do this during performance reviews and publicly.

When people know that they are appreciated for their contributions to the organization, when they can use their strengths every day, and when they know they make a difference.

"The two greatest corporate leaders of this century are Alfred Sloan of General Motors (GM) and Jack Welch of GE," says Noel Tichy, a professor. "Welch would be the greater of the two," he adds.

He has delivered extraordinary growth, increasing the market value of GE from just $12 billion in 1981 to about $280 billion in 1998.

> *When Welch leaves at the end of the year 2000, GE's stock*
> *could trade at $150 to $200 a share, up from $82, and the*
> *company could be worth $490 billion to $650 billion.*

Company is committed to providing the tools and support employees need to grow and develop in their current position and manage their own career.

HR leaders should obsess resulting creative productivity—increasing the creative commercialization opportunity of their talent investments. To become a profit center, they need to:

i.   Provide the outstanding staffs and development program: Recruit and select the most qualified individuals for any of job openings.

They should be becoming people who inspire company to make a difference in the business.

HR leaders assist employees at all levels develop skills needed for their professional enrichment.

The Human Resource leader promotes a work environment which attracts talented, high caliber staff and which challenges each of employees to perform at the highest level of achievement and contribute in meaningful ways to the company objectives.

The success of the company depends on an outstanding staff, and working together collaboratively, etc.

A successful HR leader is able to improve the employer brand, which is a key to attracting and retaining the best talent.

Bad hiring decisions are usually not the fault of the interviewer. They are caused by the fact that we are making these decisions based on bad information. The solution is to get more information about the applicant before they interview candidates.

Dependable information about the applicants can help us make a better decision about who to hire. By getting more information about how an employee will act on the job, we can increase the probability of making a good hire.

Candidate of a leader should have strong background and proven record in change management to show a valuable asset as the company may press harder to complete its transformation. He/she must have the right experience and leadership skills to realise the full potential of the company.

HR leaders are aware of their blind-side, their tendencies for avoiding or over-doing, and they are accomplished objective problem solvers.

They recognize that there are multiple ways most situations can be perceived; they seek the objective viewpoints that can best assist the enterprise in problem solving and decision making efforts.

Knowledge and awareness enables HR leaders to lead in the variety of circumstances in which they find themselves.

Let's be frank, there are a lot of HR leaders who do very little to help their businesses succeed. They enjoy demonstrating their preference for weak candidates.

They only want to hire the junior. They felt threatened by the super-competent successors and hadn't the confidence to know that they must always hire people smarter than themselves.

HR leaders in business today almost always work for great business leaders. The leaders hold HR to the same high standards as they do everyone else. They expect them to be committed, capable, independent leaders who have a point of view on how to drive business success.

Poor HR leader can be seen by his/her inability to hire good former employees. Every good HR leader has alumni, eager to join the team again; if they don't, smell a rat.

HR leaders challenge their business leaders by telling them what they don't want to hear, by offering opposing views, but pushing them to see their own behavior in a new insight.

HR leaders are recruiting the best employees for the organization's needs. They want talented employees who fit company culture. To achieve it, the recruitment strategies will include:

1. Provide appropriate training in recruitment techniques. HR leaders assist staffs actualize their full potential.

    Oil spill worker charged with raping a co-worker.

    A lack of screening of oil spill cleanup workers left him free to rape a colleague.

    The British Petroleum (BP) representative told only drug screenings, not background checks, were being conducted on the cleanup workers.

    "We're not going to know who we're dealing with if we don't do background checks on these people," said a Mississippi county sheriff.

    An investigation into the incident reveals that basic background checks were not done on those hired to remove oil from the beaches.

2. Provide mechanisms that assist assessors in making good decisions and ensure the decisions are fair, free of bias, and transparent.

    Internal recruitment can provide the most cost-effective source for recruits if the potential of the existing pool of employees has been enhanced through training, development and other performance-enhancing activities such as performance appraisal.

    HR leaders develop performance indicators to assist employees in achieving and maintaining agreed levels of performance. They identify the performance measures, critical milestones and requirements of success for the total organization and functions.

HR leaders ensure that individual and team performance is acknowledged.

3. Provide employment packages to attract outstanding staff.

The strategy may retain employees which includes flexible schedules, extended leaves, job sharing, on-site daycare, eldercare assistance, and concierge services, etc.

Companies which are approaching world-class status were three to five times more likely to report highly effective human-resources programs than other firms.

On other hand, companies that fail to develop effective recruiting, training and retention programs risk diminished employee performance.

The opportunity for personal development is one of the more important variables in personnel selection and retention.

World class companies focus much more on linking learning and development initiatives to the critical skills and competencies.

HR leader provides a framework for comprehensive employee development opportunities and to support the company achieving excellence.

Talents and abilities can be developed through passion, education, and persistence.

Research shows that the more money people have than others, the more likely they are to report being satisfied with their lives.

The higher their salary than the norm, the happier they tend to be.

People tend to value their own wealth more—and are happier—when it compares favorably to everyone else's.

It's not simply how much money they make that contributes to satisfaction, but how much more money they make than others (their neighbors, colleagues at work or friends from college).

The higher their rank, the greater their sense of happiness and self-worth would likely be.

People care about whether they are the second most highly paid person, or the eighth most highly paid person, in their comparison set. They may not care of the amount they receive as far as the value is higher than their co-worker.

Focusing on growth, HR leaders demonstrate an increased interest in promoting employee engagement. This includes attempts to recruit, socialize and retain a committed workforce.

The recruitment proposition forms the basis for workplace satisfaction and identification with organizational goals and values.

ii. Low resignation rate: HR leaders find out the most effective and efficient way to attract, motivate and retain employees to complete the goals and mission of the company. They need to focus on creative ways to recognize employees, i.e. benefits, career path, compensation, flexibilities, etc.

They will identify the marketplace for talent—external labor and talent markets and internal movements through promotions and career paths.

The best-performing organizations achieve 67% less voluntary staff turnover.

Companies must be able to attract and retain the best employees. They must aim to create an environment where employees feel appreciated for their contributions.

A meaningful strategy provides guidelines for how various reward programs should be designed and managed.

The purpose of rewards strategy is to define the critical requirements of company's compensation and reward programs so they enable the company to effectively manage the people resources.

The programs can include salaries, variable cash compensation plans, long-term or equity based plans, employee benefits and services, recognition programs and other programs, and practices that influence the actions of employees.

A reward strategy should articulate in simple but powerful terms how the company will invest its resources, reinforce its core principles and values, and create a competitive advantage.

When employees have high levels of well-being and job satisfaction, they perform better and are less likely to leave their job—making happiness a valuable tool for maximizing organizational outcomes.

Reducing employee turnover is also dependant on work environment. People want to enjoy their work. Make work fun. Demonstrate respect for employees at all times. Listen to them deeply; use their ideas; never ridicule or shame them.

At the time of the deal, MySpace was one of the fastest growing Web properties adding millions of users within a few months. But in the last two years it has lost momentum to fast-growing rivals like Facebook and Twitter and has become something of an albatross around Murdoch's neck.

It has steadily seen its visitor numbers drop.

It has also lost several top executives including co-president Jason Hirschhorn. Hirschhorn, with fellow co-president Mike Jones, replaced former CEO Owen Van Natta just four months earlier.

Company may offer competitive salary and benefits, flexible schedule options, and tuition assistance to achieve resignation rate at the lowest level.

iii.   Focus on strategic work force planning: Activities related to strategy provide the most high-end impact for HR to demonstrate its value.

To help line leaders get better at growing their organizations, HR leaders should provide a strategy of designing and staffing the growth-related organization.

Heavy US reliance on private security in Afghanistan has helped to line the pockets of the Taliban.

It is because contractors often fail to vet local recruits and end up hiring warlords.

Private security contractors in Afghanistan have empowered warlords, powerbrokers.

iv.   Retain higher: Key employee retention is critical to long term health and success of the business.

When a key person left the organization without sharing his/her understanding of how to get things done; unshared knowledge loses value.

Companies with world-class organisations require 46% fewer new recruits than typical companies.

Employee retention matters, because it affect the organizational needs such as training time and investment; lost knowledge; mourning, insecure coworkers and a costly candidate search aside, failing to retain a key employee is costly.

Retaining best employees ensures customer satisfaction, product sales, satisfied coworkers and reporting staff, effective succession planning and deeply imbedded organizational knowledge and learning.

v.   Fill faster: A HR leader needs every effort to fill vacant positions as quickly as possible, many factors determine the time it takes to fill a position including the period of time the position is posted, the number of applications received, and the schedule of the person responsible for screening and interviewing applicants.

Companies with world-class organisations fill positions 11% faster than typical companies.

Hiring good, hard working candidates is a big challenge for HR leaders.

The secret to finding a good employee faster is in discovering their inner character, what drives them, what makes them tick. Once we know a little bit about who they are, we can then move on to determine if they have the work experience and or skills necessary to perform the job.

HR leader positions are some of the hardest to fill because the pool of qualified talent is so small.

That's why we need to develop HR executives internally. A lack of planning and a shortage of HR talent within the company diminish the continued effective performance of the HR function.

Study found HR leaders are not succeeding in developing their staffs to take on top-level HR positions. Companies hire externally to fill their top HR position. Even large corporate employers have replaced their top HR leader with an external hire.

A vacancy requires the identification or confirmation of a set of position descriptions and the relevant selection criteria.

In Japan, 76 percent of employers had trouble finding the right workers, the highest reading among the 36 countries and territories.

Many companies which have successfully developed HR talent identify key elements, including creating a development program, garnering executive support, ensuring accountability, identifying the right competencies and growing through stretch assignments.

Sleepover

Sleepover is part of a major rethink, a personal reevaluation of how a company or organization equips its people to lead. The rethink has anything to do with succession. Sleepover will offer great impact, if HR leaders consider:

a. Re-appraisal: Self-reflective on 'steroids.' See strengths and weaknesses.

   Re-appraisal can be done by reflecting in various specialized works that express its traits (characteristics) in comparison with previous periods. It may require redefining its object, method, and tool.

   HR leaders are looking to human capital management solutions to cut administrative labor costs—and change the historical view of HR from an administrative necessity to a strategic component leading the competitive advantage charge by managing and optimizing a company's most important strategic asset.

b. Personal connection: Bond with the team. Sometimes there's a tendency to say, 'Well, this is an officer of the company. They've been here 20 years. They can figure it out.'

   HR leaders should devote as much as 30 percent of their time for succession planning and development.

   The benefit is that each function can provide the other with knowledge that helps them to contribute.

Personal connections create a powerful combined team approach that maximizes ability to meet the needs of businesses.

c. Explore new ideas: Look beyond it to alternatives.

Creativity is linked to an open mind.

Any kind of organization must change to thrive in the new era.

HR leaders should make sure they're really on the right path in a world that they view as being very different in the future than it has been in the past.

In addition to talent acquisition and leadership development targeted to growth, HR leaders must dramatically increase their external focuson markets, customers and new ways to serve themif they are going to be strategic players going forward.

d. Invite external 'thought leader': A HR leader joins the executives and other HR leaders from different industries to learn, grow, and excel, to debate/discuss leadership with top leaders.

Indonesian President Susilo Bambang Yudhoyono met with former Polish president Lech Walesa.

Walesa, a 1983 Nobel Peace Prize laureate, is scheduled to deliver a presidential lecture at the Presidential Palace.

The true role of a leader is to lead people in new directions. To spark this kind of leadership, companies may bring in exciting outside speakers to lead discussions of issues and teach skills HR leaders will need.

The leader may find tremendous value in renowned thought leader forum, and has the opportunity to connect and share knowledge with fellow senior HR leaders.

e.   Foster programs to bring in personal coaches for high-potential talent.

At a time when many view training as a burdensome cost center, GE continues to treat human resources as a sacred art, spending $1 billion a year on training and devoting weeks or months of each year to evaluating talent.

"Their investment is formidable," says Brooks C. Holtom, a management professor.

f.   Increase exposure to the world beyond the organization.

Organizations can make themselves to pressure for change by encouraging leaders to surround themselves with devil's advocates, by cultivating external networks that comprise people organization with different perspective and views; by visiting other organizations to gain exposure to new ideas and methods; and try by using external standards of performance, such as competitor's progress or benchmarks, rather than the organization's own past standards of performance.

As a good example, GE sent 30 of its top people to more than 100 companies worldwide.

g.   Reconsider the rule that employees can't sit on corporate boards.

With few exceptions, corporate Boards of Directors have historically been composed of people who have close relationship with employers.

Employees with good education, expertise and track records that qualify them for board membership remain at a disadvantage when competing with other candidates.

This is because those who make board appointments tend to look at candidates within their own personal and professional networks.

These networks have not included employees; thus there are few or no employees on their radar screens.

h. Solicit management suggestions from a broad range of organizations. 'Wallowing in it,' to decide how a company should shape and measure its leaders.

Suggestion systems are changing to meet today's need for employee involvement to motivate employees and get them involved in the successful operation of the business.

A suggestion program not only allows employees to have an impact on the achievement of corporate and organizational goals, but also offers them the opportunity to develop to their full potential.

Companies should maintain a stance which takes into account long-term business results; it is likely to provide them with a sustainable competitive advantage. It could make them emerge as preferred employers in the long term; improve employer band image.

They will need their top talent more than ever to tide them through the downturn. The best employer always retains top performers by suitably continuing to reward them and protect overall organization performance.

Training

HR leaders spend time away from work and gained some knowledge and share it to employees. Not only expecting budget from the organization to ensure the people get appropriate training. If they keep on spending money, the investment in human capital probably is not justified.

The take home learning attitude actually will help the bottom line to grow.

It is a learning process that involves the acquisition of knowledge, sharpening of skills, concepts, rules, or changing of attitudes and behaviors to enhance the performance of employees.

HR leaders well know employees need training, and they know that not having it is costing them something. There are three kinds of training, i.e.:

a. Universal training: The impact of *universal training* programs is improving knowledge, and attitudes. This training includes activity that leading to skilled behavior.

Universal training normally focuses on values, culture, attitude, etc. It's not what we want in life, but it's knowing how to reach it; it's not where we want to go, but it's knowing how to get there; it may not be quite the outcome we were aiming for, but it will be an outcome.

When any type of training is rolled out to the workforce, adequate communication needs to be carried out that talks about the topic and the importance of that topic to both the individual and the company as a whole.

Universal training offers new or changed behaviors of the trainees. The employees will make the connection between the topic and its application and usefulness to them. For instance:

i. Observing on finance for non-financial leaders (i.e. FOREX training course). They would glaze-over during the discussion on bond ratings and price-to-earnings ratios.

The training was intended to impress upon the employees that their organization was not fiscally healthy and they needed to assist as much as possible in changing the situation so that the company could be sold.

ii. Universal Military Training is required to response to modern warfare, i.e., warfare carried out by mass conscripted citizen armies.

The case against universal military training is usually based on the belief that its results are undesirable both for the individual and, in the long run.

Most people who oppose obligatory peacetime training concede that such training might improve the efficiency of the military establishment.

iii. Universal training for citizenship and public service.

According to human capital theory, firm financed training cannot be explained if skills are of general nature.

Investments of companies into general training can be observed and mostly referring to imperfect labor market issues. Companies invest heavily into universal training although it is assumed to be general.

iv. Occupational training: The occupational training is a training program which is designed to increase employees' skill level in their occupation or area of expertise.

In today's workforce there is a need to constantly retrain and upgrade skills.

For instance: Secretarylobbying, negotiation, etc; Engineer: technical writing and presentation skills; Supervisorappraisal, communication, leadership, time management, etc.

HR leaders require to define specificity of training may be defined based on skill-weights approach. Occupational training involves education or re-skilling of employees to learn skills necessary for their profession.

Occupational training and learning is important to satisfy the business needs. It will also help ensure employees can provide new qualifications to support their occupation needs.

Occupational training is designed for professional people/ employees who wish to obtain further training and experience in their field.

A study found the more specific the skill requirements are, in an occupation, the smaller is the probability of an occupational change during an employee's entire career.

b.   Professional training: It is about work-related training which is necessary like new techniques, new methods, new tools, new materials, new sources of power, and uses of automation, and professional certification, etc.

HR leader identify each individual's required core skills. He/she may use the unique scorecard as a frame of reference. It will determine the required core skills for each person. The required skills should be those that would directly impact the person's ability to excel in his/her scorecard.

Professional training leads to unique accountability. He/she will be focus on his/her job, eliminate redundancy, overlap of accountability, and duplicate work.

It means eliminating waste of time, energy and resources. This translates not only to savings of human capital, but also to greater results.

Once the required skills are identified for each employee then HR leader can determine the existing level of competency in the skill and put an expected value that indicates whether progress is achieved or not.

It's recommended to use a simple and effective method of focusing on: the amount of effort it takes an employee to get the job done and the amount of supervision the employee needs.

An employee is fully competent when he or she can do a quality job applying the core skills with less effort than is required by a standard performer, and with minimal supervision.

In training, companies typically send both the successful and the unsuccessful employees on to the next phase of the process—the next course in the series or back to the job, ostensibly to put their new skills into practice.

When investment comes to training, too often we assume that because the trainees liked the training, they actually understood it and are going to use it to the company's benefit.

A Return on Investment (ROI) initiative doesn't have to be costly and time consuming. It can be as simple as testing for knowledge prior to attending the training, and then testing again after the training.

If the skills that are taught are soft skills such as communication skills or teambuilding, it would be more helpful to use pre—and post-observations rather than tests.

HR leaders are actively engaged as strategic business leaders in the organizations. They ensure that they are in the best possible position to understand the customer and market-driven factors that affect their businesses; effectively influence and contribute to the strategic decision making process; adapt quickly to and facilitate change in their organizations; and manage and influence organizational culture.

Employees want to grow and develop their skills. The vast majority of employees don't just want a job to pay the bills, but rather a career that makes use of their strengths while helping them develop their weaknesses.

People development is undoubtedly a time-consuming, albeit a worthwhile, proposition. Often, it can also be a challenging and frustrating undertaking, depending on each particular case and the amount of work involved.

Assessing unskilled employees and helping them improve their skills as people developers is therefore a critical task for organizations in general and Human Resources leaders in particular.

Today's emphasis on business expansion is creating growing pains for many HR leaders.

The HR leaders are expected to be accountable for the company's future. They are challenged to have a direction how to sustain the growth of companies' already expanding corporation, i.e. organizational structure look like in future that support companies' vision, new technologies will be needed, skills will line leaders need for the growth and the world changes that to be encountered.

They should demonstrate their capability of identifying and investing in organizational and individual actions that create value. HR leaders who contribute in a strategic role will make impactful decisions, and collaborate on business challenges in a systematic, strategic manner.

6th

RESPONSIBILITY

All organization elements to recognize that the workforce is not just HR leaders' problem, and that line managers and HR leaders have joint responsibility for developing talent throughout the organization.

Traditionally, HR leaders have limited involvement in the company's business affairs and goals. The HR leaders are often only concerned with making staffing plans, providing specific job training programs, or running annual performance appraisal programs.

HR leaders should know orientation of the businesses, so they can add value to business decision-making processes from a people management perspective.

This business orientation also potentially added value to the corporation as a whole by requiring higher levels of teamwork among the HR function, senior management, operating units in the field, labor unions, and external advisers.

With the growing importance of Human Resources to the success of the business, HR leaders and their departments have become more involved in the business.

75 percent of the respondents say that HR effectiveness is measured by its contribution to business results

HR leaders must be business professionals with extraordinary HR capabilities that drive results. While they have opportunity to participate in critical business decisions on a daily basis, we also play the critical role of being advocates for employees as well.

Human Resources leader seeks to achieve the company objectives by aligning the supply of skilled and qualified individuals and the capabilities of the current workforce, with the company ongoing and future business plans and requirements to maximize return on investment and secure organization success.

When HR leaders fail to assume responsibilities; they act irresponsibly. They fail to make reasonable efforts to prevent employees' misdeeds; ignore or deny ethical problems; don't shoulder responsibility for the consequences of their directives; deny their duties to employees; and hold followers to higher standards than themselves.

When HR leaders and employees set clear expectations about the results that must be achieved and the methods or approaches needed to achieve them, they establish a path for success. The expectations given to HR leaders include:

a.   Exhibit high quality products and services: Quality has also been found to be the most important competitive differentiator in the eyes of the customer.

HR leaders recognize that the collective efforts of employees contribute to the overall mission of the organization and that they should encourage opportunities for those efforts to be acknowledged.

Reducing top performer flight is top of mind for many HR leaders. The inability to retain top performers during can have a dramatic effect on the organization's future growth prospects.

In order to attract and retain the best employees, we must aim to create an environment where employees feel appreciated for their contributions.

Service comes into play with our daily priorities. We'll reap what we sow, so sow good seed. Good seed is paying attention to our vision and mission statement, understanding where we want to go and what we want to achieve, and making that a priority.

HR leaders must give it the time and energy that it requires. It will take sacrifices to get where they want to be.

HR leaders encourage people to emphasize on customer focus. Customers are playing an ever-expanding role in organization success. Organization should "be laser-focused on building and protecting the company's most precious assets—customer relationships."

Customers feature prominently in vision statements, scorecard measures, innovation efforts, employee performance standards, reward programs and other important areas of business operations—a focus that organizations hope will have a positive impact on the bottom line.

Poor HR leaders often stop the clock as soon as the candidate says yes, while good leaders don't see recruitment ending until the candidate actually shows up for work.

New hires, candidates who were not selected and candidates who declined offers are customers too.

To make sure customer satisfaction at the highest level, HR leaders will initiate following actions:

i.   Recognize the customers' needs, wants and desires. They ask the customers directly or set up focus groups to query them.

ii.   Get connected with them: HR leaders focus instead on the accomplishments of the company's objectives, many of them are now using social media tools, like Facebook or Tweet, to collaborate across business units around the world.

iii. Get referrals from customers: HR leaders provide important feedback on how employees and organizations measure up and identify the areas where improvement will provide the greatest returns.

Create value for costumers: HR leaders must ensure that top talent is allocated to the strategic roles that create the most value—those that drive the company's strategic capabilities and create value for customers.

Internet search and advertising giant Google Inc fired an engineer recently for violating users' privacy, the company said.

The engineer, David Barksdale, was accused of accessing information about teenagers he had met in a Washington state technology group.

HR leaders demonstrate their responsibility by:

1. Professional responsibility: Represent their profession to their organization. As such, they must hold themselves accountable for their decisions and ensure their actions further the credibility of their profession.

2. Professional development: Continuously expand their knowledge of the profession and the organization in which they work.

HR leaders must give time and energy that is required to accomplish their duties. It may take sacrifices to get where they want to be.

In order to contribute productively to high-level discussions of corporate strategy, HR leaders must have a firm grasp of the key concepts, and strategy.

Knowledgeable HR leaders who are working in partnership with line leaders can have a powerful impact on an organization's success.

The HR Leaders will provide employees with intensive training in strategy, enabling you to participate equally in the boardroom and contribute to the decision-making processes in your organization.

b. Have a commitment to excellence in communications: Provide open communication to ensure the sustainability of the organization.

HR leaders attribute much of their HR organization's success to excellent communication.

They should keep employees' eyes on.

A group of British Muslim has launched a campaign to improve the image of Islam in Britain. The campaign was conceived after an opinion poll found that most Britons associate the religion with extremism.

The group has displayed posters—all around London—of Muslims, with captions that reflect positively on Islam. But critics say the campaign is one-sided, and even misleading.

"We wanted to highlight our concerns by promoting a positive image of Islam which is rarely seen in the mainstream," Remona Aly, from the Exploring Islam Foundation, says.

HR leaders will need to be more externally focused and skilled at building networks and productive alliances with other groups and institutions, become more analytical and able to document the benefits associated with effective HR policies and practices, and be skilled at managing in an increasingly transparent society and information savvy workforce.

Information is power, but few people are seeing information and then changing their behavior based on that information.

Line leaders and employees need to know from HR leaders about employee performance and workforce differentiation, and communicate it.

A barrier to effective communication is potentially destroying morale. HR leaders set the standard of truth for every employee they lead. The moment people take leadership positions, they have an opportunity to place the highest premium on truthfulness.

The need for every form of communication HR leaders put forth to be an accurate representation.

Truthful information is quality information to the CEO, Board of Directors, and employers, that bring them to quality decision making on strategic plans.

HR has to bring value to the discussion. If they have little or nothing to offer, they will not keep your seat at the table.

In an age of perpetual digital connectedness (i.e. e-mail), people seem so disconnected. The leaders organize get together meeting (i.e. cycling, etc) to encourage employee well-being.

A research found that college students today have significantly less empathy—the ability to understand and share the feelings of another—than students of generations past did.

It may have something to do with our increasing reliance on digital communication and other forms of new media.

It's possible that instead of fostering real friendships off-line, e-mail and social networking may take the place of them—and the distance inherent in screen-only interactions may breed feelings of isolation or a tendency to care less about other people.

Researchers found that from 1985 to 2004, the percentage of people who said there was no one with whom they discussed important matters tripled, to 25%.

The study suggested Americans had one-third fewer friends and confidants than they did two decades ago.

c.   Promote effectiveness: The HR leaders' primary goal in a company is to ensure that the business has the right talent and skills at the right time, in the right place and in the right role.

43 percent rated HR planning and policy effectiveness as only average while a mere 6 percent rated it as excellent.

It's not surprising to find that the best HR leaders show a continuous focus on improving their organizations' human capital.

A study found that world-class organisations are those in the top 25% in terms of efficiency and effectiveness.

Companies should precisely define their talent needs against their markets and their strategies.

These talent needs can relate to dramatically new product categories, investing for long-term growth in emerging markets, or virtually any other element of a company's strategy.

Effective Talent Management will require HR leaders to:

i.   Provide premium standard of test and assessment: Dedicate to promoting high standards of excellence.

We shouldn't hire someone unless we're 100% sure that he/she is the right person. It's better to wait and get someone that we know is a good fit. Pay them adequately. We shouldn't be trapped into 'if we pay peanuts, we get monkeys.'

Baseball great Roger Clemens was indicted for lying to Congress when he denied using anabolic steroids or other performance-enhancing drugs.

Clemens, 48, was charged with one count of obstruction of the U.S. Congress; three counts of making false statements and two counts of perjury.

"In truth and in fact, as Clemens well knew when he gave this testimony, Clemens knowingly received injections of anabolic steroids while he was an MLB (Major League Baseball) player," the 19-page indictment said.

The greatest differences between good and poor organizations are found in performance appraisal practices, compensation practices and training practices.

In the area of performance appraisals, good organizations tend to encourage higher levels of employee involvement in the appraisal process.

They are also more concerned with evaluating results, rather than the methods used to achieve them.

And although individual performance remains a primary focus, group performance is more likely to be part of the appraisal process in highly entrepreneurial firms.

HR leaders fairly evaluate employees, based on their achievements and for appropriate placement, and provide them with various forms of support so they can be devoted to their work.

ii.   Provide solution that is reliable and easily used: Promote solution that is humble and simple, give incredible technical support, and promptly respond the questions and complaints.

More proficient IT use lets companies operate with 35% fewer HR employees, while they are still providing improved productivity and strategic alignment across the company, a study says.

HR leader is committed to providing effective people solutions to the company in ways which improve human effectiveness and the organization's bottom line.

Companies with no common HR software applications also spend 18 percent more on HR overall than those with a high level of common software applications.

The research highlights that HR costs materially increase with each additional HR application. Companies that do not standardize their use of common applications spend more on HR per employee than companies that make high use of common applications.

Most HR leaders have taken new roles and responsibilities due to company expansion and the emphasis on corporate objectives. It will result in heavier workloads, and the need to work harder and smarter.

*"You are seeing HR being valued much, much more in organizations,"
Joe Vocino of Mercer Human Resource Consulting says. "More and more, we are seeing HR right at the CEO's side at the time of strategic decisions, acquisitions and divestitures."*

HR leaders do not sit back and wait for something to happen. If they aren't getting clarity from their CEO, they ask for it proactively. They will put commitment to making it happen.

Therefore, human resource departments had to transform themselves from cost centers to tools of corporate strategy

Performance Management

Performance Management means activities that are required to set the foundation for rewarding excellence.

HR leaders have come under increased pressure to prove contribution in a manner that relates to real business outcomes.

Randy MacDonald, senior vice president of HR at IBM, suggests that all good HR people will risk being fired at some point in their careers when they have to stand up for what they believe in.

HR leaders have responsibilities that include performance management and/or organizational development. They create strategic partnership with line leaders to effectively manage employee and organization performance.

Performance has been largely delivered on the promise of cost reduction. But the best are no longer solely focused on cost reduction, but also quality product/service delivery.

World class companies operate with 15 per cent fewer staff11.5 compared to 13.5 HR staff per 1,000 employees.

Many companies have performance management programs, but few are satisfied with them. They frequently see the process as too time consuming for the benefits that result. Measuring organization performance, HR leaders should demonstrate following requirements:

a.   Input measures: Applying Human Resources for productive use in the company.

   61% agree that information is collected for assessing performance.

   It reflects organizational costs per employee, includes:

i.   Training investment: One of the most important roles of HR is the recruitment and training.

   "If you are going to invest a billion (dollars) plus. You have to make sure that investment generates sufficient returns to make it worthwhile," said Mirko Bibic, Bell's senior vice president.

   The more sensitive and active HR leaders are in promoting, training, and in general being open and listening to the needs of employees, the greater the value the company will receive from its workforce.

   HR leaders drive top performer retention by providing a systematic mechanism for employee development career planning and career planning.

HR leaders provide a means to identify the value of dollars invested in training related to the costs of training and the benefits achieved in increased sales, customer satisfaction, and productivity.

Forty-three percent (43%) of organizations currently employ a systematic process for employee development.

HR should focus on is the direct relationship between investment in the company's workforce and the success of its business; they take assessment of the relation between the cost of staff training and development with the productivity and longevity of stay of employees within the company.

HR leaders should assess the investment in human capital by considering the cost of training programs per employee, and determine how much more revenue this has brought to the company.

To get the figures for Return On Investment (ROI) analysis, keep track of training costs, including the cost of design and development, promotion and administration, delivery (staff or technology), materials and training facilities, trainee wages, and training evaluation.

And after training, keep track of monetary benefits, including labor savings, reduction in lost workdays and workers' compensation costs, productivity increases, and lower turnover costs.

Unfortunately, just over half (55 percent) of organizations are reporting on workforce costs.

To calculate the return on investment in HR, one should look at the relationship between the sales value derived from each training day and the total number of the training days involved, and dividing the result by the <u>total cost</u> of training.

ii. Remuneration: People are paid and in return there is an expectation that they provide the company with value.

61 percent of respondent found their total benefits package to be adequate.

Companies need to have employees who generate high levels of revenue. Overpaying employees who cannot generate high revenues or fail to complete tasks effectively and efficiently may lead to losses.

Companies with consistent levels of high revenue per employee usually indicate a company with solid management and production operations.

iii.   Staffing cost: Staffing the business is expensive, particularly when we have a number of job vacancies to fill.

In case of staffing decisions, we need to be aware of the costs, and decide the most cost effective way to take care of the staffing needs.

In order to measure the effectiveness and efficiency of the recruiting function, we calculate the cost per hire.

Cost per hire is calculated by adding up all of the expenses associated with recruiting and then dividing by the number of new hires.

Less than 32 percent of companies tracked the cost to hire a new employee.

b.   Output measures: HR leaders are measuring the efficiency and/or effectiveness of the organizations. These measures are generally output-oriented, focus on internal HR processes and activities, and are used to make improvements to HR-specific policies and procedures.

26% of HR leaders cannot measure the business impact of people management programs on their organization.

Human Resources Management measure is utilized to calculate the impact it has on organization's goals and mission.

54% agree that progress toward goals is measured.

The output of HR leaders' activity includes:

i. Products and services produced: The products and services produced by employees are measured by objectives or standards.

Employee job quality is a barometer to the success of operation, and a way to control employee's output.

It becomes necessary for the HR function to follow more of a business orientation philosophy. By this philosophy, the HR function is charged with the responsibility of advising and counseling line managers in people-related business issues.

75% of HR executives advise top management on organizational structure.

HR leaders understand that the factors to ensure competitiveness of the organization are quality product, quality customer service, and quality delivery.

ii. Financial performance: Performance plans that demonstrate the organization's ability to accomplish in particular fiscal year that contributes to the company profit.

Financial performance is observed through balance sheets, cash flow reports, and income statements.

To assess the value that HR can bring, we must look at the role that HR plays in increasing a company's profits. HR leaders' financial performance is characterized by:

1. Profit per employee: Profit divided by number of employees. This is a measure of the profits that is generated by employees working for the organization.

Human Resources Management is important to the success of a business, and the company should carefully compare profits per employee for the organization with other companies which have similar business.

Most of companies still measure their performance using systems that measure internal financial result. They don't take sufficient notice of the real engines for its wealth creation, i.e. the knowledge, relationship, reputation, and other intangibles created by talented people.

The superior performance of successful companies demonstrates the value of intangible assets.

Companies can redesign the internal financial performance approach and set goals for the return on intangibles by paying greater attention to profit per employee rather than putting all of the focus on returns on invested capital.

HR leaders can create wealth either by increasing profit per employee, by increasing the number of employees earning such profits, or combination of both methods.

2. Revenue per employee: A commonly used measure of management efficiency is revenue per employee. The best run companies have high revenue per employee figures.

The turnover generated by employee in the organization is indication of how much revenue people produce.

Revenue per employee is to determine how productive employees are in a business.

Steve Jobs is the most successful Apple's CEO. He is selected as a smartest CEO, because of his capability to constitute tech savvy today.

He has combination of alchemy of intellect, ambition, and that uncanny ability to peer around corners.

He is a visionary, a micromanager, and a showman who creates such anticipation around new products that their releases are veritable holidays. And Jobs is a pop culture icon like no other business executive.

Job has succeeded to turn Apple which was close to bankruptcy becoming a company with market cap of $250 billion and is the world's most valuable tech company.

HR leaders support employees to increase their revenues. This can be delivered through a variety of different approaches such as greater productivity e.g. increasing employee engagement; new products and services e.g. increased innovation; increased customer spend e.g. improved customer service; or entering new markets e.g. appropriate talent.

Where there is a potential to increase revenues, HR leaders have a role in helping the organizations build investment to HR.

This formula indicates how productive each employee is in generating revenues for the organization.

From the difference between revenue and costs, employees' productivity can be clearly seen. Human Resource productivity will act to broaden the gap between revenue and costs.

c. Outcome measures: It considers how people respond. People interact and respond to what they are required to do, how they do it, and how they are managed.

This measurement shows how the organization efforts are related to business outcomes such as on customer engagement, revenue, growth, profit generation, etc.

HR leaders should be able to assure maximum employees retention rate and minimum resignation rate.

Resignation rate affects the cost of losing and replacing key employees. It means loss of skills and expertise and a need to incur costs by hiring new staff.

HR leaders believe that providing career advancement opportunities as well as career development program are the two most important mechanisms for retaining high performers.

Very few companies measure the correlation between staff training and employee turnover.

There are also other elements, such as morale and job satisfaction, which are too subjective to measure.

18 percent of organizations ascertain hiring manager satisfaction.

The HR function's primary customers are the employees of the organization. A powerful predictor of an organization's ability to attract and retain its employees is indicated by employee engagement.

Employee engagement is the degree to which employees are intellectually and emotionally committed to the larger cause of the organization.

It has been shown that employee engagement is positively correlated with business financial results and is a strong lead-indicator of high tenures and productivity.

Performance Management is one of the key processes that helps employees know that their contributions are recognized and acknowledged.

Only a third of survey participants have all employees completing performance reviews; 12 percent have no performance appraisal process at all.

HR leaders insist that workforce success become a measured accountability of line leaders. The line leaders would be evaluated on workforce successhow well the workforce impacts the success of the organization.

Performance Management is an ongoing process of communication between line leaders and employees that occurs throughout the year, in support of accomplishing the strategic objectives of the organization.

The communication process includes clarifying expectations, setting objectives, identifying goals, providing feedback, and evaluating results. Employees, who work with line leaders whose good Performance Management, will find following circumstances:

a.   Feel valued: In the successful organization, contribution is seen as important matter. The recognition considers that its people are its most important asset has traditionally been part of the corporate culture.

Contented, happy employees directly influence a company's productivity.

b.   Feel supported: Focus more on the efficiency and effectiveness of programs that support the bottom line.

Employees are valued partners, with the right to fair labor practices, competitive wages and benefits and a safe, harassment-free, family-friendly work environment.

For the leaders themselves they should be encouraging collaborative behavior—not setting teams off against each other; equally they should be actively discouraging a silo mentality.

c.   Be recognized for their high performance Employees know that those contributions will be recognized and acknowledged. High performers do not feel like they are carrying the low performers. Employees function better when fueled.

Top HR executives at world-class companies are 115% more likely to report to the chairman or CEO.

A HR leader shows continuous focus on improving their organisations' human capital. Human capital is collective knowledge, skills and abilities of people that contribute to organizational success. leaders foster innovation and ideas and prepare employees to succeed in work place.

HR leaders allow employees from competing together. It opens an opportunity for employees to explore and exploit their own capacities to achieve their future desires.

This does not mean that employees do not get the work done if they are not given extra for what they earn, but a sound reward system makes all the difference.

While HR leaders seek to understand what other companies do or to develop the 'form' that will do everything they want; line leaders are frustrated with the 'over grading' of employees, but are seldom engaged in modeling the desired process or clarifying the performance expectations. Good employee performance management should consider following issues:

a.   Provide performance ratings: Setting clear performance expectations, it helps the employee know what needs to be done to be successful on the job.

Through the use of objectives, standards, performance dimensions, and other measures it focuses effort.

This helps the department get done what needs to be done and provides a solid rationale for eliminating work that is no longer useful.

b.   Link performance processes to career development and learning management

97% of HR leaders believe that a systematic career development process positively impacts employee retention and engagement.

By defining job-mastery and career development goals as part of the process, it enables the employees to understand clearly how the current position supports their growth and the opportunities they need to explore.

c.   Drive continuous improvement: Through regular check-in discussions, which include status updates, coaching, and feedback, it promotes flexibility, allowing us and the employee to identify problems and set action plans to improve the lacks.

By knowing the performance of employees and organization, HR leaders have an opportunity to develop their own action plans for partnering with line leaders in developing plans for their organizations and employees.

Accountability

Human Resources leader must be fully aligned with the CEO in creating and implementing the vision and mission statement for an organization.

66% of HR leaders are not viewed as strategic partners by the Top Management.

Human Resource function has good impact on general business performance. In fact, an organization's competitive advantage largely depends on the way it manages its largest assetits people.

There always seems to be annoying conflicts line leaders, employees and Human Resources leaders over the management process.

Guatemalan police arrested Alejandro Giammattei, the former head of the national prison system, accusing him of orchestrating the executions of seven prisoners during a 2006 government raid on an infamous jail.

The jail had ostensibly been controlled by prisoners for a decade with guards only patrolling the perimeter while allowing inmates to build private houses, restaurants, video arcades and even hard-drug laboratories on the inside.

The raid, carried out by thousands of police and soldiers backed up by helicopters. The authorities said the prisoners were heavily armed.

Authorities bulldozed the part of the prison farm with churches, pool halls and telephone banks where prisoners extorted people on the outside.

Line leaders are accountable for the business results achieved through good human resources management, the HR leaders are accountable for HR compliance, and both are accountable for the overall effectiveness of the Human Resources Management program.

Half of the respondents agree that Human Resources Management (HRM) accountability is shared between the HR leaders and line leaders.

When responsibilities exceed rights, companies go nowhere. When rights exceed responsibilities, companies go bust.

Today's global business environment demand equal responsibility and accountability from HR leaders and line leaders.

HR leaders greatly increase the value of the HR function to the business.

Competencies can be described as traits such as knowledge, personality, skills, abilities, and attitudes. The competencies required by HR leaders have changed over the years, depending on how the HR function was expected to work with its customers.

HR leaders require a wide range of skills and competencies, and yet The HR leaders may not get the breadth of development needed to prepare them for strategic leadership.

HR leader is responsible for directing the organization's journey to world-class status and for creating an organizational culture committed to all that is necessary for achieving continuous improvement.

According to animal rights activists, the number of animals at Kiev Zoo, Ukraine's Biggest Zoo, has almost halved in the last two years; they accuse the zoo's authorities of shoddy management, corruption and neglect.

The deaths have prompted outrage and denial, with activists accusing the zoo of negligence and corruption and authorities pointing to an anonymous killer as the culprit.

The animal was underfed, kept in poor conditions and stressed by constant changes to the staff of handlers.

They criticized officials of carrying out shady schemes to privatize the land the zoo is located on in the center of the Ukrainian capital.

In order for leaders to position themselves favorably for the upturn, they must create a sense of meaning and purpose at their work for those they lead and develop a sustainable culture that is ethically strong and successful.

We demonstrate our commitment by taking actions that achieve desired performance, improve efficiencies and own their responsibilities. There are clear consequences to our actions. HR leaders are accountable for their action, includes:

a.   Measurement: HR can only determine its value to the organization by measuring it. The performance measures are becoming better linked to individual, group and organizational success.

85 percent of companies have no economic data exists to justify how HR decisions impact the bottom line.

Effective measurement is crucial to deliver effective HCM. Comprehensive human resources measurement policy enables the organizational management to collect consistent information about the employee population, which alleviates decision-making and ensures that management and development activities remain relevant with overall business strategy.

W. Edwards Deming, says: "When you can measure what you are speaking about, and express it in numbers, you know something about it; but when you cannot measure it, when you cannot express it in numbers, your knowledge is of a meager and unsatisfactory kind."

HR management can make business decisions that are based on cold facts rather than 'gut feeling,' and use the exact figures to back up business cases and requests for resource.

b.   Provide opportunity: There is always opportunity to build a more valuable work force.

Employees will be much more inclined to be positive and energetic about their jobs if they have trust in line leaders.

Employees must also ensure that they are demonstrating their capabilities, seeking feedback, asking how they can help the company to be more successful, and helping their leaders understand what they need to be successful.

Saudi Arabia ordered at least one BlackBerry smart-phone service to be blocked.

India's security establishment has taken a hard-line view on Research In Motion's (RIM) stance that it does not possess a 'master key' to intercept data traffic on BlackBerry and has warned services that cannot be monitored will be shut down.

The United Arab Emirates claims it does not have the same kind of surveillance rights to BlackBerry messages. It has threatened to clamp down on some services unless they get more access.

Saudi Arabia, India and the United Arab Emirates together represent only about 5 percent of the 41 million BlackBerry devices in service worldwide.

c.   Development: Training and education, in what the employee is interested in learning, is one of the key factors in retention and motivation.

Yet 56% of HR leaders still do not believe that their workforces are adequately prepared to meet their organizations' future plans.

Training will add value to employees by providing them with the tools to efficiently and effectively apply their knowledge/ skills to the organization.

d.   Availability of workforce planning and analysis: Workforce Planning is the planned strategic process of linking business directions with planning for resources, growth strategies, together with planned activities including succession planning, work design and staff development.

Workforce planning is a critical step in planning for staff and achieving the goals of the University's Strategic Plan. It is the first step in the human resource planning cycle and links up to preparing to recruit, attracting staff, recruiting and selecting staff and developing staff.

e.   Internal mobility and career development: Career development is now the primary responsibility of individuals in organizations. Employees have to proactively prepare their future in the organization.

Two-thirds of organizations have tied or plan to tie employee career development planning to learning management in order to facilitate training.

A recent study indicates that HRD Directors consider career development to be their least important function.

The responsibility for learning and for the development of career paths has been downloaded to the individual employees.

f.   Self-learning culture: HR leaders develop environment that focus on self-learning. This ability is currently one of the important goals of today's business.

A study showed that over 80% of managing directors believed Human Capital Management to be vital for the fundamental success of a business.

Training, workshop, or seminar is not only the way to development employees. The organization should shift company-centered development to self-learning capability.

HR leaders foster approach to development by emphasizing self-learning culture and are keen to promote its benefits to individuals and the organizations.

g.   Reward: A meaning of the size of the reward, usually related to the depth of the appreciation. Unless each reward is greater than the last, we risk being seen as less appreciative than we really are. HR leaders think about companywide acknowledgements, such as an employee-of-the-month program, as well as innovative rewards, raises, and promotions.

HR leader should, therefore, formulate an employee reward and recognition policy that is fair, transparent and justifiable.

A reward considers honoring the outstanding performance by expressing our appreciation and offering our trust. Offer our trust by offering more responsibility and greater challenges.

By giving the outstanding performer an opportunity to demonstrate further outstanding performance, we give both the performer and the organization opportunities to achieve together. It includes:

1.   Reward a star employee periodically. A star employee delivers competent and committed employee.

We can make a provision of Monthly or Quarterly Award for the best employee, Awarding 2 or 3 best workers each month. The award can be in terms of gifts or money.

Israel granted honorary citizenship to an Indian woman who braved gunfire to save an Israeli boy from the 2008 Mumbai terror attacks that killed both of his parents.

Sandra Samuel rescued 2-year-old Moshe Holtzberg from a Jewish center targeted by Islamic militants. She found him by his parents' bodies and rushed him to safety.

Samuel has been caring for him in Israel since then. He is in the custody of his extended family.

2.   Make a personal phone call or visit to each employee weekly or at least monthly.

3.   Acknowledge or affirm their accomplishments: A high-performance, results-oriented culture within our organization with motivated employees who take pride in and find a sense of accomplishment from their work.

One of the most effective ways to express appreciation is often one of the most overlooked: saying thank you.

Even if most of the duties one performs are a normal part of the job, hearing 'thank you' in a spontaneous and timely way can mean a lot to anyone. It should be done often, and can be done privately or publicly in front of co-workers.

HR leader should, therefore, formulate an employee reward and recognition policy that is fair, transparent and justifiable.

With her father away on military service in the Middle East, Chelsea Jusino was resigned to attending her high school graduation without him.

But when she donned her graduation gown and went to the ceremony at a baseball stadium in Clearwater, Fla., she got a surprise.

After Gary Schlereth, principal of Countryside High School, spoke to the students about adulthood, he introduced a video on the stadium's JumboTron screen. There was Chelsea's dad, Edgar Jusino.

"Chelsea, I know due to certain circumstances, I have not always been there for you and that I have missed many important dates in your life," the elder Jusino said.

"I want you to know that I will always be there for you in your hardest, most difficult, most lonely times. I will be there to pick you up when you fall. Wipe your knees and hands. Clean your feet. Wipe your tears. Give you a shoulder to cry. Give you a hug, with a kiss."

By using proper measurements enables HR leader to:

1. Assess his/her performance: Make sure employees understand what is critical for the business to succeed and recognize they will be rewarded based on those achievements.

    HR leaders teach the employees to inspect or to evaluate their own work for quality with the understanding that they know what high quality work is.

    High performing HR leaders are credible and proactive—have a point of view, are willing to challenge assumptions, make things happen.

    Like line leaders who reports dollars associated with operation, HR leaders must be held accountable for reducing dollar loss as a result of turnover, the HR equivalent of waste.

    A litmus test is also required to see whether a business is in good shape is to measure the engagement of employees and ask them for regular feedback.

    When we replace an employee, we need to start the process all over againwe start with raw goods and transform it into a value-added product. Manufacturing calls this as re-work.

    HR leaders must report and be held accountable for terminationsvoluntary and involuntaryas costs of re-work.

    Organizations with an advanced people management strategy that is well aligned to overall business objectives and strategy outperform those organizations that have no people management strategy by 32%.

    When effective strategy, leadership, and integration are all pulled together within the organization, a dichotomy between HR leaders and laggards becomes clear.

    HR leaders emphasize talent strategy in place, dedicate line leaders responsible for strategy and programs, and integrate talent processes, systems, and data. On other hand, a laggard has nothing to do with people development.

Overall, people management leaders outperform laggards by 37%.

2. Create HR policy-based research: Provide information, research studies, articles and case studies to find more effective strategies for assessing and developing Human Resource practices.

   Using millions of Twitter messages, or tweets, from the popular social networking site, researchers at Northeastern University in Boston have created a Twitter Mood Map to measure the moods of the nation.

   People are happiest in the morning and in the evening, with happiness peaking on Sunday morning and dipping Thursday night, they found. Twitter users appeared most gloomy at mid-afternoon, shifting to better moods in the evening.

3. Understand competitors: Evaluate on criteria that are used to benchmark company performance with peer group organizations.

   Benchmarking is a systematic process of measuring an organization's products, services, and practices against those of a like organization that is a recognized leader.

   HR leaders assess the effectiveness and competitiveness of the programs in relation to peer group, industry or key competitors.

   HR leaders are using this practice to identify ways to improve product/service and align with business results.

   The University of California at Berkeley was second, followed by Stanford, according to the list of 500 institutions compiled by Jiaotong University's Centre for World-Class Universities.

   Jiaotong uses criteria such as the number of Nobel prizes and Fields medals won by staff and alumni, the number of highly cited researchers on staff, and the number of articles by faculty published in Nature and Science magazines.

It was intended to benchmark the performance of Chinese universities, amid efforts by Beijing to create a set of world-class research institutions.

High performers understand both the business and external and industry factors that influence success.

4. Recognize other world-class companies that are not competitors (generic and functional benchmarking): Get insight into the differences and similarities in HR policy across surrounding countries.

   These benchmarking will highlight areas of relative strength and weakness and gives HR leaders and Top Management valuable insight to their employer brand.

4. Information systems: Company requires credible information systems for collecting, processing, and disseminating data and for providing the feedback mechanism that is required to meet their objectives.

   Google Inc launched a website for users who want to sift through news, comments and other information on the Internet in real time.

   Google's effort underscores the importance of real-time data on social media, in an increasingly competitive Internet search arena which it dominates. Microsoft in October also announced partnerships with Twitter and Facebook to provide real-time search results.

   Technology, including the information revolution and globalization continue to exert major effects on HR.

   Many companies have claimed that the benefits of technology have not matched the cost of investment in it. The reason for this in most cases is that technology has not been used productively or usefully.

Technology per se is not productive, and does not add value unless there are people who can use it productively. IT may crush time and space.

In Australia, late guilty pleas were seen a major contributor to delays and inefficiencies in the trial process.

The 40 percent reduction in term length would apply for someone pleading guilty within six weeks of arrest, while a 30 percent cut would apply for a later plea that still comes before a trial is set.

A 20 percent reduction would be given for guilty pleas entered after trial committal proceedings.

There would be no reduction for a plea entered in the four weeks leading up to a trial.

5.   Adhere to continuous improvement: One of the qualities of HR leaders is that they seek to improvement anything they do.

Demonstrate continuous improvement that is supported by the strategic use of information systems.

HR leaders continually teach the employees that the essence of quality is constant improvement. The line leader's job is as a facilitatordoing everything possible to provide the workers with the best tools and a friendly, non-coercive, and non-adversarial atmosphere.

High performers understand, respect, and evolve the organization through improvements in HR systems and practices.

More than 80% of organizations have still not yet aligned their HR programs and activities to business results, which suggest a significant room for improvement.

HR leader should be in the front to enable the company achieves an international standard of people management excellence.

The Human Resource leader is not focused on compliance, but provides the tools, training and assistance needed for line leaders to fulfill their responsibilities.

Profit

We all need to remind ourselves that we're in business for profit.

A successful organization should seek opportunity of getting large cost reductions, as well as increased revenues, higher capacity utilization, higher sales per employee, and returns on invested capital (ROIC).

HR organization that uses technology might be spending more money.

But this increased spending more than pays for itself by enabling improved efficiency and effectiveness human resources (HR).

With the help of improved technology usage, world-class HR organizations spend 13% less than other.

HR function will operate with fewer staff and also show improved performance across a range of metrics tracking effectiveness and strategic alignment.

Leo J. Taylor, executive vice president for human resources at Pulte Homes, says that he hopes to have pared his workforce-management staff from 30 down to 20, after reaching $20 billion in annual revenues. "I want one HR professional for every $1 billion in revenue," Taylor declares.

HR leaders must have a strong understanding of operation and finance. Once the initial cost savings are calculated, they have to track the long-term productivity and savings.

HR leaders could be evaluated on financial contributions, such as cost saving initiatives; customer satisfaction that reflects workforce success; improvements in business processes that lead to greater efficiency and accuracy. Successful HR leaders contribute high profit for the organizations, i.e.:

a.   Optimize cost: HR leaders conduct cost and impact analysis that assures employees practice the desired behaviors, produce the desired results and provide cost-effective outcomes.

HR leaders have responsibility to ensure that the organization does not unnecessarily spend money where the returns cannot be justified or the resources are unavailable.

The best-performing companies spend 25% less on HR than other, less successful organisations.

ABC has helped determine the full cost of agency activities, the proper distribution of costs, and has even influenced service rates. An additional benefit to the system is that it has encouraged strategic thinking.

Activity Based Costing (ABC) is a method of cost management that determines the true cost, including overhead, for a service or product.

Finding the true cost allows agencies to discover cost improvement opportunities, prepare and actualize strategic and operational plans, and improve strategic decision-making.

It involves identifying activities, determining activity costs, determining cost drivers, collecting activity data, and calculating the service cost.

Nowhere is workers' rage as palpable as in Bangladesh, where even Sheikh Hasina Wajed, the prime minister, called the current minimum wage 'not only insufficient, but inhuman.'

"There are no industrial relations," says Korshed Alam, a Dhaka-based labour rights activist. "The whole attitude is arrogant and feudal. Owners and government think they are helping the workers. The workers are not treated like workers—they are treated like beggars."

b.   Cost cut: When the economy goes into a downturn what corporations focus on changes. It shifts from a focus toward growth and hiring to one where CFO's run the agenda and cost cutting becomes 'king.'

The best-performing companies spend 25% less on HR than other, less successful organisations.

HR leaders continue to support the organisation in reducing costs and being as efficient as possible. This can be delivered in direct savings or managing risks e.g. helping managers to make balanced decisions.

According to a survey, 43 percent of respondents said they would cut their budgets. Another 40 percent of respondents said they plan to implement hiring freezes. About 40 percent of companies polled said they won't fill jobs lost to attrition.

It may require creative ways to cuts HR costs; in which the following ideas may be worth exploring:

i.   Bring the salary of new hires to the lower level: Low salary may result in a much lower job offer or losing the job offer we worked so hard to obtain.

Surveys indicate job seekers will continue to have a hard time getting work.

To secure talent, we should consider the salary history of the employee is taken into consideration.

Specifically, attention should be given to the candidate's previous experience as it relates to the responsibilities and required skills in the new classification.

Consideration of past experience and corresponding salary will help us to establish a salary rate in our deliberations.

ii.   Reduce employee's salary: Pay cut is never good news. It's the employer's prerogative to set pay rates for employees and to periodically adjust those pay rates (up or down) unless otherwise defined or limited by an employment or union agreement.

In the event an impending salary reduction, a prior notice or warning to the employee is recommended. Likewise, when a pay reduction is necessary to reduce costs to save the business during difficult economic times, an employee may consider a job with a lower pay rate to be a better alternative to a layoff.

Clearly communicate to all affected employees the economic conditions and the resulting employment actions being considered.

iii.   Freeze the employee's salary: A pay freeze on management salaries should be made effective first, prior to be implemented to employees.

HR leaders bring essential cost savings and work practice efficiencies in order for the company to grow and remain competitive.

Employees claim their compensation that they have earned in exchange for their labor, is their right. In an economy where employees are said to earn what they work for, it is contradictory and unjust to call this anything but unwaged and uncompensated labor.

Only 7% of organizations had already instituted a blanket salary freeze for this period, while 5% were considering it and 12% were considering a freeze for specific employee groups.

iv.   Freeze recruitment: The freeze is one element of sweeping changes to the size and scope of the organization. The ban on new recruitment is likely to see expense reduction.

Jon Terry at PwC said: "Pay and promotion freezes, changes to pension schemes, cuts in recruitment and slashed training budgets, combined with poor communication, have eroded the bonds of trust between some employers and their employees."

The effect of long-term hiring freezes is particularly damaging to the recruiting function, because 'no hiring' generally means that a majority of recruiters will be laid off.

Recruitment and promotion freezes are always temporary in nature. Even if the freeze lasts a number of years, at some stage new employees must be hired and merit-based promotion should be reinstated.

It affects lost revenue. Across-the-board hiring freezes mean that critical revenue-generating and revenue-impact positions go unfilled.

Obviously, when there is no one in a revenue-generating position, there is a lost opportunity to generate revenue if the position remains vacant.

v. Freeze promotions: Whenever there is a downturn in economic conditions, one of the first knee-jerk reactions that many CFO's and Top Management take is placing a freeze on all hiring, pay raises, budgets, and promotions.

There was a more positive attitude to promotions with none of the respondents considering a freeze on promotions in 2010. This compares to 12% in 2009.

vi. Suspend training and development program.

vii. Suspension of the automatic replacement of employee who are retired in normal condition.

viii. Freeze salary increase: HR leaders see that an immediate reaction to the downturn was to reduce or freeze salary increases.

ix. Withdraw benefits, i.e. allowances, health insurance, pension program, tax, etc

x. Reduce workforce, i.e. early retirement, lay-off, flattening the organization

In the time of budget cuts, downsizing, and an aging workforce, workforce planning becomes extremely important to increasing the organizations' overall ability to achieve its missions.

xi.   Jobs cut: Companies will rely on hiring freezes and budget cuts instead of lay-offs to get through the recession. It gives job growth remains flat.

About 70 percent of those surveyed said they expect a continued weak environment for hiring in the second quarter of 2009.

The respondents went on to say that they plan to keep their payrolls flat or will eliminate jobs. Most of them did not add any new jobs.

xii.   Outsource the particular workforce: Outsourcing has become a critical component of a cost-effective delivery strategy. Successful outsourcing begins with internal processes, including HR transformation, pragmatic scoping of the HR outsourcing project, gap analysis and change management.

HR outsourcing was not new. In 1999, British Petroleum agreed to outsource almost all of its HR processes to Exult.

c.   Demonstrate effectiveness: HR leaders realize benefits that go well beyond financial returns. They are able to increase the focus of the people on key performance drivers, and strengthen their commitment to success throughout the organization.

World-class companies operate with 15% fewer staff.

d.   Productivity: A measure of efficiency with regards to the use of Human Resources within the organization. Productivity is simply the value of the outputs the organization produces divided by the costs of producing those outputs.

HR leaders need to focus on productivity. The leaders first identify which people programs (training, compensation, recruitment or employee relations) can dramatically increase employee productivity.

Then they focus their time and resources on those productivity increasing services and programs.

So if we haven't already done it, begin tracking our company's revenue per employee, profit per employee or employee output per dollar spent.

We should do a competitive analysis by comparing our figures to the product competitors and to our own 'last month's' performance. Then, begin 'merciless criticism of our current approach in order to improve our results everyday until they are the highest in the industry.

We have to prove that HR function increases productivity, product quality, customer satisfaction, margins, sales or product development speed.

The level of productivity should be a factor in our organization's business

Improving the over-all productivity of the workforce requires that HR develop initiatives to continuously increase the dollar value of employee output while maintaining or reducing the average labor cost per unit.

The formula for productivity is simply—Productivity equals to Outputs / Inputs.

HR must accept that it is their job to influence line leaders within the organization to increase the productivity of employees.

To increase productivity, outputs must increase more than costs. There are two basic ways to accomplish this, decrease costs while maintaining output, or increase output while maintaining low cost. Things HR leaders can do to increase productivity include:

i.   Retention tools: Employee retention, especially of the most desirable employees, is a key challenge in organizations today.

Knowing what makes employees unhappy is half the battle when you think about employee work satisfaction, morale, positive motivation, and retention.

If employees feel safe, they will tell us what's on their minds. Our work culture must foster trust for successful two-way communication.

Competitive salary, competitive vacation and holidays, and tuition reimbursement are three basic examples in employee retention.

ii. Referral programs: This will reduce cost (charges of external consultants and searching agencies) of hiring a new employee and up to an extent we can rely on this resource.

World-class organizations fill professional positions 35 percent more quickly than their peers.

On every successful referral, employee can be given a referral bonus after 6 or 9 months of continuous working of the new employee.

By this we can get a new employee at a reduced cost as well as are retaining the existing one for a longer period of time.

iii. Metrics (to increase accountability) and rewards that are tied to performance and productivity.

iv. Take survey or interview: Identifying what motivate, challenge and frustrate employees.

v.   Performance Management programs that drop poor performing line leaders and employees and offer incentive systems that focus on rewarding great people.

vi. On the job learning and growth opportunities, i.e. job rotations and special projects, offer rewards for sharing best practices between employees.

vii.   Increase cooperation: Provide measures and rewards that encourage cross functional communication.

viii. Appropriate forecasting and workforce planning.

The ultimate measure in productivity is called people profit. It is a ratio between profit and total employee costs. The organizations that generate more dollars of profit per dollar spent on employee costs are the most productive.

e.   Cost saving: Many organizations need to find ways to reduce their overheads.

HR leaders provide processes and programs that align with the corporate strategic business plan to reduce operating costs, increase productivity and increase retention.

For some employers, this means redundancies and for others, adopting alternative ways to make the necessary cost savings whilst trying to maintain their existing staff in whom they have invested time and resources.

Indeed, some larger organizations have actively sought to avoid redundancies where possible and maintain their staff training and development programs so that they will have the staff in place when the economy becomes more buoyant again.

49% of employees understand their employers' decisions over reward and working hours because times are tough. Many HR leaders encourage organization cost saving program includes:

i.   Review salary increase to the expected level

ii.   Flexible working opportunities: i.e. working from home, job sharing or varying or reducing hours of work, shift shifting.

HR leaders have differing expectations of how and when they should work. While it may be acceptable to call contacts in one location in the evening or during their vacation, others may consider it intrusive or unprofessional.

iii. Review benefits, i.e. insurance, transportation, scholarship, etc

Only five percent of companies polled are willing to cut employee benefits.

About 78 percent of respondents reduced health care coverage.

iv. Apply HR solutions/program that enable employees to do digital/automatic transactional activities

World-Class HR organizations 87 percent more likely to use common HR applications, rely on fewer benefit and compensation plans.

v. Introduce sabbatical policy, i.e. allowing a period of unpaid leave.

vi. Opportunity to buy extra annual leave.

vii. Reduce absenteeism, i.e. review sickness, encourage healthy lifestyle

viii. Control overtime, i.e. ensure job planning and workforce assignment, convert overtime to leave.

ix. Encourage innovations and creative thought.

x. Simplify the organization, i.e. Introduce shared service unit.

xi. Restricting the authority of spending for hiring, advertisement, or purchasing.

xii. Slow down the promotions.

xiii. Distract employees, i.e. encourage multi tasks, bring in the working time control machine to the individual workplace, prevent work redundancy.

xiv. Review punishment policy for misconduct behavior or wrongdoing, i.e. application of tough punishment.

In China, any official who was reassigned or demoted as a consequence of serious misconduct would have to wait for any career advancement opportunities.

> *Geng Zhixiu, who was removed as director of Jinan Railway Administration in April 2008, following a fatal railway accident that left more than 70 dead, was appointed security director of the Ministry of Railway last March.*

xv.   Outsource the particular tasks, i.e. Hire new employees through a recruitment partner, or outsource administrative jobs.

xvi.   Emphasize referral program for recruitment: i.e. utilize alumni networks.

xvii. Talent transfer: Give away high caliber professional for economic gain.

xviii. Review HR practices: Policies, procedures, rigid rules, lack of strategic management decisions, absence of statewide HR data, lack of workforce planning or the ability to plan for the future, etc.

> *"Complexity increases costs. World-class HR executives are simply more effective at targeting areas where complexity reduction offers the greatest impact," said Stephen Joyce of Hackett.*

> *"This focus on complexity reduction is a significant factor in how they cut costs, operate with significantly fewer staff, yet provide more strategic benefit to their companies."*

xix.   Bring in skilled employees: i.e. do not hire fresh graduate, only hire candidates with experiences and certain level of competencies.

xx.   This practice will reduce cost of people development program.

xxi.   Review cash reward: A result of the recession, there would be less emphasis on the cash element when rewarding employees.

Zero defect policy: Zero-defect is effective for quality management. Once line leaders accept zero defect policy as his or her personal performance standard, error will no longer be tolerated and defects will go away; defects can be prevented.

Defect will cause wastes (material time, energy, and money) and un-necessary work repetition.

They know that cutting waste translates to saving time and money for the organization.

xxii. Deliver a recruitment process with rigor, speed and accuracy.

A research supports that the more engaged employees are, the longer they stay with and the more valuable they are to the corporation. The research consistently indicates that engaged employees are more likely to recommend their employer as a place to work and have pride in the organization.

xxiii. Reduce redundancy in roles and responsibility: Define clearly the roles and responsibilities and required skills.

When people management technology usage and the overall business impact of technology are correlated, several potential areas of focus emerge to both increase internal talent mobility (i.e. finding new opportunities for top performers within the organization) and decrease voluntary turnover (i.e. flight).

Reducing top performer flight is top of mind for many HR practitioners.

HR leaders prevent a situation that could create resentment among career HR people. They must be a hero for their own staffs.

They, therefore, develop new skills in which HR people will be able to well-perform in a transformed function.

xxiv. Review bureaucratic procedures: The more complex the job, the more complex the demands.

xxv. Improve response time and customer service, i.e. tracking response times and the over-all customer service rate

xxvi. Application of IT: Web technology, data-entry tasks and other transactions could be pushed to line leaders or employees without having to train them how to operate HRIS software.

HR leaders encourage smooth pay run with a minimal error rate; create a single, centralized Web-enabled HR database, real-time connection for the routine transaction.

HR could bundle up all of the data-entry tasks for recruiting or learning management into HRIS and move these tasks from a $40-per-hour generalist to a $7-per-hour clerk.

Organizations with fully integrated talent processes, systems, and data outperform those organizations that have not integrated by 41%.

xxvii. Redeploy the talent: Redeployment means rapidly moving the most productive workers out of low return divisions and jobs and into higher return ones.

The shifting of great people into the right job can have a dramatic increase in productivity and without the need for any additional hiring.

HR needs to learn how to rapidly redeploy talent.

Redeployment means rapidly moving the most productive workers out of low return divisions and jobs and into higher return ones.

The shifting of great people into the right job can have a dramatic increase in productivity and without the need for any additional hiring.

HR leaders need to begin a redeployment program. This means a proactive effort to identify top performers that would have an increased impact if they were moved to higher growth divisions or more impactful jobs.

Under redeployment, HR leaders should identify the talented people and proactively persuades them to move (or just moves them) into jobs where they can have a larger impact.

Conversely, low performers in key divisions and jobs must be transferred to where they might make the most productivity impact or should be moved out of the company.

xxviii. Become a competitive advantage: During tough times executives become increasingly competitive; they're almost always more competitive than HR leaders.

If a HR leader is to survive budget cuts he/she must demonstrate that his/her programs and approach provide the company with a distinct competitive advantage in the marketplace.

It means HR leaders must be able to demonstrate that 'the way we do it' is different enough and its results are superior enough so that the HR programs need to be maintained or even strengthened.

HR leaders who are consistently offer the employees new opportunities and invested in the people pipeline are now at a competitive advantage.

In a fast changing competitive world, 'speed doesn't kill, slow kills.' Because the speed of change matters; HR leaders must learn to match the speed in which the products/service can improve.

HR leaders continually improve their speed of change and 'obsolete' their programs as fast as the speed the company improves its products/services and at a rate that is even faster than the competitors.

The HR leaders need to do competitive intelligence and benchmarking against their competitors. They must prepare a competitive analysis showing how and where HR programs are superior.

More importantly, demonstrate how HR leaders help the organizations maintain an advantage in sales, productivity or product development.

Factors that influencing HR leader can contribute to business profit, i.e.:

i. Employee engagement: Companies should create a strong sense of ownership with their employees. Therefore, equity ownership remains a critical element of a total system of rewards.

    World-class organizations have 61 percent fewer voluntary terminations per thousand employees, and they fill professional positions 35 percent more quickly than their peers.

    Ownership provides more than just a 'monthly paycheck' relationship with employees; it reinforces a mutual commitment to the long-term success of the company.

    Attractive and competitive compensation is to create a sense of ownership, a stake in the long-term value of the company or a tool to attract and retain critical talent.

    The companies use it to create a balance between operational results, and strategic value creation.

    A goal of HR leaders is to create the type of environment where employees are engaged in that mission and vision of the company.

    Creating an engaged employee is the responsibility of both Human Resources leaders and the line leaders.

    Most organizations leave the task of creating employee engagement to the HR leaders.

    The Top Management who gets disconnected with the day to day rigmarole of employee engagement, and thinking or presuming that it is what the HR function exists for.

ii.   Employee loyalty and commitment: Employees know what they are responsible for and see how their work is linked to the broader strategy, goals and priorities of the organization.

HR staffs are able to spend 223 percent more time than their peers doing analysis for standard reports and less time collecting and compiling data.

Poor HR leaders work very long hours. They think this is a brand of heroism but it is probably the single biggest hallmark of incompetence.

But good leaders are passionate about becoming excellent people because they value people.

To work effectively, we must prioritize and we must pace ourselves. The HR leaders who boast of late nights, early mornings and no time off cannot manage themselves so they would better not manage anyone else."

More than 50% of employees are (currently) looking to change companies.

iii.   Strategic capability: Optimize employees' performance levels and so that the human potential can be explored fully.

Top Management recognizes the importance of the HR leaders to mission accomplishment, especially in terms of recruitment and staffing, employee development, and employee relations.

A HR leader able to show his/her confidence when he/she speaks, the company listens.

The dangers to an older woman and the babies she is carrying are stills significant.

Doctor Bishnoi Anurag, from India, is continuing the practice of allowing older women to receive fertility treatment.

He says: "It is very dangerous to go on a airplane—it can crash. It is very dangerous to ride a bike—you can always bash or someone may bash into your motorcycle—but people do it. Why? Because, they want to reach their destinations."

"It's the same in these cases. They want to realize their dreams, their destination, so they take risks."

He says he has successfully impregnated a 70-year-old woman

The HR function has moved from a transactional one to a strategic one due in part to awareness at the C-level that HR leaders adds value to the business and impacts the bottom line.

Today's HR leaders lead a critical corporate function that requiring a broad and deep level of expertise and leadership skills. They play a seminal role in driving growth and innovation.

Almost 75% of HR executives advice Top Management on the company's organizational structure, and only 9% think that HR should have full responsibility

HR leaders describe the competencies that define 'how' things should be done and how they reinforce the values of the organization.

As high performers, they effectively and efficiently administer the day-to-day work of managing people inside the organization.

iv. Resilience and adaptability: Resilience is the ability to overcome challenges and turn them into opportunities.

HR leaders provide employees with a variety of development programs aimed to increasing resilience.

According to a survey, 71 % people said resilience as very important when determining who to retain.

Resilience, that demonstrates the combination of adaptability, flexibility and strength of purpose is a criterion for professional advancement.

In the condition of uncertainty and intense competitiveness, organizations that instill resilience in their up-and-coming leadership will have a clear advantage.

While Charles Darwin argued that competition was the major driving force of evolution; a researcher identifies the availability of 'living space,' rather than competition, as being of key importance for evolution.

Living space refers to the particular requirements of an organism to thrive. It includes factors like the availability of 'food' (earnings) and favourable 'habitat' (work place or organization).

A German think tank is arguing that the country's retirement age will eventually have to be lifted to 70; since low birth rates and growing life expectancy leave no way around increasing the retirement age.

The government decided in 2007 to gradually lift the legal retirement age from 65 to 67 from 2012 through 2029.

Raising of the retirement age to 67 has been an issue of heated debate, and opponents argue there already are too few employment opportunities for older people.

Rather than survival of the fittest, a healthy approach to adaptation and success creation is good for companies to become more resilient.

A pilot project teaching sex education in schools is being rolled out across the Philippines. But the scheme is opposed by the powerful Catholic Church.

In the Philippines, a conservative, predominantly Catholic country, even older students learn little about how to make babies, or—of more urgency according to many officials and health workers—how to prevent making babies.

The pilot scheme is introducing sex education into the school curriculum from the ages of 11 onwards.

The former education secretary, Mona Valisno, saying it would empower schoolchildren to 'make informed choices and decisions.'

Self-confidence is believed to be a key characteristic of the resilient. Companies need to improve their capability to cope with disruptive competition, and to continuously reinforce strengths and resolve weaknesses so they can recover more quickly from mistakes.

Promoting resilience matters because of the huge economic and social costs of corporate decline and failure.

Managing a resilient organization requires the HR leaders a greater willingness to access information from multiple sources for richer content, and to avoid guidance by those with a vested interest in the status quo.

A cross-functional decision making may offer better results.

Both groups (HR and operational managers) reinforced the need for HR to increase professional skills in consulting and managing change.

v. Innovation capability: Innovation is a critical source of competitive advantage. Companies create its own innovation capabilities creation trajectory, according to its strategic intentions, and supported on different clusters of organization capabilities.

Fidel Castro said Cuba's economic model no longer works.

"The Cuban model (Soviet-style communism) doesn't even work for us anymore."

Castro's words reflected an acknowledgment that 'the state has too big a role in the economic life of the country.'

Innovation capabilities are created in some organizational capabilities that enable people to support innovation strategies and activities.

HR leaders should have the ability to mould and manage different key organizational capabilities and resources that successfully stimulate the innovation activities.

vi. Comply with legislation: Policies and procedures communicate the values of the organization and provide employees with a consistent process to follow.

"The call to prayer in Egypt has recently become a very chaotic process involving a war of microphones and sound disruptions that do not suit the spirituality of calling for the prayer," said Minister of Endowment Hamdi Zaqzouq.

"The unified call for prayers will bring back its spirituality, because its main aim is to attract people to praying and not repel them."

The government decrees that the now-'chaotic' call by thousands of men must instead be delivered by one muezzin broadcast over a system linking 4,500 mosques.

HR leaders understand and how to comply with legislation relating to employment. The HR policies and practices that company adopts must take into account the laws and regulations.

HR leaders must constantly remind themselves that the organizational culture is set by their own personal behaviors and trustworthiness.

Companies provide employees access to their files, employees often also have the right to make a copy of any document in the employee file. This should not be an issue, as the employee already should have seen and signed most of the documents in the file.

If company allows employees to see their personnel folders, it would be smart to allow them access. Having an open employee file rule builds trust. On the other hand, barring employees from reading about themselves can send a negative message.

Steve Bolze, president and CEO of GE Power & Water, calls it 'a chance to get to know each other better.'

vii. Lead the people side of the business: Company is to build a work environment that maximizes the productivity of all the diverse people involved.

Landon Donovan, American soccer player, said he will take responsibility if a woman's claim that he made her pregnant proves true. "If I need to take responsibility, then I will provide the appropriate support."

Companies, with high trust level, give employees unvarnished information about company performance.

HR leaders should explain the rationale behind management and HR decisions (such as compensation and promotion); and encourage employee involvement and information-sharing. They also are unafraid of sharing bad news and admitting mistakes.

A successful HR leader is able to combine the technical, managerial and behavioral aspects of change to reach business objectives. Therefore, setting goals and monitoring performance are essential.

Authorities in Mexico have fired nearly 10 percent of the federal police force as President Felipe Calderon seeks to rein in powerful drug cartels and curb widespread corruption among Mexican police.

"Because they failed to carry out duties established in the federal police law, 3,200 policemen were fired," Deputy Police Chief Facundo Rosas said at a press conference on Monday.

High performers are effective business partners in building winning strategies by linking people and organization practices to competitive requirements.

HR leaders are faced with a wide range of challenges that vary drastically based on an organizations size, maturity, industry and globalization.

The HR leaders sponsor a culture of risk taking. They inspire employee to elevate ideas, even if they're risky or could potentially trigger a backlash.

HR leaders give potential successors opportunities to exercise and build their leadership skills. The culture may insist to:

a.   Empower employee to become a leader, with responsibility for his or her own organization.

The problem with leadership development is that talent sourcing, organizational structure and corporate culture are acute, systemic and intensifying in the company.

"The personal connection is something I may have taken for granted before that I don't want to ever take for granted again," Jeffrey R. Immelt, the chairman and CEO of General Electric, says.

Companies often lack succession plans that reach beyond their C-level officers and their direct reports.

HR leader has a fiduciary responsibility to the shareholders to ensure that the most effective leader is in place, and sometimes that means replacing the present one.

b.   Give back up: HR leaders will 'have their back' if their risk taking doesn't turn out favorably. The leaders should plant an understanding that when they succeed, they get the credit. When they fail, the leaders take the blame.

Fidel Castro, the former Cuban president, said the persecution of gays, who were rounded up at the time as supposed counterrevolutionaries and placed in forced labor camps, was a 'great injustice' that arose from the island's history of discrimination against homosexuals.

He said he was not prejudiced against gays, but "if anyone is responsible (for the persecution), it's me."

"I'm not going to place the blame on others," he said.

c. Be humble and open to inspired thoughts from wherever they may come: Check ego and do more listening than talking.

Michael Strianese, L-3 Communications, said: "I just don't run the company from sitting at a desk in New York City," he told the summit. "I think our folks that do the work like seeing some of the corporate folks around and recognize that we are regular people too."

7th

ENTREPRENEURSHIP

Entrepreneurs are people who can see opportunity what most people do not, and demonstrate the ability to change an ordinary circumstance to become a stepping stone to achieving great success.

The word entrepreneur is derived from the French word 'entreprendere' which means to undertake. An entrepreneur is someone who undertakes to organize, manage, and assume the risks of a business.

The changing nature of Human Resource Management fostered the development of entrepreneurial activities in human resource management.

Entrepreneurial activity was demonstrated through an entrepreneurial philosophy, treating other departments within the firm as customers when they utilized the services of human resource departments.

Entrepreneurship involves a process of value creation in which an individual or team brings together a unique package of resources to exploit an opportunity. The key steps involved are:

a.   Identify opportunities: Human Resources has always had a service role in the firm, but this role needed to change to a new role for Human Resources as business partner.

Various activities within Human Resource Management reveals that some activities are cost centers (i.e. benefits administration), but others do create value, i.e. recruitment, selection, performance management, and training can add significant value to a company.

"Competition plays in driving greater investment, innovation, and choice in the market," MTS Allstream's Chris Peirce said.

b. Develop business concepts: In the media competition, everyone is rewarded for producing enjoyable and affirming content. Output is measured by ratings and page views, so much of the media, and even the academy, is more geared toward pleasuring consumers.

c. Determine needed resources: HR is now looked upon as more than a strategic implement. It is becoming a source of excellence in companies that understand people as the resource that distinguishes value in the marketplace.

d. Acquire resources

The Philippine airline whose flight attendants danced a safety demonstration to Lady Gaga said they were 'surprised' after a video of the routine became an online sensation.

Cebu Pacific Airlines, a budget airline long known for entertaining passengers with amusements such as mid-air trivia games, said they had wanted to make the safety demonstrations 'fun and exciting' to get passengers to pay attention.

Instead of the usual bored flight attendants robotically buckling seatbelts, passengers on a recent domestic flight watched as women wearing bright orange shirts and stylish pants ran down the aisles of the plane, smiling broadly.

e. Manage and harvest the venture: Entrepreneurs have established the habit of doing things they don't necessarily like to do, but because they recognize that it's an absolute requirement to accomplish those goals, they do them.

Human Resource Management (HRM) practices partially mediated the relationship between corporate entrepreneurship and company performance.

Entrepreneurship affects organization performance, both directly and through its effects on Human Resources Management practices.

A study found that HRM practices explain a significant level of additional variance (9 per cent) in company performance.

Strategic Human Resource Management (SHRM), therefore, is seen as crucial for innovation and entrepreneurship in the company.

The successful entrepreneurs are able to identify better and more cost-effective ways to provide Human Resource services. They also have demonstrated the ability of Human Resource Management to add value to the company.

The field of Human Resource Management typically has not been associated with entrepreneurial activities. In fact, some observers might argue that entrepreneurial Human Resource Management is an oxymoron.

Standard

Companies around the world are producing goods and services with global market oriented. It will raise their awareness and appreciation of international standard. It becomes a critical factor governing the ability of the company to secure competitive advantage in the market.

'Intrapreneur' has become commonly used to describe people who act in an entrepreneurial way in corporate setting. They set standards for the best achievement of the organization and employees. A few important standards include:

a.　　Quality standard: People often use 'quality' to refer to excellence or perfection products or services of products and services. Quality shows the extent to which the product or service meets the defined requirements.

M. Night Shyamalan's The Last Airbender currently holds the lowest Rotten Tomatoes ranking of the year.

Paramount's $280 million live-action version of the beloved Nickelodeon series received only a 6% rating based on a ranking system that pools the reviews of film critics into a tidy little score.

Probably the place where The Last Airbender will go down most notably in cinema history is "worst ROI". The reason is: It was a halfway decent movie; a flawed movie.

The acting was pretty terrible. The movie was too short (100 minutes); it should have been about 20 minutes longer and the time would be used to develop the characters.

The movie was far too solemn and took itself too seriously; the thing missing was humor.

Quality standards indicate a minimum level at which the organization is operating in business. This is attractive to employers, customers, and prospective employees.

b.   Ethical standard: Making ethical decisions can be difficult because long-range social responsibility considerations may conflict with immediate needs. Or, ethical principles may seem even to be in conflict with one another. Finally, at times we are forced to choose among bad options.

When placed in these kinds of situations, Human Resources leaders aspire to weighing their options and making the ethical decision they feel they can, based upon an attempt to be socially responsible.

Obama made clear that, although Stanley McChrystal was faithfully executing the White House's war plan, the conduct revealed by Rolling Stone magazine amounted to insubordination that tests the sacred principle of the American military-civilian divide.

Obama said, "Does not meet the standard."

Standard is required to provide guidance to organizations. The standard will help organizations meet their obligations as well as to develop their employees to optimize their goals.

Quality

In general, definition of quality is the degree to which a set of inherent characteristics fulfils requirements. Hence, quality is our product/ service satisfies customer—meeting customers' expectations.

Company places an emphasis on quality, and continually seeking to enhance the business.

HR leaders view quality standards and approaches are relevant to HR.

Unique and increasing HR involvement becomes a management reality. HR leaders' role in the quality effort is to help all employees develop a new mindset—a shared commitment to quality in everyday work. Quality awareness will enable employee to learn dealing with errors, i.e.:

a.　　Able to detect errors: HR leaders place quality inspection at the end of the assembly process, checking the quality of product/service before it is delivered. Detection of errors is important and helping employees and the leaders learn that poor work could not and must not be delivered to customers.

　　　Ability to detect error at the earlier stage will minimize complaint and optimize satisfaction of the customer.

　　　An Upson County couple is suing a grocery store chain in federal court, claiming that the husband found a used tampon in his bowl of cereal.

According to the complaint, Thomas and Lynn Roddenberry said they bought a box of Chocolate Chip Crunch cereal from the Save-A-Lot store in Thomaston in October 2008.

A day after buying the cereal, Thomas Roddenberry said he discovered the tampon in his bowl after taking a bite of the cereal.

The man said he spit out the cereal, immediately became nauseated and went to an emergency room.

b. Able to prevent errors: Employee who are responsible for error prevention ensure that customers received high-quality products and services by focusing on the entire value chain and insuring that inputs were of high quality.

BP's CEO Bob Dudley, understands the only way to quiet the critics, keep politicians and regulators at bay and avoid financial disaster is to improve safety and prevent disasters like the Gulf Mexico oil spill from happening again.

He's just taken an odd and flawed approach to accomplish it. In a leaked internal memo, Dudley told staff the sole criterion for rewarding employee performance in the fourth quarter will be improvements to safety.

Awareness of quality dramatically affects attention to quality and help companies produce goods and services that enable to meet and exceed customer expectations.

Quality is maintained and elevated through quality planning, quality control, and quality improvement. In conjunction with this effort to improve processes and products, world-class companies utilize an activity called benchmarking.

Organizations and companies succeed, or fail, based on the quality and effectiveness of employees. Today's successful companies recognize that to compete in global markets, they must have world class Human Resource leaders who are actively participating in strategic and operational decision.

c. Adapt to error free-work: All employees share a commitment to quality and act accordingly. When it's well established, with minimum supervision, if employees with a quality designation are not found in the organization, yet the commitment to quality remains.

Company must be able to deliver the most elusive of customer-oriented goals; delivering not just a satisfactory experience, but actual delight.

Today's business is facing customers with intensifying pressure to reduce costs. They want it free, they want it perfect and they want it now; if that's the definition of delighting a customer.

Increasingly, companies are looking to technology to delight customers with better service, lower costs or even a better product, as well as to help gauge the success of their efforts.

"The first thing we have to do is get the measurements in place to find out who's satisfied and, if they're not, why," says Michael Tryon, COO of Metal Management.

If the companies do not adapt to the incremental improvements, particularly intangibles such as customer experience, can be much harder to gauge.

'Zero defect' is the primary goal of every world-class company. In order to achieve zero defects, the world-class company is educated in and has fully implemented statistical quality control (SQC), sometimes called statistical process control (SPC) or quality at the source.

When every employee has a personal responsibility to monitor quality, the costs of quality employees are consequently reduced.

Top Management should encourage the shifting in responsibility for quality from the top of the organization to the empowered and committed employees.

The skilled employees know what decisions should be made in their work areas to make quality happen, and when given the opportunity, they make those decisions.

HR leaders must see quality standard as business partners, which need to introduce quality improvement program through training, team building, cultural change and changing working patterns, etc.

They should be committed to providing a quality, timely and efficient service which reflects the organization's objectives. It will ensure delivery of excellent products and services in all aspects of employment.

Quality standards, particularly those around HR, demonstrate to employees and organization that we are good HR leaders and it help to recruit and retain employees.

There are major quality standards and techniques implemented in business world, including ISO 9000, the European Foundation for Quality Management, Total Quality Management (TQM), 5-S, and Six Sigma.

Whether they are reengineering the pay and benefits of the company or implementing Total Quality Management (TQM) programs, Human Resources leaders play a central role.

This involves comparing the firm's performance, either overall or in a functional area, with that of other world-class organizations. The use of TQM techniques, according to some analysts, is the most striking differentiator between world-class and non-world-class companies.

The quality framework focuses on three quality dimensions: relevance, accuracy and availability.

All quality costs (prevention costs, appraisal costs, and cost of defects—both internal and external) are evaluated and held to the lowest reasonable sum.

Human capital investment provides a framework that helps organizations to improve performance and realize objectives through the effective management and development of people.

Ethics

It is important to remember that morals are rules or principles which guide human conduct.

HR leaders who want employees to behave ethically must exhibit ethical decision making practices themselves. They have to remember that leading by example is the first step in fostering a culture of ethical behavior in their companies.

Emma Jones, the estranged daughter of a U.S. pastor who has threatened to burn copies of the Koran believes he has gone mad and needs help.

"As a daughter, I see the good-natured core inside him. But I think he needs help." "I think he has gone mad," she added.

Ethics can be defined as the application of moral values to business situations.

No matter what the formal policies say or what they are told to do, if employees see leaders behaving unethically, they will believe that the company wants them to act in a like manner.

A survey found 37% of American adults said they had been bullied at work.

Workers who are abused based on their membership in a protected class—race, nationality or religion, among others—can sue under civil rights laws. But the law generally does not protect against plain old viciousness.

The New York state senate passed a bill that would let workers sue for physical, psychological or economic harm due to abusive treatment on the job.

If New York's Healthy Workplace Bill becomes law, workers who can show that they were subjected to hostile conduct—including verbal abuse, threats or work sabotage—could be awarded lost wages, medical expenses, compensation for emotional distress and punitive damages.

There are conflicts in the way business conducts its affairs and the way that the public perceives business should conduct its affairs.

Different people have different description about what constitutes ethical behavior.

Ethics is concerned with analyzing what is right or wrong in people's behavior or conduct. Ethics and morality are terms that are often used interchangeably in discussions of good and evil.

HR leaders play an important role in establishing their ethical tone. If they behave as if the only thing that matters is profit, employees are likely to act in a like manner. They are responsible for setting standards for what is and is not acceptable employee behavior.

It's vital for leaders to play an active role in creating a working environment where employees are encouraged and rewarded for acting in ethical manner.

The term ethics is usually applied to persons, and 'morality' applied to acts and behavior, meaning customs or manners.

For one homeless Australian man who considers begging for money a full-time job, the long hours on the street have landed him a middle-class salary, The Daily Telegraph reported.

Ken Johnson, 52, spends up to 16 hours a day, seven days a week, sitting at a Sydney intersection that can net him $400 a day from generous pedestrians, and has brought him a steady income since the late 90s.

"I'd be really disappointed if I did a long Friday and I only had $250," Johnson said.

Work ethics is behavior characterized work habits, values, and attitudes. Work ethic referred to a positive attitude toward work; i.e. work value, job satisfaction, loyalty, self concept, organizational commitment, beliefs, work performance, attitudes, and role conflict. Work ethics traits include:

a.   Attendance: Available—always present; be punctual—arrive/ leave on time; give information—notify in advance of planned absences; avoid excessive absenteeism and/or lateness.

As CEO-designate in Temasek Holdings Pte. Ltd, Singapore, Goodyear pushed to instill a tighter sense of discipline within the company, say people at Temasek.

People who didn't show up on time for internal meetings were fined for each minute they were late, they say. Typing messages on BlackBerrys during meetings was prohibited.

b.　Positive character: Display integrity—keep confidential records, material or information; statement concerning individuals; money or financial accounts, show exceptional job performance, loyalty, honesty, trustworthiness, dependability, reliability, initiative, self-discipline, and self-responsibility

Employers are refusing to hire Generation Y workers because they lack a work ethic and spend too much time talking to friends in work hours.

"Employers come to us about Gen Y, saying they're looking for a staff member but they don't want anyone in that 20s age bracket because they find they don't understand common courtesy in the workplace," Kristy-Lee Johnston, director of Footprint Recruitment, said

Persistence and tenacity go hand in hand. We must have tenacity; some call it 'thick skin.' HR leaders have the ability to keep going through all resistance, no matter what it is. That is where persistence comes in.

c.　Advance teamwork: Respect the rights of others; respect confidentiality; be participative; cooperative; assertive; display a customer service attitude; seek opportunities for continuous learning; demonstrate mannerly behavior; deal appropriately with diversity; respect equality, challenge discrimination, does not engage in harassment, abuse and violence of any kind.

"If I said fish live in the sea, they'd say no," Barack Obama, U.S. President, on Republicans who have consistently opposed him.

d.   Good appearance: Appearance matters, *"What they see is what you get," fashion consultant Georgia Donovan said.* Employee should display appropriate dress, grooming, hygiene, and etiquette. *"Everything we put on represents a choice we've made about how we want others to perceive us, and treat us," he said.*

A survey found 49% of female MBA graduates have tried to advance in their careers by sometimes engaging in at least one of 10 (ten) sexual behaviors, including crossing their legs provocatively or leaning over a table to let men look down their shirts.

Inappropriate dress should bring HR leaders the importance of dress code policies and harassment training.

Since the line between work attire and provocative has become more blurred the importance of harassment training becomes a good solution.

When employees are faced with images/issues out of the norm, the leaders may encourage them to respond and behave appropriately.

e.   Positive attitude: Demonstrate self-confident; have realistic expectations, etc. Entrepreneurs demonstrate strong internal motivation. The motivation that drives their behavior comes from two sources: internal and external.

Internal factors include constructs like needs, desires, motives, and will power. External factors include any type of motivational influence from the environment such as rewards and punishments. For entrepreneurs, the most important motivational factor is the internal one.

"There's a definite correlation between happiness and productivity on the team," says Jackie Donovan, director of Fairway Market.

"Happiness at work is closely correlated with greater performance and productivity as well as greater energy, better reviews, faster promotion, higher income, better health and increased happiness with life. So it's good for organizations and individuals, too."

The happy worker really is the productive worker.

The happiest employees are 180 percent more energized than their less content colleagues, 155 percent happier with their jobs, 150 percent happier with life, 108 percent more engaged and 50 percent more motivated. Most staggeringly, they are 50 percent more productive too."

The greatest differences between entrepreneurial and non-entrepreneurial companies are found in performance appraisal practices, compensation practices and training practices.

In the area of performance appraisals, firms with a more entrepreneurial orientation tend to encourage higher levels of employee involvement in the appraisal process.

They are also more concerned with evaluating results, rather than the methods used to achieve them. And although individual performance remains a primary focus, group performance is more likely to be part of the appraisal process in highly entrepreneurial companies.

f.   High productivity: In general, productivity refers to the relationship between what we put in to a business (inputs) and the final result (output).

Argument that increasing employee productivity is often thought to be based on salary and promotions is not always the case.

A study concluded that in a large number of cases, salary has less to do with motivation.

Principle of management, that dictates how to maximize employee productivity, emphasizes HR leaders to prioritize areas of focus in which include personal motivation and work environment.

The first key factor in leveraging Human Resources to produce the most is found through motivational incentives.

Second factor is creating a work environment in which employees are productive, that will increase profit for the company.

In terms of Human Resources, productivity is more difficult to measure, understand and define.

What influences the productivity levels of employees is wide variety of skills, characteristics and attitudes. This includes formal training and qualifications, motivation levels, initiative, team skills, attention to detail, judgment, multi-task abilities, communication skills, general attitudes and work ethos.

g.   Show or model the job and work to increase workers' sense of control over the work that they do, i.e. follow safety practices; conserve materials; keep work area neat and clear; follow directions and procedures; make up assignments punctually; initiate changes and improvements.

Employees who have a high sense of control determine the positive and negative events and outcomes in their workplace. And employees with a low sense of control are experiencing higher levels of powerlessness.

HR leaders recognize knowledge provides strategies to facilitate self-empowerment. The good feeling and sense of control that employees have is a driving factor to self-motivation.

h.   Organizational skills: Display leadership skills; appropriately handle criticism, conflicts, and complaints; demonstrate problem solving capability; maintain appropriate relationships with supervisors and peers; follow chain of command, manifest skill in prioritizing works and management of time; demonstrate flexibility in handling change.

Personal effectiveness is the key to Human Resources function.

HR leaders encourage higher levels of employee involvement in the appraisal process. They are also more concerned with evaluating results, rather than the methods used to achieve them. Human Resources Management requires an orderly approach, which includes:

i.   Clear communication: Display appropriate nonverbal—eye contact, body language and oral—listening, telephone etiquette, grammar—skills; prevent to use profane, obscene, or abusive language.

HR leaders need to focus their efforts (both individually and organization) on continuous communication and feedback.

Keeping employees informed through clear, precise communication is vital to the organization. Clear communication is keeping everybody on the same page.

j.   Good citizenship: Respect community; prevent any kind of environmental harm; proper use of tools and resources; no possession of firearms, explosives, or weapons; keep distance against drugs and alcohol; and ownership of properties.

People are calling for better use of the power that corporations seem destined to have in today's business.

A study found 72% to 82% of Americans strongly agree that business has gained too much power over too many aspects of American life.

Other findings revealed that the community continues to give companies low marks in citizenship. Companies should owe something to their workers and the communities in which they operate and should sometimes sacrifice some profit for the sake of making things better for their workers and communities.

Because of the change in community's expectation, gap between desired and perceived corporate citizenship, companies need to be alert to any disconnect between the activities they engage in to demonstrate their good citizenship and the corporate mission and core values.

Otherwise, an attempt to be a good citizen is likely to be viewed by much of the public as self-serving and having a hidden profit motive.

It may not be possible for any set of work ethics/rules to cover every situation or behavior that may occur in the workplace. Work ethics/rules help every employee understand what is expected of him/her and indicates what types of activities are to be avoided.

HR leaders recognize the importance of ethical behavior. The best leaders exhibit both their values and their ethics in their leadership style and actions. Their leadership ethics and values should be visible because they live it in their actions every single day.

People who enjoy their work would be regarded as having a better work ethics than people who did not enjoy their work.

Violations of work ethics may result in some form of disciplinary action, depending upon the seriousness of the offense involved. All offenses which lead to discipline are not of the same degree of seriousness.

Harassment

Harassment in the workplace can be clarified as any conduct that creates significant anguish to another employee, with the intent to bother, scare or emotionally abuse a victim, including:

a.   Directed at an individual or group

*The predominately Muslim country is under mounting
international pressure to end the use of children by Koranic
teachers to collect money, rice and sugar after a prominent
rights group said the practice was similar to slavery.*

*"We have arrested seven Koranic teachers who have sent
children to the streets to beg," Senegalese police spokesman
Mbaye Sady Diop said. "They were handed over to the
prosecutor to do his job."*

Other form of such harassment happens if a man directs
harassing conduct to females that typically does so precisely
because he wants to direct such conduct to females and is not
at all in directing it to males.

b.   Offensive, intimidating, humiliating or threatening:
Harassment occurs when a person conditions the granting
of a benefit upon receipt of sexual favors from a subordinate
or punishes the subordinate for refusing to submit to his or
her request.

*"I was treated like a slave by the family who hired me and
ended up being beaten and threatened with rape," said
19-year-old Bangladeshi housemaid Shimoli. (Alastair
Lawson, 2004)*

HR leader is strictly liable for acts of harassment
committed by a person who has the power to make (or
recommend) significant employment decisions affecting the
subordinate-victim, such as hiring, promotion, discipline, or
discharge.

c.   Unwelcome and unsolicited: The challenged conduct must
be unwelcome in the sense that the employee did not solicit
or incite it, and in the sense that the employee regarded the
conduct as undesirable or offensive.

*Babette Perry, New Jersey pharmacy technician, says she
was traumatized when a masked gunman burst into her store*

demanding OxyContin is suing her employers for arranging the mock holdup.

She says in a lawsuit that she was not told in advance of the training drill in December 2007 at the Hampton Behavioral Health Center.

She was diagnosed with post-traumatic stress disorder.

Such unwelcome sexually determined behavior as physical contact and advances, sexually colored remarks, showing pornography and sexual demands, whether by words or actions.

Otherwise, sex-related conduct was 'voluntary,' in the sense that the complainant was not forced to participate against her will.

When a woman sleeps with a man willingly and subsequently if there is any rift in their relations she cannot claim that she was sexually harassed.

Each employee has the right to be free from improper or offensive conduct at work. It includes religious harassment can stem from jokes, teasing or coercion about religious beliefs, practices or clothing; gender harassment has to do with conduct, behaviors and conversations that demean someone because of her gender; age harassment is any negative treatment on the basis of age, including exclusion, restrictions or coercing someone to retire early; racial harassment victims are subject to offensive stereotyping through words, jokes and gestures.

Harassment can even occur based on one's national origin, when a person's gestures, comments, symbols and accent are under attack.

It's HR leaders' duty both to prevent workplace harassment and to take swift action to remedy it. Threatening is an action of intentionally or knowingly putting other person in fear.

Herkimer County man is facing an aggravated harassment charge after police say he called the Sears store in the Sangertown Square Mall to complain about services and ended up threatening the manager with a gun.

50-year-old Jeffrey White, of Ilion, never ended up going to the mall and never actually had a gun, but the Sears manager called police after being threatened over the telephone.

Although it is difficult to define with precision how severe conduct must be before it may be considered offensive for sexual harassment. Sexual harassment and other forms of harassment in the work place may involve:

a. The employee, who is harassing another employee, can be an individual of the same sex. Sexual harassment does not imply that the perpetrator is of the opposite sex.

b. The harasser who might be the employee's supervisor, manager, customer, coworker, supplier, peer, or vendor. Any individual, who is connected to the employee's work environment, can be accused of sexual harassment.

c. The victim is not just the employee who is becoming the target of the harassment. Other employees who observe or learn about the sexual harassment can also be the victims and institute charges. Or anyone who is affected by the conduct can potentially complain of sexual harassment.

In harassment, HR leaders must demonstrate appropriate steps; that need commitment to take immediate action and make sure the consequences for the perpetrator are severe. Harassment also takes in various forms include:

a. Verbal harassment, such as derogatory comments, jokes or slurs.

An African student in India who runs a news and current-affairs website from the city of Bhopal accused companies like Coca-Cola of airing racist commercials on Indian TV that portrayed Africans as primitive savages.

The Indian lemon drink LMN, produced by the Parle Agro Corporation, has a blatantly racist subtext in its TV spot that shows two Africans digging in the sand for water. When they spot a tap nearby, they wrench it off and start using it as a shovel.

Spot for BP's Castrol engine oil, shows two young Indian men being magically transported from place to place: a beach, a lion-infested jungle—and a cauldron being carried by smiling African cannibals.

Indian marketers have a field day in putting 'blacks' where they've always 'belonged,' at least in the average Indian mind-sets," wrote S.K.Y. Banji, an Ugandan who has lived in India for more than four years.

b. Physical harassment, such as unnecessary or offensive touching, or impeding or blocking movement.

HP was under fire for spying on journalists and board members in order to determine the sources of leaks to the press.

The embarrassing incident had forced Patricia Dunn, the company's then chairwoman, to step down.

c. Visual harassment, such as derogatory or offensive posters, cards, calendars, cartoons, graffiti, drawings, messages, notes or gestures.

Spears' former bodyguard, Fernando Flores, filed a sexual harassment lawsuit alleging that the singer made multiple unwelcome passes at him exposed herself on numerous occasions.

The suit states that Flores reported an incident in which Spears called him up to her room "for no other purpose or reason than to expose her naked or near naked body to Plaintiff."

According to the suit, Flores' supervisor, Josh McMahan, shrugged off the incident, saying, "You know you liked it." Flores also apparently voiced his issues several times, but "his complaints were ignored or mocked, and no action was taken to rectify the situation."

Provocative dress might be also seen as one of the causes for sexual harassment where others are tempted to tease.

Lugi Bobbio, mayor of Castellammare di Stabia in Italy, insists that he is not trying to ban miniskirts altogether. But only those skirts, which are so short that they show women's underwear.

The mayor states that he only added the miniskirt ban in order to stop the display of female flesh in public areas other than beaches. Police will check the hemlines of women's skirts, and if found to be against the ordinance, the proposed fines would be up to €500.

Miniskirt bans have been proposed in Kenyan, Uganda, and other UK are as well as in Chile. Some of those proposals went through and others did not. Many job places are also banning miniskirts.

One of the newest areas of the law relates to online harassment, often called 'cyber-stalking.' This is a different avenue for harassment because there is no physical proximity to the victim and not even any verbal communication.

Line leaders are the front line when it comes to managing employee performance and needs from work. They have to provide a strategy to preventing harassment, includes:

a.   Provide guidance for addressing harassment situations: HR leaders establish sexual harassment awareness training that enables employees to learn and apply the important skills of handling sexual harassment issues and complaints.

The training thoroughly addresses the elements of how to prevent unacceptable behavior; that includes a detailed overview of what sexual harassment is, explains legal definitions, discusses sexual harassment prevention, and shows how to handle sexual harassment complaints and maintain a positive work environment.

b. Provide employees with a work environment free of any type of harassment: Each employee should exercise good judgment in their relationships with coworkers. Each employee has the right to be free from improper or offensive conduct at work.

A researcher found that chimps wage war to conquer new territory.

Male members of one group mysteriously vanished, and another group then expanded into what had been their land.

The group dissolved into civil war, resulting in killing and land takeovers.

It seems, chimps, like humans, go to war. "Even if that were true," says Mitani, the researcher. "We operate by a moral code chimps don't have."

Employees are prohibited to harass co-workers.

It is important to remember that about 5 percent of population will be totally crazy. But they're unnecessary mentally ill.

Crazy in the sense of "Thinks it is a good plan to joke with the flight attendant about seeing a bomb in the restroom."

According to a survey 26 percent of American adults suffer from a diagnosable mental disorder.

It's just normal life. There is nothing we can do about the crazy 5 percent except ask the law enforcement to keep an eye on them.

HR leaders and employees must take action to address and prevent harassment. Behavior that amounts to harassment can also be the subject of criminal and/or disciplinary proceedings.

A report says that 4.4 percent of inmates in prison and 3.1 percent of inmates in jail report being victimized sexually by another inmate or staff member.

The report found that female inmates were more than twice as likely as male inmates to report experiencing sexual victimization by another inmate.

Among inmates who reported victimization by another inmate, 13 percent of male prison inmates and 19 percent of male jail inmates said they were victimized within the first 24 hours after being admitted to a corrections facility. In contrast, the figure for women was 4 percent for prison and jail.

"Tens of thousands of rapes are occurring in America's prisons each year," Pat Nolan, vice president of Prison Fellowship.

HR leaders prohibit harassment or a work environment that is abusive to employees because of their race, gender, color, religion, disability or national origin.

The Crom Corporation and Crom Equipment Rentals violated federal law when they allowed the racial harassment of black employees, the U.S. Equal Employment Opportunity Commission (EEOC) charged in a lawsuit.

The EEOC also says the Florida-based construction companies unlawfully suspended an African American employee for complaining about severe racial insults, threats and physical abuse.

According to the suit, a white employee at Crom's Holly Hill, Fla. location, locked a black coworker in a tool shed and then spray-painted the shed door with the word 'Jail.'

The EEOC said that the same white employee also put a hangman's noose around the black employee's neck, hung the noose in his work area, and threatened to decapitate him.

Another African American employee was offended when he saw the noose hanging at the Holly Hill site. Crom was aware of the harassment but didn't stop it, according to the suit.

Instead, the EEOC said, Crom suspended the black worker after he complained about the noose and rewarded the white offender with a higher-paying position.

"It is shocking and sobering that such cruelty can still occur at an American workplace," said EEOC Acting Chairman Stuart J. Ishimaru.

Discipline action is generally one of the last steps in any harassment procedure. It should follow only after we have conducted a thorough and prompt investigation, interviewed all involved parties, and carefully weighed the evidence.

Morality

Morality is a sense of how we should or should not behave. It refers to the underlying codes of right and wrong. Morality covers the vast arena of human conduct that examines our interaction with other human beings.

Women and children came first when the Titanic sunk but not when the Lusitania was torpedoed, a study has claimed.

The Titanic took more than two hours to sink when it hit an iceberg four days into its maiden voyage from Southampton to New York, on 14 April, 1912; killing more than 1,500 people.

But the liner Lusitania sank in 18 minutes in 1915 when it was torpedoed by a U-boat during World War One; with the loss of nearly 1,200 lives.

Time pressure seems to have been the key in determining who lived and who died.

The study says that on the Lusitania, selfish behavior dominated, and on the Titanic social norms and social status (class) dominated, contradicting standard economics.

Morality is not only about ethical principles, commandments or laws, but primarily about the proper response to the human person's essential dignity.

The difficulty with morality is the concept relativity. We have to find a subset of rules that promotes behavior that doesn't injure people.

Companies are bound by law to treat the people they employ fairly and not to discriminate against identified groups.

Legislation is needed that involves accepted moral principles, and acts to moderate standards within the organization.

Conformity to all legal requirements does not necessarily ensure the best treatment of employees. For, the law itself may not be fair; it may not cover all eventualities; and it may not always offer a clear guide to action. The unethical practices of HR are, but not limited to:

a.   Exploiting 'already cheap' labor markets. Developing nations (commonly called third world countries or poor countries) are the focus of much debate over the issue of exploitation.

Critics of foreign companies allege, for example, that companies such as Nike and Gap Inc. paying their workers wages far lower than those that prevail in developed nations (where the products are sold).

Bangladeshi garment workers, who make clothes for western brands such as H&M, Gap and Marks & Spencer, greeted a recent 80 per cent pay rise by rampaging angrily through the capital Dhaka burning cars and looting shops.

For the world's lowest—paid garment workers, the increase in the minimum wage, effective from November, takes their pay from $23 to $43 (€33, £27.50) a month. It was their first pay rise for four years, a period of soaring food and fuel prices.

"This is not enough for the survival of workers and their families," said Amirul Haque Amin, president of Bangladesh's National Garment Workers' Federation.

Some in the United States propose that the U.S. government should mandate that businesses in foreign countries adhere to the same labor, environmental, health, and safety standards as the U.S. before they are allowed to trade with businesses in the U.S.

They believe that such standards would improve the quality of life in less developed nations. But on other hand, this would harm the economies of less developed nations by discouraging the U.S. from trading with them.

However, the common response to the argument that corporations exploit poor laborers by lowering working standards, wages, etc. is that they only have incentive to do business in these nations if there is this alleged exploitation.

If activists were to achieve their goal of raising work standards, it is likely that the corporation would no longer have profit incentive to invest in that nation.

The result would probably the corporation pulling back to its developed nation, leaving their former workers out of the job.

b.   Using child labor: The full-time employment of children who are under a minimum legal age.

Children living in the poorest households and in rural areas are most likely to be engaged in child labor, that work which exceeds a minimum number of hours, depending on the age of a child and on the type of work.

Canadian prisoner Omar Khadr told interrogators he was an al Qaeda terrorist and described pulling the pin of a grenade that killed a U.S. soldier in Afghanistan.

Khadr was 15 when captured during a firefight at an al Qaeda compound in Afghanistan in 2002.

He was raised in a family of Islamist extremists who spent holidays with Osama bin Laden, trained their boy to use bombs and guns and encouraged him to kill Americans.

Human Resources leaders should encourage that line leader performs Human Resource auditing. An HR audit is a study that proves to the line leaders has ensured that everything is running as it should be in the organization.

They must safeguard children against harm such as exposure to hazardous, unsanitary, or immoral conditions, and overwork.

An estimated 165 million children between the ages of 5 and 14 are involved in child labor.

Millions of them are engaged in hazardous situations or conditions, such as working in mines, working with chemicals and pesticides in agriculture or working with dangerous machinery.

HR leaders recognize children need a good quality education and training if they are to acquire the skills necessary to succeed in the labor market.

c.　Longer working hours: Long hours frequently result from poor team development, ill-defined goals and unrealistic deadlines.

A 50-year-old Sri Lankan woman who worked as a maid for a large family in Saudi Arabia for five months was allegedly tortured by some of the family members hammering nails into her body.

X-rays showed there were 23 nails embedded in her body, some of the nails had been heated prior to insertion.

"Some of the nails were 2 inches long," Dr. Prabath Gajadeera of Kamburupitiya Base Hospital said.

"I had to work from dawn to dusk. I hardly slept. They beat me and threatened to kill me and hide my body," she said.

Unclear goals and unrealistic deadlines can have a big impact on efficiency and often contribute to excessive hours on the job.

Goals are often vague, confusing or even contradictory. Investing some up-front time in goal definition can lead to teams that don't need to work long hours because they aren't wasting their time."

Deadlines frequently are the result of wishful thinking. Companies need to take the time to figure out how fast they can move and what is, or is not, realistic. That prevents people from working long hours trying to meet an arbitrary milestone.

Among the white-collar workers, the long working hours were accompanied with other stressful work issues such as career problems, excessive business trips, strident norms, and changes of work places.

Among the blue-collar workers, they were accompanied with those such as irregular midnight work, insufficient manpower and long-distance driving, etc.

Or with additional sudden events, including work-related emotional anxiety or excitement, rapid increase of workload, unexpected work trouble or environmental changes of work places.

In many organizations, leaders are overworked, stressed out, and frustrated by competing demands and pressure from their customers.

Ironically, an overworked leader may also neglect employees are underutilized or inefficient because they do not have enough responsibility or information to perform their tasks to the best of their abilities.

A study suggests that individuals who work more than 10 hours a day are about 60 percent more likely to develop heart disease or have a heart attack than those who work just seven hours a day.

It was shown that two-thirds of them were working for long hours such as more than 60 hr per week, more than 50 hr overtime per month, or more than half of their fixed holidays before the attack.

d. Increasing work stress: Stress in the workplace can make people dread walking into the office every morning, and make them worry about their jobs at night. Stress affects not just morale, but a company's bottom line.

Alarmed that its children are falling behind those in rivals such as South Korea and Hong Kong, Japan is adding about 1,200 pages to elementary school textbooks, bringing the total across all subjects for six years from 4,900 pages today to nearly 6,100.

"There's a sense of crisis," said Hiroaki Mimizuka, a professor of education at Ochanomizu University in Tokyo, who thinks the new guidelines are a step in the right direction. "With the year-by-year weakening of the competitiveness of our economy, there are serious concerns about whether our education system is working for a country with few natural resources, whose most valuable resources are its people."

It is also argued that work conditions in these developing-world factories are much less safe and much more unhealthy than in the first world. For example, observers point to cases where employees were unable to escape factories burning down—and thus dying—because of locked doors, a common signal that sweatshop conditions exist.

e. The use of disputed and dubious practices in hiring and firing of employees

249

Employees use to survive under exploitative and irresponsible working conditions that are perceived to be the norm. At times workers are satisfied simply with wages being paid on time, whilst other violations are sidelined for their fear of losing their jobs and their needs to meet their families' basic needs.

HR leaders must get involved to raise awareness of labor rights violations, to promote responsibility and hold companies accountable for unscrupulous business practices.

f.   Repress employees the right to organize and bargain collectively as well as the right of association.

A U.N. report cites political repression as one of the main forces preventing Egyptian youths, who make up a quarter of the population, from participating in the country's development.

They also criticized restrictions on freedom of expression and demonstrations and interference in political activities of university students.

The report presentation described a 'culture of fear' among youth and recommended police stop intimidation that prevents citizens from expressing opinions or engaging in political activity.

g.   Labor exploitation: Companies are in fact exploiting people by the terms of unequal human standards (applying lower standards to third world workers than to their world ones).

People choose to work for low wages and in unsafe conditions because it is their only alternative to starvation or scavenging from 'garbage dumps', this cannot be seen as any kind of 'free choice' on their part.

The idea of morality is not only matter related to religious or philosophic idea, but involving business and leadership implications.

Value Creation

Entrepreneurship is a key driving force for organization productivity and competitiveness. Company contributes to higher value added. These results arise when enterprises innovate and exploit opportunities.

Development of entrepreneurship is cardinal and most crucial to the industrial development. It is the process of encouraging a prospective entrepreneur to set up on industrial unit whether production, processing or servicing.

Many innovations arise from companies that continue developments. The companies built entrepreneurial teams, continued to seek and exploit new opportunities, and infused entrepreneurship in their organizations.

HR leaders must contribute value. They are capable to handling people effectively that at least as core a business function as handling money effectively.

The leaders promote evidence that entrepreneurship has important economic value. And entrepreneurial companies produce important spillovers that affect employment growth.

Entrepreneurs respond effectively to other incentives including the opportunity to achieve recognition, and the satisfaction of creating new products or improving existing ones.

The majority of Americans do not favor making affordable high-speed Internet access a government priority, according to a study.

53 percent of those surveyed said that expansion was not an important priority.

A debate has arisen about shifting of priorities in a tough economic environment or the uncertain benefits of the Internet access to all Americans.

Value creation distinguishes great corporations from others that eventually disappear from the corporate success.

Within enterprises, there is a need for creative entrepreneurship and value creation. Some enlightened corporations have fostered value creation within their organizations by providing opportunities for innovation, intra-organization venture financing, and ownership in employee-initiated projects.

More needs to be done are to motivate the involvement of employees through tangible and intangible means.

HR leaders should have commitment to promote the exchange of knowledge of, experience in, and approaches to innovation, entrepreneurship, and value creation in organizations as a strategy for business excellence and growth.

Spirituality

Entrepreneurs see religious faith is as important as profit. HR leaders should accommodate the gathering of employees who use to practice their religious service and pray about the business.

Company can believe that by encouraging employees to attend the religious service, business will prosper.

When employees practice such rituals, their attitude towards their work might get transformed.

"The more people becoming religious the more they are honest, with a better heart. And the more they are responsible," Weng-Jen Wau of the Boteli Valve Group in Wenzhou, China, says. "Also when they do things wrong, they feel guilty—that's the difference," he explains.

Religious faith is now seen as a source of business inspiration.

Employees attend on-site religious fellowship service, where they read the holy book and pray for each other.

If employees become religious or spiritual, it would have a very big impact, and would really help the development of the company. On other hand, many employers aren't excited about spirituality or religiosity in business; because they don't see the payoff.

"If they can't see benefits immediately, they stay away from it," an expert says. "They don't want to make sacrifices."

In today's spirituality life, employees demonstrate qualities of the transcendence (the transcendent character of the individual that can be seen in the organization growth.

The degree to which the transcendent is enlivened sets the frame for the organization and its behavior.

Transcendence means a state or condition in which spiritual ecstasy is experienced.

Plans to build an Islamic cultural center near the World Trade Center site moved forward after New York City's Landmarks Preservation Commission voted to allow the demolition of a building that would be replaced by a mosque.

"Let us not forget that Muslims were among those murdered on 9/11 and that our Muslim neighbors grieved with us as New Yorkers and as Americans," Mayor Michael Bloomberg said. "We would betray our values and play into our enemies' hands if we were to treat Muslims different than anyone else."

Transcendence as a way of thinking, with its emphasis on balance and self-other integration, offers the promise to bridge global divides and facilitate the formation of global-minded leaders.

Happiness At Workplace

When employees are unhappy, they are less efficient, less effective and more likely to squander work hours or quit. To maintain employees' work satisfaction, HR leaders should learn how to treat employees exclusively, includes:

a. Status: Most individuals attain the status of employee after a job interview with a company.

    If the individual is determined to be satisfactory fit for the position, he/she is given an official offer of employment within that company for a defined starting salary and position.

This individual then has all the rights and privileges of an employee.

The higher their rank, the greater their sense of happiness and self-worth would likely be.

People care about whether they are the second most highly paid person, or the eighth most highly paid person, in their comparison set. They may not care of the amount they receive, unless the value is higher than their co-worker.

An individual's rank was a stronger predictor of happiness than wealth. The higher a person ranked within his/her age group or neighborhood, the more status he/she had and the happier he/she was regardless of how much he/she made in dollars.

In terms of life satisfaction, rank is a better predictor than absolute wealth. Money may be enough to purchase status—and a little bit of happiness.

A research shows ranking scales were more powerfully associated with satisfaction—that is, whether they are happier or not if they make more than their neighbor/co-worker or if they make more than others in their profession.

b.   Recognition: HR leaders encourage recognition activities that generally build positive morale in the work environment.

Switzerland remains the world's most competitive economy, while the United States has fallen from second to fourth after losing the top spot last year, according to the World Economic Forum.

The WEF said America slipped in the ranking due to a build-up in U.S. macroeconomic imbalances, a weakening of the country's public and private institutions and concerns about the state of its financial markets.

Employees are the keys to the organization success, but few believe they know whether their people are well managed or if they are prepared to fortify and enhance the transformations facing the organization.

Recognition is a communication tool that reinforces and rewards the most important outcomes people create for the business. When we recognize employees effectively, we reinforce, with our chosen means of recognition, the actions and behaviors we most want to see people repeat.

At the Bellagio Casino and Hotel in Las Vegas, employees with dubious pasts may be hired under a program that begins with work at local fast food restaurant.

After eight months of successful employment, these successful employees are promoted to a more prestigious position at Bellagio at almost double their salary.

Bellagio has found that a largely untapped labor market, ex-convicts, composes a particularly motivated and committed work force.

An important tool for motivating employees is praise. This can be taken as useful method of giving an employee a sense of worth in relation to the actual work being done. Praise has shown to increase productivity.

One of the reasons, why people seek opportunity from other enterprises, they want to grow. It's not merely matter of 'seat' or position, but might be recognition.

HR leaders recognize that the collective efforts of employees contribute to the overall mission of the organization and that we should encourage opportunities for those efforts to be acknowledged.

World-class companies rely on 16% fewer HR workers, with 11.88 per 1,000 staff, compared with a global average of 14.11 per 1,000.

In order to attract and retain the best employees, they must aim to create an environment where employees feel appreciated for their contributions.

HR leaders develop their people to become future leaders in the organizations. If they succeed in development program, they will have enough leaders to occupy any position in the corporate. Otherwise, if they fail to do it, it will become a 'Black Hole' or predator for the organization.

c.   Value: A study indicates companies are rethinking overall salary increase projections but top performers continue to be treasured.

They are also rethinking their approaches to compensation, hiring, and reward practices. They allocate a higher part of their salary increase budgets to reward exceptional performance.

Research shows that the more money employees have than others, the more likely they are to report being satisfied with their lives.

The higher their salary than the norm, the happier they tend to be.

People tend to value their own wealth more—and are happier—when it compares favorably to everyone else's.

It's not simply how much money they make that contributes to satisfaction, but how much more money they make than others (their neighbors, colleagues at work or friends from college).

Companies are going in for strategic hiring as a way to selectively recruit some of the very best talent.

In compensation practices, companies with a more entrepreneurial orientation tend to base pay rates on market comparisons more so than on internal equity concerns.

The companies frequently provide a lower base pay, but are significantly offering greater opportunities in the form of performance-based pay incentives.

Technology

HR leader is committed to provide effective people solutions to the company in ways that improves human effectiveness and the organization's bottom line.

HR leaders who leverage technology, are 110 percent more likely than their peers to use a high degree of functionality in their HR applications and 178 percent more likely to make management decision-making the primary use of their HR application.

HR leaders also more frequently rely on technology include resume capture, applicant tracking, paperless payroll, requisition tracking, and employee self-service.

Technology is a key to how world-class companies streamline processes, cut costs and staff, reduce error rates, stay more productive, deliver information more effectively, and make better strategic decisions.

World-class organizations clearly benefit from their increased focus on technology, and are more than three times as likely as typical companies to offer employees online access to health and welfare systems.

HR leaders take a very different attitude and approach towards technology than their peers. They understand it better, and work hard to ensure that they derive as much value from it as they can.

World-class companies possess the knowledge and technology to provide products and services of continually improving quality.

The more we can automate details and transactional stuff (HR systems, payroll, benefits, even parts of recruiting and substantial parts of training) the better.

A research found that world-class HR executives and their peers dedicate almost exactly the same amount per employee on technology.

Since world-class organizations operate with 35 percent fewer HR staff per thousand employees (10.5 versus 16.2), this actually translates into a 53 percent higher technology investment per HR staffer.

Technology can provide important leverage to help companies cut costs and increase the efficiency of spending.

"The efficiencies initiative is an important thing to do. I see technology as leverage for that," Zachary Lemnios, director of defense research and engineering, said.

His office was already working hard to get new technologies to troops on the battlefield more quickly.

"We take every one of these seriously," he said.

World-class companies spend almost exactly the same amount on technology per employee as their peers.

But their improved ability to leverage technology is a critical enabler that helps world-class executives spend 27 percent less per employee on HR than their peers, operate with 35 percent fewer HR staff, and also provide higher value to their organizations, with improved HR productivity and strategic alignment virtually across the board.

If we don't develop people with these future challenges in mind, we will have another generation of leaders who can't understand why being a good service provider isn't enough. We must build awareness and an orientation around these needs.

In the absence of clear metrics, several CEOs still struggling to assess the value of investments in business automation and technology suggested an inward focus.

The human costs of maintaining multiple data centers, packaged applications, customizations, operating systems, programming languages, hardware/telecom standards, etc., contribute to a marked increase in total IT cost.

Reduction of unnecessary IT system complexityhardware, software and networksdirectly reduces complexity, liberating time and money for investment in value-adding activities.

Innovativeness

Innovation is defined as adding something new to an existing product or process. The key words are adding and existing. The product or process has already been created from scratch and has worked reasonably well.

When it is changed so that it works better or fulfils a different need, then there is innovation on what already exists. Innovation is the successful exploitation of new ideas.

An innovator is someone who pushes the boundaries of the known world—a change agent who is relentless in making things happen and bringing ideas to execution.

In many ways, innovation is a key to our success, no matter what our business is. The minute we stop innovating is the minute we become mediocre.

Proactive behavior is concerned with implementation and doing whatever is necessary to bring a concept to fruition.

If we apply knowledge to tasks we already know how to do, we call it 'productivity'. If we apply knowledge to tasks that are new and different, we call it 'innovation'. Innovation is the introduction of an invention into a use that has economic value.

Entrepreneurial innovation is an important source of economic growth. HR leaders identify the risks, returns, and other characteristics of entrepreneurship that bear on its attractiveness. Innovation requires an emphasis on developing new and unique products, services and processes.

An invention is a new product.

Companies tend to include innovation in their employee evaluations and encourage risk-taking behaviors. Building a greater tolerance for failure into the appraisal process and evaluating performance over a longer period of time complements the entrepreneurial emphasis.

All innovation begins with creative ideas. Creativity is the starting point for innovation. Creativity is however necessary but not sufficient condition for innovation. Innovation is the implantation of creative inspiration.

Entrepreneurship is creative activity applied to initiating and building an enterprise or organization to achieve goals, seize opportunities, overcome barriers, or solve problems.

Until now creativity has generally been viewed as fuel for the engines of research or product development, not the essential leadership asset.

Creativity is marked by the ability to create, bring into existence, to invent into a new form, to produce through imaginative skill, to make to bring into existence something new.

Creativity is not ability to create out of nothing, but the ability to generate new ideas by combining, changing, or reapplying existing ideas. Some creative ideas are astonishing and brilliant, while others are just simple, good practical ideas that no one seems to have thought, of yet.

Creativity is an attitude, the ability to accept change and newness, a willingness to play with ideas and possibilities, a flexibility of outlook, the habit of enjoying the good, while looking for ways to improve it.

Creativity is also a process. Creative person works hard and continually improves ideas and solutions, by making gradual alterations and refinements to their works.

Very few of creative excellence are produced with a single stroke of brilliance or in a frenzy of rapid activity.

Connectivity

HR leaders unite people. They also unite people with workplace, and create healthy working environment. They establish HR polices that are aimed to strike a balance between work and personal welfare.

Relationship tends to be taken for granted at operational levels. Inter-organizational HR practices are relatively weakly prioritized and are not clearly identified and supported in the way that intra-organizational practices are. Connectivity within the organization includes:

i.   Co-dependent: Mutually dependent, dependence on the needs of another. If there is negative relationship between team fluidity and team flexibility, it should be attenuated in more task interdependent teams.

      Leaders are much more collaborative in the way they approach problem-solving. It should be much more of a team kind of approach.

      Pakistan has accepted $5m (£3.2m) in aid from its rival and neighbour India, as donors pledged more money for the flood-hit country.

      Abdullah Haroon, Pakistan's UN Ambassador, welcomed the offer saying the disaster transcended any differences the two countries had.

      India's UN Ambassador, Hardeep Singh Puri, said the donation of $5m in relief supplies was an initial offer and his country was ready to do more if needed.

ii.   Interdependent: Cooperate to achieve something that can be achieved independently. HR leaders should understand how the different departments or units within their organization depend on the performance of others.

      It's broadly characterized by collective activity that requires mutual inquiry and learning. It may lead to the widespread use of dialogue, collaboration, horizontal networks, valuing of differences, and a focus on learning.

      Having good social relationships may be every bit as important to a healthy lifespan.

      People with strong social relationships were 50 percent less likely to die early than people without such support.

Other characteristics associated with interdependency, i.e. ability to work effectively across organizational boundaries, openness and candor, multifaceted standards of success, and synergies being sought across the whole organization.

HR leaders must seek to describe and understand the interdependency of the multiple elements of the organization, to discover new relationships, to explore the consequences of alternative decisions, and communicate unambiguously within the organization and with the customers.

Entrepreneurs are willing to consider alliances than are traditional corporate-types, in part because of their willingness to take risks and also because they're frequently involved with fledgling ventures with limited resources.

Hundreds of protesters rallied worldwide, against the imprisonment and possible execution of an Iranian woman convicted of adultery, Sakineh Mohammedie Ashtiani.

The case has drawn international attention. Ashtiani was convicted of adultery in 2006 and faces the possibility of execution.

The London protesters said Iran has unfairly sentenced others to death, including 18 gay citizens. o

Leaders should help people maintain relationships as a way of keeping the organization healthy.

Think you don't care what your neighbors are up to. OPOWER, a software company that promotes home energy efficiency, bets you do.

Instead of showing you a plain power bill, OPOWER collects energy data from the home and displays it in a chart that compares your energy use to that of your neighbors in aggregate. Such exposure causes 60 to 80 percent of people to change their energy behaviors, the company says.

The company puts a 'smiley face' on the energy-consumption readouts of people who used relatively less energy than their neighbors.

A research found OPOWER's energy reports lead to about 2 percent reduction in energy consumption.

HR leaders should show connectivity with employees and with the company.

Leaders may emphasize top-down control and deference to authority.

"The personal connection is something I may have taken for granted before that I don't want to ever take for granted again," Jeffrey R. Immelt, the chairman and CEO of General Electric, says.

Teamwork

Most of the companies view people are their greatest pride and resource.

The most difficult task for HR leaders is to get people to work together to achieve a common goal. Of the resources available to them (capital, information, knowledge and people), the most difficult to lead and leverage is people working together in support of, and in contribution, to one another.

Google Inc has acquired Angstro, a startup that sorts news and information across social networks.

Palo Alto-based Angstro has developed applications to find photos on Facebook, combine Caller ID with LinkedIn profiles and other tools for Twitter.

The Angstro deal underscores the importance to Google of social networks in an increasingly competitive Internet search arena which it dominates.

No one accomplishes anything in an organization alone and without the help and contribution of someone else.

As in the team, employees combine various skills, ideas, knowledge bases and perspectives. Teams usually increase individual productivity and workplace satisfaction.

Simply being on a team can be a key source of employee motivation, status and pride for having been selected to participate.

Team output is generally higher in quality and quantity than individual performance. To be successful, people in the team need to consider following success factors:

a.   Identification of the goal.

      An African Union summit has been held in Kampala with calls for tougher action against the extremists in Somalia.

      Ugandan President Yoweri Museveni pleaded for Africa to unite in a strong military response to Islamic militants in Somalia who claimed responsibility for the bombings.

      "Who are these guys who do not respect the A.U.? Where do their loyalties lie? Whose interests are they serving? These terrorists can be and should be defeated. Let us now act in concert and sweep them out of Africa," he said.

b.   Acceptance of role and responsibilities: We want line leaders concentrating on business and day-to-day management of people, with some sensitivity to complicated HR items, but not to try to be expert in all of them. We don't even want them tied up for long worrying about where to find the right sort of expert for the challenge they're suddenly facing.

c.   Foster involvement, such as in decision-making, conflict resolution, communication and participation: Dependent is broadly characterized by the circumstance that only people in positions of authority are responsible for leadership, i.e. concentration of decision-making authority in a few senior positions, seniority and position levels as an important source of status, etc.

d.   Ability to trust others: Research shows zero-tolerance policy have been found reducing connectedness.

e.   Recognize other's strengths and weaknesses in a manner that encourages positive working relationships.

The best way for implementing entrepreneurship is by means of teaming up the right sort of people for the purpose of task completion. Teamwork always gives the impression that the employee is contributing directly to the success of the company.

Teamwork increases the good will and creates a positive spirit among the employees that in turn enables them to drive towards the companies' objectives.

In a decision-making process, an entrepreneur can access to various options provided by the team members. It accommodates individual's thought and paves the way for innovation.

Challenge .

Entrepreneurs have courage to seek challenges. Entrepreneurs are risks takers. Risk-taking involves a willingness to pursue opportunities having a chance of costly failure.

HR leaders do not attempt to hide behind the attitude of 'I'm just the HR leader.' CEOs want and need HR leaders who aren't afraid to step up to the plate and demonstrate some initiative and risk taking.

In many cases, the expect leaders who can solve problems in various areas of the organization.

They identify, assess, and prioritize potentially unfavorable situations and circumstances to minimize risks.

Companies provide strategies which will minimize economic and legal consequences. They are able to effectively control non-desirable outcomes.

For the Human Resource leaders, a few risks include workers compensation insurance, recruiting, safety, training, coaching, policy and procedure development, employee complaints of harassment or discrimination, and uniform termination procedures.

Entrepreneurs are individuals who are willing to take risks, to develop new products, and start new businesses. They recognize opportunities, like working for themselves, and accept challenges.

HR leaders need to show achievements; they seek to perform at their best. Who stops being better, stops being good. They are open to feedback, are goal oriented, seek to be unique, and strive for accomplishments based on their own efforts. They also take risks, not extreme risks, but calculated risks.

When former Xerox CEO Anne Mulcahy received the prestigious Corporate Innovator Luminary Award by The Committee of 200 in Washington, D.C., in 2006 she won praise for her turnaround effort rescuing Xerox and for her place among 10 female CEOs in the Fortune 500.

Not incidentally Anne was a former Xerox VP of HR. In 2008, U.S News & World Report selected her as one of America's Best Leaders.

Human Resources Management (HRM) practices are important driver of success. Human Resources Management makes to company's ability to accept risk, be innovative and be proactive.

Companies should be able to attract a large number of entrepreneurs in the service sector and assisting newer areas of activity. It will provide the leaders to take opportunities on leadership roles early in their career.

Companies must become more entrepreneurial in order to identify new opportunities for sustained superior performance. Entrepreneurship involves organizational learning, driven by collaboration, creativity and individual commitment.

An order of Benedictine nuns has signed a major record deal with the company behind Lady Gaga, it has been revealed.

The Nuns of the Abbaye de Notre-Dame de l'Annonciation, from France, won a global search of more than 70 convents across Europe, the US and Africa.

The reclusive order, based near Avignon, was deemed to have the finest Gregorian Chant singers.

The Reverend Mother Abbess said: "At first we were worried it would affect our cloistered life, so we asked St Joseph in prayer. Our prayers were answered, and we thought that this album would be a good thing if it touches people's lives and helps them find peace."

HR leaders encourage employees and organization to seek opportunity. They include innovation in the employee evaluations and encourage risk-taking behaviors.

It will allow building a greater tolerance for failure into the appraisal process and evaluating performance over a longer period of time complements the entrepreneurial emphasis.

Al Qaeda is appealing for financial donations for the third time in a little over a year in a sign that the terror network might be short on funds.

A message posted on a militant website Wednesday repeats a June 2009 appeal by the group's top Afghanistan commander, Mustafa Abu al-Yazeed, was killed in an airstrike in May. He said then that many militants in Afghanistan were unable to fight because they lacked money and equipment.

An entrepreneurial orientation requires employees to think and act in new ways, taking individual responsibility for change while also cooperating with teams. Employees must be more opportunistic, creative and achievement-oriented, yet tolerant of ambiguity and willing to take risks.

Spending money and using resources to supply a product is risky, because costs are incurred before consumers decide whether they will purchase the product at a price sufficiently high to cover the costs. Profits are the financial incentive and the income that entrepreneurs receive in return for their effort and risk if they are successful.

Understanding the roles of entrepreneurs, profits, and losses is important to employees, business owners, and costumers. Wages and employment opportunities at a business depend on the business' success in earning profits and avoiding losses.

In addition to financial losses, other disincentives to which entrepreneurs respond include the responsibility, long hours, and stress of running a business.

Entrepreneurs accept the risks in organizing resources to produce goods and services because they hope to earn profits.

Entrepreneur is someone who's been able to identify a problem and come up with a solution to it before somebody else did.

Entrepreneurship is willingly working together, risking, creating, implementing, driving and following through innovative idea that seeks to maximize value from opportunity.

8th

AUTHENTICITY

Authenticity describes a character of being ourselves; being the person we were created to be.

Authenticity is an important value for HR leader.

HR leaders lead with their whole selves—their hearts as well as their mind. Any leader who has failed in life, generally he has not failed to lead other people. They've failed to lead themselves.

HR leaders lead with their whole selves—their hearts as well as their mind. Any leader who has failed in life, generally he has not failed to lead other people. They've failed to lead themselves.

The HR leaders should build their authenticity in both the business and lives. They are doing the right thing; acting with integrity, bringing their best to work, being a positive role model, etc.

A lack of authenticity and incongruence leads to a breakdown in trust and is considered unethical and hypocritical. While good ethics are good for business (though sometimes hard to prove), bad ethics are undoubtedly extremely bad for business.

Authenticity isn't a destination—it's a journey. HR leaders in their journey must focus on defining and expressing authenticity through employees and line leaders' experiences that are authentic, intentional, and wholly integrated. The HR leaders must have a sense of purpose that is in aligned with the company's vision.

a.   Understand the purpose: HR leaders should know what really motivates them.

HR leaders are highly passionate about their jobs and their organizations.

Without purpose, the authority and motivation may not be required for HR leaders to be sitting at the board room table.

Successful companies must have a cause that is bigger and broader than the organizations itself. A successful leader has to truly believe in a vision and a mission that can be combined to form a cause. He or she must be identified with the cause.

Andrea Jung, the CEO of Avon Products, was a star and on her way to the top of Neiman Marcus. At age 35 she walked out

She said: "I didn't want to spend the rest of my life making luxury goods for upper-class women." So she walked out without another job and wound up at Avon Products. There she found her passion—to help women achieve their self-sufficiency.

'Walk the talk' is an important jargon. HR leaders derive their authority from having a genuine, inspiring sense of purpose.

Authenticity emphasizes HR leaders to knowing and acting on what is true and real inside their soul, employee, and organization.

b.   Practice core values: Having values means seeing the corporation as an organization where the HR leaders contribute to its objectives.

HR leaders make sure employees understand the value they bring. They know how the rest of the organization works to have credibility through financial knowledgewhich involves numbers; product and industry knowledge—how it connects with key HR areas like compensation; and functional knowledge—includes sales, marketing and operations.

To build enduring organizations and motivate employees to provide superior customer service and create sustainable value for the organizations, HR leaders should know themselves, lead with integrity and demand conformance to higher ethical values.

The leader must be closely aligned with the culture they hope to lead.

The culture might be reflecting interests of employees and organization.

HR leader whose own culture that is inseparable from a company's culture is likely to be much more effective.

HR leaders inspire employees to model organization values. This is typically done by displaying behaviors that is giving the organization the tools they need to measure success.

c.   Establish enduring relationships: Employees expect a connection with the leaders, but many line leaders fear getting close to employees and hide behind a false persona.

HR leaders do not deny emotional/relationship side of work and business. It's never 'just business' to the people whose lives are affected.

Walmart has decided that it can't live with a $7,000 fine for the death of an employee in a 2008 trampling incident in Long Island, New York.

The company has spent more than $2 million in legal fees to battle the fine.

It agreed to improve safety measures, offer large charitable donations and create $400,000 fund to help customers injured at the store.

As a part of the settlement, Nassau County prosecutors agreed to suspend its criminal investigation.

The HR leaders seek a purpose for leadership beyond self-interest, which helps them create partnerships.

Communication should give rooms for employees can let the management know about their needs and aspirations.

HR leaders have consciousness that helps people communicate honestly and openly. This approach expands emotional intelligence by developing awareness of the connection between feelings and human needs.

The leaders provide a method of resolving difficult conflicts so that people feel heard. By deepening awareness of needs, we contribute to trust, safety, and improved communication.

When people are understood at a deep level, they're able to release their attachment to their positions, explore options and make requests that meet everyone's needs.

The HR leaders are able to deal with conflict that reframes how people communicate so that strong emotions are not a liability, but an opportunity to discover more satisfying options.

One of the most important qualities that HR leaders have is the power to communicate effectively and authentically. When we know the art and science of effective communication, all of our business relationships are enhanced.

d.   Demonstrate self-discipline: A leader doesn't let ego or emotions reign but is 'easy and predictable' to work with.

A HR leader is a self-reliant learner who remains a knowledgeable. He/she develops employees who learn and use the skill of self-help, know their learning needs, be able to explore options in learning, think divergently, make decisions, and evaluate his/her own role in the workplace and in the organization.

Authenticity demonstrates confident, hopeful, optimistic, and deeply aware of how to think and behave.

HR leaders display a high level of integrity and be committed to building the organization through purpose, value, heart, relationships, and self-discipline.

We must allow ourselves to just be ourselves—a real person—rather than believing we have to act out the role of HR leader.

In today's business, there is unethical meltdown in leadership and cite major corporate failures. The degradation in ethical leadership coupled with cultural challenges emphasizes the need for leadership that is authentic.

Many leaders have sacrificed the future of the organizations and the employees in an effort to chase immediate opportunities for personal gain. And the leaders have been grossly undermined by the loss of trust.

Lasting values in organizations are built upon authentic, reliable, and passionate leadership. Authenticity can make a difference in the lives of the employees and organizations they serve.

Building authenticity is a choice and a journey.

Authenticity and undisputed credibility are pivotal for sustainable success in the current climate, and for the future. HR leaders need to follow these steps to build their authenticity, include:

a.   Be a good role model: HR leaders strive to be people of influence, but people often overlook the significance of authenticity in crafting and expanding their influence.

Authenticity enables HR leaders recognize that they aren't perfectand they're OK with their imperfection. The leaders gain influence because employees become more OK with their own imperfections.

That doesn't mean the employees lower their standards or fail to deliver with their responsibilities. But they recognize that they have flaws and need the employees to complement and complete what they bring to the table.

Any one can become a role model, and being a positive role model enables and encourages us to raise the bar.

Positive role models are passionate, optimistic and enthusiastic. They focus on solutions rather than problems. By doing so, we gain respect, enhance self-belief and improve our well-being measurably. In turn, we become more productive and raise our profile in the business.

HR leaders lead by example which can foster respect, loyalty and commitment; and set the tone how the employees they leads should behave.

We need to spend more time developing future leaders within the company, who have the character, values, wisdom, and depth to lead the organization in the future.

The HR leaders believe that there are employees who have the capacity to grow under the right circumstances, include self reflection, conscious personal development, willing to become a mentor/teacher, ever last learner, loving family, have a significant life experience, etc.

HR leaders strive to be people of influence, but people often overlook the significance of authenticity in crafting and expanding their influence.

b.   Think positively: By choosing to think positively, we've a greater chance of getting more of what we want. This is not just about 'positive thinking.' HR leaders, who are optimistic gain more support from employees, lead more successful lives and feel freer to behave more authentically.

The more real we are to our employees, the more relatable we are. The more people can relate to us, the more they trust us—and the more they want to work with us to achieve our goals.

We should not assume people know how we feel about difficult decisions. Part of our job is to share your inner world, to share our thought process and our feelings.

HR can get better at eliminating the negative effects and capitalizing on the positive to improve their performance.

c.   Do the right thing: Authenticity in HR function is about telling the truth. It's often said that honesty is the best policy: actually, it's the only policy.

When HR leaders behaving with integrity sits at the top of their to-do list, they increase feelings of self confidence and well-being. By doing the right thing, even when nobody else notices, their authenticity quotient is raised significantly.

Leadership development is almost entirely about self-development. The HR leaders are willing to take themselves through an inner journey of who they are and integrate their discoveries into their daily lives.

They are aware of their effect on employees; they dive deeply into how they make meaning of the organization.

The deeper that dive, the more compassion they have for themselves and for organization.

Authenticity is the degree to which HR leader is true to his/her own personality, spirit, and character.

The closer we come to knowing ourselves and acting accordance with knowledge, the more authentic we appear to people.

Authenticity demonstrates self awareness and self-regulated behaviors, and fostering self development.

HR leaders show their impact on the organization performance. By increasing employee's awareness that facilitates development of skill, attitude and behavior required to optimize their growth and performance.

They create organization context that allows people to continuously learn and grow. Leadership is not about traits and characteristics. But about how their life experience guides their passion to lead. It gives them the authenticity to be something they were.

Authenticity is what our customers intuitively crave and what our businesses claim to understand better than most.

Integrity

Integrity is the integration of actions and inner values. Inner value will tell us uncomfortable feeling that occurs when our actions conflict with what we know to be true.

A person of integrity is the same on the outside and on the inside. Such an individual can be trusted because he or she never veers from inner values. Honest dealings, predictable reactions, well-controlled emotions, and an absence of tantrums and harsh outbursts are all signs of integrity.

A HR leader must have the trust of the employees and therefore must display integrity. He/she will be a person who is centered in integrity and be more approachable by employees.

An Italian Catholic diocese has denounced homosexual priests for their 'double life' and said they should not be in the priesthood.

The Diocese of Rome was responding to a magazine article on three homosexual priests that gave details of alleged sexual encounters and trips to clubs.

The diocese said 'the honour of all the others' was sullied by their behaviour.

Most leaders today genuinely try to get things done for good and even altruistic reasons. They are nonetheless often perceived as being driven by money, materialism, and self-interest.

Maturity

In order for Human Resources to remain viable and relevant, they must see themselves as leaders, and their actions should be inherent with it.

Top Management has been longing for HR leaders to lead company's efforts to take care for their employees. They will truly affect the bottom line. It will drive results and provide an engaged workforce who will produce more, and provide exceptional customer service.

Human Resources maturity can be defined in terms of how much delineation exists between **position, person** and **performance.** HR leaders display maturity that is characterized by:

a. Not care who gets the credit as long as the job gets done: HR leaders don't draw attention to themselves; they express appreciation for the contributions of others.

Since the leaders hire people better than them, they don't worry about them doing better than them because they take credit for good hiring. They know that having the best people working for them will make them look better.

When HR leaders find misalignment in an individual's work-life map, they practice humility by avoiding blame.

A conflict or negative experience should be paraphrased, with no blame or finger pointing, so that the entire team can learn what could have been avoided or what would have been a better response to the issue.

b. Willing to put the mission ahead of their personal agenda: HR leaders know that what they have done as individuals is far less important than what they can accomplish with and through others.

HR leaders ultimately create and develop and business philosophy in the organization that values its people, invests to nourish and support development through continuous training, coaching and mentoring.

The organizations who do not set a positive encouraging mechanism to develop this business philosophy, they are never benefited by unlimited creative power of people because they don't believe in inspiring people, raising their morale and restore a sense of purpose.

To lead people to deliver their best a encouraging environment, HR leadership has to play a very crucial role in organization.

c.   Are gratified by the achievements of employees: HR leaders realize that there's plenty of success to go around, and they help those around them reach for the stars.

Traditional management is underlined. The life expectancy of such company in the Fortune 500 has declined from around 50-60 years to just 15 years, and is heading towards 5 years, unless something changes.

Today's company with traditional management, only one in five workers is fully engaged in their work.

Radical management is two to four times more productive than traditional management.

d.   Give credit where it's due: HR leaders know that there are no 'little people' in the organization; every person's contribution is significant. The leaders know how to say "Well done," and they say it often.

Magnanimity means giving credit where it is due. The HR leader ensures that credit for successes is spread as widely as possible throughout the company. Conversely, the leader takes personal responsibility for failures.

This sort of reverse magnanimity helps employees feel good about themselves and draws the team closer together. To spread the fame and take the blame is a hallmark of authenticity.

e.   HR leaders should be generous and merciful to their opponents, as well as to those who are weaker than themselves.

Business has been focused on external measures of achievement, with little attention to cultivating the inner capacities of intelligence, intuition, wisdom and compassion.

There should be an opportunity to truly integrate core human values into how we lead: We need to rediscover and reconnect with our inner capabilities.

Real source of competitive advantage lies in people. But on the other hand, many Top Executives continue to devalue the Human Resources (HR) function.

Pakistan's President Asif Ali Zardari said the international community was losing the war against the Afghan Taliban.

"I believe that the international community, which Pakistan belongs to, is in the process of losing the war against the Taliban," Zardari said. "And that is, above all, because we have lost the battle for hearts and minds."

"If you protect the population from Taliban threats, and if you bring them schools, health clinics, clean water and other services, they'll turn away from the insurgents," Evan Vucci, a photojournalist, says.

Humility

More than just niceness, humility reveals that the leader understands that no one person can create a great organization.

Humility is truthfulness; we acknowledge both our talents and our failings. Humility comes from the word humus, earth. Humble people are down to earth. They are honest in evaluating their strengths and their weaknesses.

Humility is not self-deprecation, impoverishment, shame or humiliation. It is not co-dependence, inferiority or passivity. Neither is it lack of personal caretaking or responsibility.

Humility is recognizing that we see a tiny fraction of ourselves and life, and that everything is much greater than our physical senses and human awareness indicate.

Humility believes there is a deeper dimension in spirit, and that higher consciousness can lead us there.

Humility means that we remain curious, open-minded and teachable, and thus in a process of continual growth.

To build enduring organizations and motivate employees to provide superior customer service and create sustainable value for their organizations, we need HR leaders who know themselves, who lead with integrity and demand conformance to higher ethical values.

"Leadership is a long journey into your own soul." General Electric Co. CEO Jeff Immelt says. "If leaders start to think it's all about their fame and power and glory, in the end they're going to do the wrong thing, and they're going to lose it along the way."

When we develop greater humility, employees feel like they're being listened to and acknowledged. The authenticity has willingness to hear more because we listen more.

This gives them access to more input and ideasand all of that plays into problem solving and the organization success. Humility gives us an enlarged sense of how we can get things done. HR leaders practice humility by demonstrating:

a. Make decision that balancing multiple priorities and multiple stakeholders with multiple needs. Most of us find a balance between utilizing some degree of instinct, and some degree of analysis. We might be highly guided by data, but trust our instincts.

Being real also relates to knowing how to use our intuition and emotional intelligence (EQ).

A high level of EQ improves influencing skills and personal impact. Intuition can inform our decision-making processes in ways that enable greatly improved outcomes. In short, think less and feel more.

b. Observe productive mistakes: Knowing from the start that we might be wrong, we might be right—fearlessly going ahead with what we think is right, but monitoring the results of the decision. Keep our minds open. That allows nimble course correction. And that can lead to better results.

We accept disappointments, loss and tragedies for the lessons that we learn from them. Humility is reinforced with failed expectations.

HR leaders, who admit they have a lot to learn, possibly make mistakes, and that they can't run the company alone earn respect and engender responsible attitudes in employees. Key practices of good leadership stem from humility—and inspire responsibility.

The kind of humility which HR leaders have is not the sort which leaves them bent and bowed. It is of the type which means that the organization and employees run their PR for the leaders.

Humility leaves us open to hear and therefore learn more. Most HR leaders possess humility and professional will.

Leading from good to great does not mean coming up with the answers and then motivating everyone to follow your messianic vision. It means having the humility to grasp the fact that you do not yet understand enough to have the answers and then to ask the questions that will lead to the best possible insights.

HR leaders focus on observing, listening, understanding and forgiving rather than judging and condemning. The HR leaders who act with humility aim to achieve a shared vision with everyone in the organization. They want to understand the perspectives of those at the frontlines and adapt to accommodate those perspectives.

Humility means that we do not take more than we need, and we willingly share what we have.

HR leaders are able to demonstrate passion and humility at the same time. They show excitement when they describe their accomplishments and ambitions.

"Passion is always attractive," Janice Howroyd, the head of Act-1 Group, says, "and humility becomes the thread between passion and skill." "The most shameless act of self promotion that we can engage in is being humble."

Because others find humility so attractive, the virtue serves many purposes.

The leaders manifest humility by routinely crediting others, the external factors and good luck with their companies' success. But when results are poor they blame themselves.

HR leaders believe there is no way that humility can be an essential ingredient to success as a leader. Success as a leader breeds more arrogance than humility and is not necessarily a deterrent.

Authenticity is characterized by those who are deeply aware of how they think and behave, being aware of their own and other's values perspectives, knowledge and strength, aware of the context in which they operate, and are confident, hopeful, optimistic, resilient, and have high moral character.

We have a responsibility to honour, respect and care for ourselves, employees and the organization. Humility engages us to protect and nurture people and the organization.

Humility is the most attractive trait in a HR leader. Being humble allows us to keep our two-way communication channels open. We are open to feedback, change, and improvement because we don't believe we know everything already.

As HR leaders, we should be humble enough to focus on constant, quantum leaps of improvement.

Humility means that we place a higher priority on our heart and soul experience, and pay less attention to our mental chatter.

The German central bank has called on the country's president to dismiss one of its board members over comments he made about immigration and Jews.

Sarrazin has criticised German Muslims, suggested the existence of a Jewish gene, and warned of ethnic Germans being outnumbered by migrants.

He states Muslim immigrants refuse to integrate. "All Jews share a particular gene."

President Christian Wulff said he was concerned Germany's image could be damaged by Thilo Sarrazin's remarks.

German Chancellor Angela Merkel said Sarrazin's remarks were 'completely unacceptable' and urged the Bundesbank to act.

Humility means that we conduct ourselves with honour and integrity.

One characteristic of Hr leaders stand out that they have a high level of self-esteem. They know who they were. Humility is defined not by self deprecating behavior or attitudes but by the self-esteem with which we regard others.

Good behavior flows naturally from that kind of humility. Generally, we can be humble only if we feel good about ourselves—and we want to help those around us feel really good about themselves too.

HR leaders learning from people who are actually doing the work.

HR leaders motivated by humility remain physically present and personally connected; they fear ignorance more than they fear confronting mistakes or problems.

Humility drives responsibility—when the leaders focus on customer needs, they train employees at the frontlines and elsewhere to move beyond self-interest too.

HR leaders who are driven by humility make a practice of asking questions to understand what others do and what they need.

They practice active listening and seek out quiet environments to interact with employees without distractions. They empathize with their associates and ultimately empower employees by reinforcing strengths and resources.

Following a string of suicides at its Chinese factories, Foxconn Technology Group raised workers' wages. Now the often secretive manufacturer of the iPhone is holding rallies for its workers to raise morale at the heavily regimented factories.

The outreach to workers shows how Foxconn has been shaken by the suicides and the bad press they have attracted to the normally publicity shy company.

"Foxconn feels it's perhaps time to look back and to learn from the tragedies and to send an important message to their employees that they are not alone, and that the Foxconn family is there to support them and to help them through their challenges," Burson Marsteller ofFoxconn, said.

Humility sows the seed of connection to employees. It creates connection to many people which makes the organization successful.

No organization will ever be successful unless they can attract others to it, either to work for it, run it, buy from it or invest in it. Arrogance drives people away, humility draws people in that is why in a leader it is so vital.

Leaders motivated by fear or arrogance remain aloof, disconnected from their employees. HR leaders with humility recognize that they are no better or worse than employees in the organization. The leaders not self-effacing but rather try to elevate everyone.

Self-worth is not a tangible concept that can be measured. However, it can be increased.

Among the most emotionally weighted issues for employees is compensation. It's related to self-worth.

HR leaders persuade employees that the value represented by pay is the value of their position, not the value of the person.

Previously salary was the sole motivating factor for corporate success. High pay may affect high delivery. Now, however, recognition of self-worth is the larger issue employers have to deal with.

Authenticity worth is high or low; it piqued our curiosity not only because of the presentation but also because it was coming from a valuable outsider perspective. Their self-worth would be undisputable if:

a.   Show concern: HR leader provides valuable perspectives on how employees should be developed and why employee empowerment, team-building, open organizational interaction, and life balance need to be in place.

Because organizations pay so little attention to how people are feeling in the workplace, and because we ourselves are so often unaware of what we're feeling, we often fail to recognize the effect that our emotions have on us, and on others.

A new college started classes this summer in Berkeley, California.

Zaytuna College's motto is, "Where Islam meets America." It's the first Muslim college in the United States.

"We want to manifest Islam in a way that's compatible with America," says Imam Zaid Shakir, who founded Zaytuna. "If we prove ourselves, even those more vocal critics will be silenced. It's up to us. The ball is in our court."

The Islamic college will reduce perception that Islam is a religion that condones, and teaches, violence and intolerance.

Employees have the confidence to go to the line leader and share useful pieces of knowledge in a way which they would be unable to do if the leader was of the more brash type.

Being a part of organization, contributing to it and supporting employees, is an integral part of building authenticity. HR leaders demonstrate their concern through:

i. Not encourage unhealthy internal competition. There will be more losers than winners. This can do a lot of damage to self-esteem, which adversely effects output.

The more they feel threatened, the more energy they spend defending, restoring, and asserting their value, and the less energy they have available to create value.

ii. Try not to concentrate solely on skills and abilities. Tap into the concerns of employees.

The biggest challenge to employees' satisfaction and effectiveness was the feeling of not being valued. Their core emotional need is to feel valued.

One of the factors that motivate employees is the ability to see tasks through its completion. Employees should recognize that their involvement in the workflow can be seen from the finished products/services, once these are complete; and gain the understanding of their importance in the achievements as a whole.

Researchers have found that the highest rises in survival level—the most extreme fight or flight response—is prompted by threat to social acceptance, self-esteem, and status.

Rupert Stadler of Audi, says: "When you talk about a credit crisis the common factor is people. It always has to do with the actions and judgments of people."

Many are afraid to acknowledge others' emotions. As HR leaders, we should let employees know we understand their perspective.

b. Give recognition

"It will be a very interesting prize, one that can influence the agenda of the day" Thorbjoern Jagland, chairman of the Nobel Peace Prize Committee.

i. A simple thank-you and see the difference in our employees work attitude.

ii. Name employee of the month: We can make a provision of Monthly or Quarterly Award (depending upon the budget) for the best employee—Awarding 2 or 3 best workers each month. The award can be in terms of gifts or money.

c. Respect people: Respect takes years to build, but it takes a second to break.

Supreme Court Justice Antonin Scalia provocatively said: "Women's equality is entirely up to the political branches. If the current society wants to outlaw discrimination by sex, you have legislatures."

i. Contemplate our words: When we want to raise our voice think carefully about what we are going to say.

ii. We shouldn't encourage employee attitude tests. They are self worth killers.

d. Pay fairly: Most employees suffer from what is known as the 'I am not worth it' syndrome. They may feel 'overworked and under valued'. Few people expect high pay. But, everyone expects fair pay.

A judge has awarded a US exhibition company $110m for salvaging artefacts from the wreck of the RMS Titanic.

RMS Titanic Inc, which displays the artefacts in museums across the world, is entitled to their full market value.

The ship sank on its maiden voyage from Southampton to New York on 14 April, 1912, killing more than 1,500 people.

The Belfast-built ship sank about 400 miles off the coast of Newfoundland, Canada, two hours after hitting an iceberg.

It was discovered in 1985 by an expedition led by Dr Robert Ballard.

RMS Titanic Inc. has undertaken seven expeditions to the wreck site 2.5 miles (4km) below the north Atlantic, and has retrieved more than 5,500 artefacts.

Giving employees anything but the best news about compensation is one of the most challenging communication tasks a company can face, and the HR leader is typically at the center of the process—striving to find the best ways to convey the message.

HR leaders make sure distributive justice refers to how employees perceive fairness in the outcome related to pay.

This occurs when employees starts to compare their pay with their co-worker and the amount of workload that they have to do.

Employees must be able to access information with regards to their pay grade, job description, basis allocation of bonus and increment.

HR leader provides valuable perspectives on how employees should be developed and why employee empowerment, team-building, open organizational interaction, and life balance need to be in place.

Character

Successful HR leaders are authentic in word and action, but there are challenges they must face to build character in the workplace.

One of the cornerstones upon which the organization is to builtis authenticity.

Character—an innate sense of fairness, honesty, respect for others, and humilityis becoming the most resonant quality for global leaders.

Authenticity and character are essential for HR leaders in a culture-driven company to be effective. It is alignment among the leader's passion, the company's mission, and the corporate culture in which everything transpires.

The HR leader should be authentic especially in facing situation that requires decision-making is a character defining moment.

HR leaders bring character too. Good leaders are well rounded. Their persona carries a sense of maturity, authenticity, and commitment. It is in this area where people fall short as leaders.

Many try to act like leaders, talk like leaders, and even command as leaders, but they are unsuccessful from within. They lack authenticity. There are challenges a HR leader will face to becoming authentic at work.

Character and motivation are the two qualities that separate loyal, enthusiastic employees from mere jobholders. Often the best hire is someone who has experienced failure.

HR leaders experience moments that shape their character or authenticitysituations that force them to transform beliefs and values into calculated action.

Those situations build and define a leader's character because neither choice is the wrong choice, just a deeper reflection of the leader and person he or she chooses to be. There are challenges a HR leader will face to becoming authentic at work.

Control

Traditional management viewed employees as '(human) resources' i.e. they assume employees are not people, but 'things' that could be controlled and manipulated and exploited.

The goal of the organization is seen as producing goods and services to make money for shareholders. It means they will achieve the goal through cost reduction, downsizing and outsourcing.

The employees are simply assumed as set of 'things' to be manipulated to achieve the lowest cost result.

Since HR leaders and Top Management are implementing the idea of doing work through employees and treating them as things to achieve particular short-term results, with the long-term philosophy of cost reduction through command-and-control.

Successful companies discovered that the energy of its employees—now many of them are highly educated—couldn't be bought or directed or commanded and controlled. Employees had to be inspired to contribute.

Steve Connell, author of Personal Brand Essence says: "Business brand is harder to control because you are a cog in a (corporate) machine with regard to your personal brand, I think you can control more than 50% of how people think of you through what you say and do."

Self-awareness and self-knowledge are critical characteristic of successful HR leaders. They foster development of the employees by displaying responsibility fir developing human capital.

The HR leaders act constantly in accordance with believes and values. HR leaders have capacity to control the organization, include:

a. Self-control: Self-assured and assertive, keen to set the agenda and to lead, but not obsessed with the need to take control of every situation.

    HR leaders are self-assured, opinionated employees with clear ideas on how things should be done and they should get out of their way and let them get on with it. The leaders hate to be micro-managed.

    Self-awareness and self-control are important factors for HR leaders to develop a mind set and the skills to understand how best to integrate other's perspectives and empowering employees for the success of the organizations.

    The HR leaders speak with open mind, take control and lead in all situations.

b.   Manage employees: Reducing high performer flight is a top priority for HR leaders.

Studies indicate that 45-50% of all high performers are actively looking for new jobs.

HR leaders explore Human Capital Management because it links to employee engagement.

The leaders do commit to the talent management process. They consistently breed the values on people. Therefore, they quickly gain reputations for attracting exceptional talent and for the loyalty they inspire in employees.

There is a strong link between lower absenteeism and better profit margins. For example, organizations with an average five days' absence per employee per year have profit margins 60 percent higher than organizations with an average 10 days' absence per employee per year.

HR leaders must take on stronger relationship building with employees as the best chance of influencing them in the right direction.

c.   Manage the tasks: Increase the strategic credibility of HR function

56% of HR leaders still do not believe that their workforces are adequately prepared to meet their organizations' future plans.

HR leaders and line leaders have to make sure their strategic plans are aligned. Employees will learn from the inconsistencies across the organization.

The HR leaders need to work in partnership with line leaders, who have direct responsibility for leading employees. Only then can they ensure they are leading by example.

The planning consists of strategic planning—the process of identifying an organization's long-term goals and objectives and then determining the best strategy for achieving those goals and objectives; and action planning—the overlap between strategic planning and implementation.

HR leaders inspire employees to forgo self-interest, encourage them to be creative, pursue ambitious goals and empower them to make decisions.

They show sincere and genuine care to the needs of employees.

A research revealed clear and positive links between the 'feel good' factor of HR people being satisfied with their contribution to the business and profit margins.

In organizations where HR people are very satisfied with their department's influence on business strategy, profit margins were 46 percent higher than for those who are not satisfied with their contribution.

d. Determine the future of the organization: Examine in strategic HR. Long term outlooks enable HR managers to predict and plan for specific areas of talent shortfall and to adopt management training programs to prepare for the demands of future growth.

When company brings in a HR leader whose background was primarily in executive search, not HR; the company may intend to secure its long-term future in a world where talent will determine success.

80% of organizations have still not yet aligned their HR programs and activities to business results.

HR leaders need to truly have an impact on their organization's success through passion, purpose and courage.

Optimism is also a defining characteristic of the HR leader.

A study found 80% of business leaders were optimistic about their business prospects, but also identified a positive outlook from their management teams

Discipline

'Discipline' is derived from the Latin word 'disciple,' which means 'to teach.'

Discipline in the workplace is the means by which HR leaders correct behavioral deficiencies and ensure adherence to established company rules.

Discipline and punishment are not the same. Discipline is a process for correcting problems in a positive, non-punitive way.

The purpose of discipline is to correct behavior. It is not designed to punish or embarrass an employee.

However, if unacceptable behavior is a persistent problem or if the employee is involved in a misconduct that cannot be tolerated, management may use discipline to correct the behavior.

The longer the undesirable behavior persists, the harsher the consequences become—including possible termination.

Badam Bagh, or Almond Garden is Afghanistan's only prison for women in the capital Kabul.

The prison is a window on a world where, outside these walls, women are constantly judged against a standard that makes many of their stories difficult to fathom.

About half of Afghanistan's 476 women prisoners were detained for 'moral crimes.'

That includes everything from running away from home, refusing to marry, marrying without their family's wishes, and 'attempted adultery.'

Sixteen-year-old Sabera frets that she is missing school.

"I was about to get engaged, and the boy came to ask me himself, before sending his parents. A lady in our neighborhood saw us, and called the police," she explains.

Employees should know in advance that poor conduct or performance will result in specific, pre-determined consequences.

Once the company regulation is formalized, HR leader immediately communicates to employees. So, they know whether they have done something wrong or not.

Discipline should be impersonal. It is applied in a particular situation which reflects the offense, not the person who committed it. It will be the same each and every time.

HR leader must ensure, discipline should not be applied arbitrarily, nor should it differ, for the same offense, from one person to the next. HR leaders consistently display three forms of discipline, include:

a.   Disciplined thought: Be competent, be knowledgeable. When HR leaders have disciplined thought, they don't need bureaucracy.

   Behind every successful leader is a vibrant culture that engages and energizes employees. In almost every case, that culture has been defined, shaped and personified by the leader.

   The HR leaders should have enough knowledge that related to the processes and activities used to formulate objectives, practices and policies aimed at meeting short and long-range organizational needs and opportunities, and focus on human capital issues.

   The knowledge includes matters relating to the HR professional's knowledge and understanding of the business and its markets, the external environment, internal assets, effective business practices, HR metrics and other aspects of strategic human resource management.

They are able to interpret information from internal sources, including finance/accounting, business development, marketing, sales, operations and information technology.

They exhibit their expertise that focuses on HR careers, communications, legal and regulatory issues, technology, metrics, outsourcing, effective practices and global issues.

HR leaders should consider giving people opportunities at very young ages to step up and lead without risking the organization. The people have to learn early. Then when they get to higher-level positions they don't repeat those kinds of mistakes.

Learning organizations allow employees to do that—they give them those opportunities, they watch them closely, and then they give them feedback.

67 percent of HR leaders are now members of the highest-ranking leadership team in their organization.

It is clearly important that HR leaders have the required competencies, such as the ability to influence, to justify their place at this level.

HR leaders have a crucial role to play in enabling and facilitating the shift, because it is essentially one of moving from a world where employees and customers are treated as 'things' to be manipulated to a world where employees and customers as thinking, feeling, and caring human beings with whom there are relationships.

Using terminology that refers to human beings as 'resources' i.e. things, is a remnant of traditional machine thinking. Such terminology unwittingly degrades human beings into things to be manipulated, exploited, and then thrown away.

b.   Disciplined action: Keep on the track of HR best practices. When HR leaders have disciplined action, they do not need excessive control.

They describe company's objective into planning and implementation.

37 percent of employees said they have a clear understanding of what their organization is trying to achieve and why.

In the action plans, the HR leaders establish a system how to measure progress of implementation over time, assess the resources that will be needed to implement the strategic plan, and assignments in which employees will be involved in the implementation process.

Company provides the organizations a balanced scorecard measurement system that enables the organizations to clarify their objectives and strategy and translate them into action.

The purpose of the HR scorecard is to manage HR as a strategic asset and demonstrate HR value to the organization and its financial success.

Only 15 percent felt that they organization fully enables them to execute key goals.

c. Disciplined people: Create disciplined environment in the workplace. When HR leaders have disciplined people, they don't need hierarchy. Leadership is all about making people disciplined, making their thoughts disciplined and action disciplined.

The US military has said it could take weeks to determine the impact of the leak of more than 90,000 classified military records.

The documents, published online at the website Wikileaks, detail the war in Afghanistan, including previously unreported civilian deaths.

The White House condemned the leak as a possible threat to national security.

The huge cache of classified papers is one of the biggest leaks in US history.

Because of HR leaders' failure, Top Management sees that talent management is a gimmick and a sham—just another buzzword designed to help HR departments build empires and spend more money.

In fact, talent management is not only the integration of recruiting, on-boarding, performance management, succession management and training. talent management is described as the processes, practices, and culture that help optimize the employee life cycle; from the time someone becomes a candidate until the time they become alumni (quit, retire, terminate).

It involves the processes, practices, cultural elements, and systems that positively impact employee retention, ownership, commitment, and results.

Direction

In a constantly evolving business environment where change and innovation are commonplace, strategic leadership is essential to the growth and competitiveness of an organization.

To better align HR leaders within their strategic leadership teams, the company should equip the HR leaders with the relevant and critical business foundations and tools necessary to position themselves as strategic partners within their respective organizations.

If there's no policy in place, it might be because the leaders of the company didn't take the initiative.

HR leaders should be capable of identifying and investing in organizational and individual actions that create value. They will display to the workplace an optimum contribution in leadership role, make impactful decisions, and collaborate on business challenges in a systematic, strategic manner.

Product and service excellence should be nurtured by direction from management, which must view and manage it as an integral, indivisible part of the company. It cannot tolerate mediocrity or even average performance. To gain high performance, HR leaders must be able to identify critical issues include:

a.   Talent management: To be competitive, organizations need the leg up with a strong HR and talent management strategy. HR leaders need to lead this vision, and give impact to the organization objectives.

A study found 54% of Gen Y was unclear about exactly the skills considered desirable by employers.

While employers show confidence that 97% of Gen Y respondents would be able take action to rectify their skill deficit.

In U.S., today's younger workers are much easier to manage. Stunned by a barrage of pink slips instead of promotions, Generation Y—people ages 18 to 30—has swallowed a piece of humble pie. Those who still have jobs have adopted new workplace attitudes.

Traditionally, when an economy enters recession businesses will choose to pull back their work hours to save money before making layoffs.

However, once it happens the remaining workers tend to pick up the slack and actually boost productivity because each employee is expected to do more.

b.   Employee engagement: Employees are clearly more engaged and motivated when they are empowered with some level of control over their careers and future paths.

While HR leaders should not be only in the business of building development plans for employees they have to provide the appropriate tools to empower employees to take control over their own careers.

97% of HR leaders believe that a systematic career development process positively impacts employee retention and engagement.

The key to engagement of employees is quality of the leaders. Organizations need to make sure their leaders have the right skills to build and maintain strong relationships with those who work for them-capturing their 'hearts and minds.'

Salary increases/raises (45%) were deemed less important than the factors of employment.

We have heard this time and again. Fair salaries are an essential base ingredient in strong employee engagement, but compensation is far from the top of the list.

c.   Become a learning organization: *Human Resources leaders must show their areas of expertise (recruiting, hiring, retention, succession planning, performance management, compensation and change management, etc) are deeply connected to and impacted by business decision.*

The Human Resources leaders should understand the challenges of the other functional areas, including finance, sales, marketing and operations. And they will learn day to day basis how their organization can contribute to the best achievement of other organization in the company.

The leaders give people opportunities at very young ages to step up and lead without risking the firm. People have to learn early. Then when they get to higher-level positions they don't repeat those kinds of mistakes.

Learning organizations allow people do, they give employees opportunities, watch them closely, and give them feedback.

They also recognize that they aren't perfectand they're OK with their imperfection. This leader gains influence because others become more OK with their own imperfections.

That doesn't mean they lower their standards or fail to deliver with their responsibilities. But they recognize that they have flaws and need other people to complement and complete what they bring to the table.

HR function is developing people through in never ending process of self analysis, capitalizing on strengths and training in alignment with business strategies. HR leaders don't merely discharge supervising function; they create a sense of purpose and direction for the people.

d.   Leadership development: HR leaders are looking for talent that can fit into the organization leadership model. The talented people are employees who have ability to work as a team's member, positive attitude and diversity of thought and background.

Every one in the company has equal opportunity to be successful, and as HR leaders, it's our responsibility to build the future leaders to fit into the organization in the company.

43% of CEOs believe their HR functions possess the right qualities to motivate and develop people effectively.

This suggests that HR leaders need to align themselves more closely with companies' strategic direction in order to increase the value they provide.

Penny de Valk of ILM, says: "It's for managers to have a leadership mindset and the findings emphasize the need to continue focusing on leadership and management development, even in a downturn, when budgets are tight."

HR leaders should be involved in cross-industry network that enable them to get exposed with multiple forums to increase their knowledge, share information, discuss strategic issues, and connect with others who face similar challenges.

They will have opportunity to participate in high-level discussions, share best practices, exchange information, and network directly with peers from a variety of industries.

e. Manage change and cultural transformation: Many organizations relegate HR leaders to a tactical and administrative role responsible for personnel, instead of a strategic function that impacts the organization's overall performance.

HR leadership and organization culture is interdependent. No organization can change its culture from good to better and best without good HR leaders.

They need to align themselves more closely with their organization's strategic direction in order to increase the value.

Commitment

In too many organizations, HR is still viewed as a necessary evil—the benefits administrators and watchdogs over hiring, promotions, compensation and other people practices. Seldom is HR a significant player in shaping the company's strategy. The HR leader should be involved and knowledgeable about their business.

Commitment is lacking in many organizations.

A study shows that two-thirds to three-quarters of U.S. employees are not engaged in their jobs.

A lack of engagement or commitment is not just in the lower levels of the organization—it is often missing in the Top Management.

HR leaders believe that commitment is critical to corporate success. Therefore, the leaders should be heartened to hear that employees can play a critical role in increasing it, include:

a. Making employees more valuable: From a highly capable employee who makes productive contributions through talent, knowledge, skills and good work habits

It is the quality of the employee recruited that plays a key roll in differentiating between a successful organizations and a 'run of mill' organization.

Only 10 percent felt that their organization holds people accountable for results.

Success is built on relationships. Relational interactions recognize that how people are treated is as important as the outcome.

Relationships require an investment of your time, however the higher quality results produced by strong relationships is well worth the effort.

HR leaders are motivated by the need to help people. able to maintain a professional distance where necessary.

Organizations that have linked employee development and learning management display following reports:

i. Better workforce alignment to overall strategy: Employees should perform to the expectations and their function is viewed as helpful to supporting the company's goals.

Employees are seen as a strategic element in the organization success. They are needed to suppress some of their initiatives to 'fit in' to the achievements.

HR leaders will recognize this as an essential part of their role and think and act outside the box.

"The CEO should find HR leaders easy to work with," says Goodwill.

They are assets to their organizations capitalize on their talent and use them strategically.

A study found more than 80-90% of HR professionals end up their career with only managing the compliance and routine administrative functions of the organization.

ii.   Improved ability to quickly respond to changing business needs: HR leaders don't sit back and wait for something to happen. If they aren't getting clarity from CEO, they ask for it. Then, they will commit to making it happen.

HR leaders are most motivated by an environment in which they are allowed to exercise their creativity in coming up with new ways of serving both their employees and their organization.

A survey shows CEOs who are 'very confident' about the potential for short-term growth display traits often associated with success—adaptability, willingness to collaborate and faith in people. 67% of the CEOs were also 'very confident' about the prospects for growth.

Change is inevitable and it's also vital for the health of an organization. *Warren Buffett has said: "Change before you have to."*

For some, it might be more appealing to use the word 'flexibility' instead of 'change,' which suggests a more palatable challenge for some. Often, when people hear the word 'change' they can become resistant.

When we make even small changes we become more open, more flexible and mentally more agile. In order to build sustainable authenticity, one of the building blocks is flexibility.

iii.   Higher revenue per employee: Human Resource leaders believe that organizations that align their HR strategies with their business strategies are more profitable.

A research identified a positive relationship between a documented HR strategy and improved revenue per employee35 percent higher than organizations where no such strategy exists.

iv.   Better internal talent mobility: Commitment is at least as important as talent because it drives talent to new levels. People drive the business. HR leaders strive for a high-performance culture, which focuses on training and development.

Many employees complain that their bosses are so busy managing up top that they don't have time to listen to their people in the trenches and don't have time to develop them.

HR leaders not only listen to their people, but also give them broad-reaching authority to do what they see fit in order to serve their internal customers.

v.   Improved workforce productivity: Even though, in some companies, HR leaders may not be productive, they remain assets to their organizations; either they could not develop required traits to become something extra than HR leader or their organizations could not capitalize on their talents and use them strategically.

"IBM needs 10 times more employees than Nintendo to generate the same revenue. It means, even though IBM is operating at a rate per employee that is 25 per cent better than the average company, it has 'headcount fat'," John Sullivan, a professor, says

Companies are in business to make money, so HR leaders should measure the impact that people have on revenue, profit and productivity.

HR reports and analytics are key priorities for both the HR leaders and CEO. HR leaders should accurately measure the impact of employees and talent management programs on the business.

26% of HR leaders cannot measure the business impact of talent management programs on their organization.

b.   Doing and learn something new: Learning paths and specific courses can be established for employees to facilitate their career growth.

By providing the proper tools to employees, HR leaders can take a more active role in reducing high performer flight while promoting growth and engagement.

Leader with humility trait is a leader who is receptive to feedback, possesses a learning orientation, and has the ability to have accurate self-insight.

34% of organizations have linked learning and performance management to enable learning and training as a key component of employee goal completion.

c.   Get engaged: HR leaders, while able to recruit top talent; they have to ensure getting the talent to stay and perform at extraordinary levels, not just at good or acceptable levels. This is about generating commitment of employees to the company's strategy—an environment of strategic commitment.

Only 15 percent felt they worked in a high-trust environment.

The role of HR leader is helping organization to compete through their capabilities and supporting employees perform through their abilities.

The HR leaders can make the difference between success and failure in the organization and they affect the lives of the employees they work with.

Employee engagement drives productivity.

d.   Be on the ground: HR leaders set the tone by their example. When faced with tough decisions, they uphold the corporate values and consistently make the right choices. Their actions reveal their true character and they inspire others to follow their example.

Authenticity isn't a goal but an outcome. It's the result of providing, consistently and over time, an authentic 'total experience' to our stakeholders: employees, customers, vendors, suppliers, and other key business partners.

"People helping people is really what we in HR are trying to do in our jobs every day," Hutchins of SHRM says.

HR leaders begin with self-awareness, especially emotional awareness. Emotions are an important clue to what an individual believes.

By tapping into the feelings a defining moment brings up, the leaders can identify what values they are struggling with, then look beyond feelings to how their values provide a foundation for understanding what is really at stake and what action to take.

The HR leader needs only to embrace their values, know how they relate to their organization's values, lead in a way that honors both, and hold employees to the same standards in the workplace.

e.   Working hard to accomplish great things: HR leaders seek to improve alignment between workforce activities and overall business strategies and objectives.

An order of Benedictine nuns has signed a major record deal with the company behind Lady Gaga, it has been revealed.

The Nuns of the Abbaye de Notre-Dame de l'Annonciation, from France, won a global search of more than 70 convents across Europe, the US and Africa.

The reclusive order, based near Avignon, was deemed to have the finest Gregorian Chant singers.

The Reverend Mother Abbess said: "At first we were worried it would affect our cloistered life, so we asked St Joseph in prayer. Our prayers were answered, and we thought that this album would be a good thing if it touches people's lives and helps them find peace."

To ensure business growth is not compromised by focusing all efforts on a single revenue stream, diversification is secured with different product lines, complimentary services, etc.

With talent, diversification is achieved by bringing in people with different skill sets, temperaments, and points of view, among others.

This alignment is typically achieved through performance management and goals. Line leaders and employees establish goals as part of the performance management process and align the goals up through the organization. Alternatively, the organization cascades goals down to the workforce.

The culture-driven leader constantly demonstrates passion and energy for the work to be done and is not alone in doing so.

f.   Adapting to change: HR leaders know that practices of driving engagement through compensation, rewards, talent practices have changedit is simply not salary increases, affordable benefit, great training and other efforts are part of the employment deal.

For instance, younger generation, the so-called 'Gen Y' place greater emphasis on self-actualization, high expectations of rapid career progression and are willing to change jobs, industries and careers to realize their goals.

A study found the three ingredients for organisational insight included business savvy, organisational savvy, and contextual savvy. It would make HR more responsive and relevant to the business.

g.   Embracing fast-paced innovation: HR leaders should keen to be innovative and creative in working methods.

Innovators add so much value to an organization. This is why Nintendo, Apple and Google focus efforts on recruiting and developing their innovators and can report impressive revenues per employee.

Many HR leaders manage the largest budget items in the organization, i.e. salaries, benefits, training dollars, etc. They should not only spend money, but bring innovation and new ways to invest and drive results.

h. Have high self-confidence and optimism: HR leaders are optimistic, with a confident expectation of resolving situations satisfactorily.

The HR leaders need to muster significant courage to rise above the typical posturing and corporate politics and truly coach their peers and the CEO to exude higher levels of honesty, trust, alignment and communication.

i. Bring the technology to get the job done in less time: The more automated the data capture, the better.

Organizations that learn how to approach change are more resilient and capable of adapting to new conditions with enthusiasm and commitment.

j. Having their ideas heard: Employees want to know their contribution is valued.

HR leaders encourage employees to speak up and voice their opinion. It enables employees to take stands on tough issues.

Employees will have courage to give feedbacks to the upper management when they perceive they are unjustly treated. This feedback channel must allow employees to come forward without fearing of repercussion from the organization or the line leader that they are reporting on.

Line leaders and employees at all levels will begin to believe that Top Management are listening and truly want to capture their hearts and minds.

Action

HR leaders must do what is right legally and morally. They do their best to help people and treat others as they would have liked to be treated. Their communication skills are very strong, clear and persuasive.

They are able to leave impact on others while interacting. They are present physically at any time giving full attention to others so that they feel recognized and motivated.

Action can't take place without authentic presence and skillful communication.

There are three key organizational and people management issues that need to be addressed effectively in order to positively impact the bottom line:

a.   Strategy that is integrated into the business strategy.

b.   People, policies, practices that help deliver the business strategy across the organization.

c.   HR function that can influence the business.

Authenticity creates a culture of commitment that inspires full engagement and unconditional responsibility in employees and organizations. Out of the engagement comes an action.

HR leaders set the tone by their example. When faced with tough decisions, they uphold the corporate values and consistently make the right choices. Their actions reveal their true character and they inspire others to follow their example.

People might be tired of insincerity and looking for something to be done. Authenticity brings our best capacity to work by allowing who we are on the inside to express ourselves on the outside.

HR leaders are more proactive and adapt their style to fit the immediate situation. Such leaders can be inspiring and motivating on one occasion, and tough about people-related or financial decisions on another occasion.

People don't want to hear our intentionsthey seek our integrity; what we say reflects who we are and what we say we do.

a.   Not wait until conditions are perfect: If we're waiting to start until conditions are perfect, we probably never will.

HR leaders recognize their strength and weakness.

HR leaders deal with any situation spontaneously with courage and confidence. They instill optimism in the people while staying grounded to reality.

They don't hesitate in telling the truths which may not be liked by others. They are masters of conflict resolution and handling anger.

The leaders reinforce the values and mission of the organization constantly. They foster the spirit of creativity and never accept defeat.

Great HR leaders have the confidence to be flexible, and this allows them to improve, innovate, not get in the way, and let evolution happen.

b.   Be a doer: Practice doing things rather than thinking about them. HR function is not only about programs and processes. It is about driving sustainable business results that matter.

If a HR leader cannot get the transactional side of HR (i.e. compensation, staffing, employee relations, training, etc) working flawlessly, he/she will not be able to advance to the more strategic areas of HR.

Ideas alone don't bring success—Ideas are important, but they're only valuable after they've been implemented.

One of the biggest misconceptions about creative work is that it can only be done when inspiration strikes.

c. Live in the present: Focus on what we can do in the present moment.

Authentic means being willing to take risks and be completely present in a situation. It also means learning more deeply about the things that really matter to us and sharing our aspirations and dreams with others.

d. Get down to business immediately: By working in close back-and-forth contact with the customers, HR leaders find that partnering with customers meant achieving customer-partner model. The customer-partner model describes a synergy that comes from achieving a shared vision.

Google ranks Pakistan No. 1 in the world in searches for pornographic terms, outranking every other country in the world in searches per person for certain sex-related content.

The country is tops in searches for 'sex', 'camel sex,', 'rape video,', 'child sex video,' and some other searches.

"You won't find strip clubs in Islamic countries. Most Islamic countries have certain dress codes," said Gabriel Said Reynolds, professor of Islamic Studies at the University of Notre Dame. "It would be an irony if they haven't shown the same vigilance to pornography."

A great HR leader must have the discipline to work toward his or her vision single-mindedly, as well as to direct his or her actions and those of the team toward the goal. Action is the mark of a leader.

The HR leaders learn how to make a difference in the company and are perceived to make an impact on the business results through their actions. They will take following actions to be successful in the organization, includes:

a. Enhance employees' capacity to acquire necessary resources: Information and advances in other technology have increased the demand for employees who can extract the most out of technology, as well as for people at higher levels to create and adapt technology to new uses.

b. Keep promises rather than breaking them: Company which are making and keeping promises for service, quality and delivery ensure credibility with customers, while keeping explicit and implied promises to the workforce builds employee loyalty and morale.

    HR leaders who make and keep promises build credibility, confidence and conviction.

c. Share useful information and insights rather than withholding them: Communication helps us expand our sense of well-being and trust in the world around us. It starts with accepting full responsibility for all of our interactions, and then looking for ways to strengthen our relationships.

    Clear communication utilizes specific methods such as self-disclosure, inquiry and conflict resolution.

    Learning to appreciate different styles and expressions helps leaders enhance relationships and coordinate complex tasks and projects.

    Energy giant BP has been accused of hiding key data needed to investigate the Gulf of Mexico oil disaster.

    Transocean, the company that owned the oil rig, alleged that BP is refusing to hand over information it needs about the explosion.

    "This is troubling, both in light of BP's frequently stated public commitment to openness and a fair investigation and because it appears that BP is withholding evidence in an attempt to prevent any other entity other than BP from investigating," Steven L Roberts, lawyer for Transocean said.

The disaster on 20 April 2010 killed 11 workers and caused the worst oil spill in US history.

d.   Respect other's beliefs, even in disagreement, rather than ridiculing them: Fairness means dealing with others consistently and justly.

HR leaders must check all the facts and hear everyone out before passing judgment. They need to avoid leaping to conclusions based on incomplete evidence.

When people feel they that are being treated fairly, they reward the HR leaders with loyalty and dedication.

Learning to appreciate different styles and expressions helps leaders enhance relationships and coordinate complex tasks and projects.

Openness means being able to listen to new ideas, even if they do not conform to the usual way of thinking. HR leaders are able to suspend judgment while listening to others' ideas, as well as accept new ways of doing things that someone else thought of.

Openness builds mutual respect and trust between the HR leaders and employees, and it also keeps the organization well supplied with new ideas that can enrich its vision.

Recently, Obama defended Muslims' right to build an Islamic centre by Ground Zero.

The plans have provoked vehement opposition from many conservatives, though Obama, New York Mayor Michael Bloomberg, the chairman of the US Democratic party and others have defended the developers' right to build there.

A growing number of Americans incorrectly believe President Barack Obama is a Muslim, research suggests.

Some 18% said the president was a Muslim, up from 11% in March 2009, according to a survey.

Forty-three per cent of those questioned said they did not know what Mr Obama's religion was.

The HR leaders must practice empathy when dealings with subordinates which may consist of different cultural backgrounds, beliefs and values.

For example, a manager must be sensitive to his/her Muslim employees during the fasting month and not to label the person as lazy.

e. Help to protect the employees, their loved ones and their property: Dedication means spending time or energy that is necessary to accomplish the task at hand.

A HR leader inspires dedication by example, doing whatever it takes to complete the next step toward the vision.

By setting an excellent example, the HR leaders can show the employees that there are no 'nine-to-five' jobs on the organization, only opportunities to achieve something great.

Floods have already killed more than 1,500 people in Pakistan and affected some 3 million others.

The government has come under criticism for its handling of the crises. President Asif Ali Zardari, who was already widely unpopular, is on a five-day European tour after rejecting calls to stay home and direct the flood response.

In the face of such calamity, the people need to feel that their leaders are standing by them.

HR leader has a critical role to play in workforce planning and overall talent management are driving forces that enable the company to get world-class performance.

Presence

Creating and sustaining a healthy corporate culture requires constant attention and active involvement. Therefore, HR leaders should actively shape and direct the development of the corporate culture.

Presence is the starting place for us as leaders—it is the ground of individual authenticity.

By settling into the present moment and relating with what is actually occurring, we can let go of defensiveness and accept responsibility. HR leaders' presence is characterized by:

i.   Provide organization that can be easily identified or recognized: Both the organization and product or services should be easily traceable, and the organization is committed to routinely and proactively provide information that is transparent and accessible to the customer.

ii.   Retain its indigenous character: Credibility, genuineness and authenticity are important characteristics that employees want from their leaders.

If the business environment relies too heavily on employee discretion, it's too easy for employees to make mistakes. And when employees make mistakes, they blame managers for not making it clear what was expected of them. Then, employees hesitate to trust managers in the future.

We must know ourselves, intimately. Know our strengths and our limitations. If we cannot be open and candid with ourselves, it will show through with others and we run the risk of being perceived as inauthentic.

It's about understanding enough about ourselves to be able to step forward with confidence.

One of the greatest capabilities we possess as humans is our ability to deceive ourselves.

To fit into company objectives, HR leaders provide activities that link business emphases with the organization's strategic focus:

a.   Have a data-based talent strategy: Provide CEO/Top Management to win on the decisive issue of talent.

When recruiting, HR leaders to look outside of the industry, and consider people with broad and unusual backgrounds.

People who are too narrowly educated will make the right decisions some of the time, but they won't have the breadth of knowledge and experience to make the right decisions most of the time.

Once we've made the right hire, it's essential to try to understand the personality of the people working for us.

"Understanding personality has become essential for leaders of the complex, knowledge-based companies operating in the global marketplace," says Michael Maccoby, a leadership consultant.

HR leaders inspire and nurture talent by ensuring that employees have the opportunity to grow within the organization and progress in their careers.

b.   Partnering with line leaders to develop business strategy: A documented strategy is also associated with more effective reward systems, better performance management systems and reduced absenteeism.

24% of executives outside of human resources viewed their HR counterparts as working at lower levels of strategic involvement.

Successful HR leaders engage in the development of the HR discipline, i.e. SHRM, HRLF, conferences, or follow experts.

c.   Provide analytic support for business decision-making: Able to quickly analyze and interpret information.

A HR leader should be long-life learner and expert in their business/area of expertise—allocate time to read about their organization, its category, how money/success is made, competitors.

"63% of all hiring decisions are made during the first 4.3 minutes of an interview."

With competencies they possess, HR leaders demonstrate their ability to make quick and well-considered decisions.

HR leaders should develop a 'dashboard of measures' to predict how future-proof and adaptable their organisation is.

HR functions of the future must also demonstrate deep organisational insight—understanding what makes the business successful.

d. Drive change management: Change won't happen overnight. Businesses transform and change, and unfortunately, not all people do.

The HR leader needs to be able to adapt to the changing conditions in ways that support the business.

Women don't get equal pay, and they're not advancing into management jobs as quickly as they should, according to a study.

A survey found women with bachelor's degrees earned 33 percent less than men. And median income for all women with post-graduate degrees was 11 percent lower than men who had a bachelor's degree.

Women are collecting bachelors and advanced degrees at 1.5 times the rate of men.

President Obama said: "Dream big and stay focused on education."

If there are so many more women graduating college than men, it means there will be more women filling high paying jobs than men in future.

Today, it has become an indispensable tool to bring about and manage change. Whether it is a change in policy, terms of employment, products, services or technologies, communication is a must.

Resistance to change, in fact, results from inadequate communication. It is also a must to generate commitment, loyalty and trust in an organization.

Communication is the key to employee engagement.

Leadership is communicating people's worth and potential so clearly that they are inspired to see it in themselves.

iii.   Be unique—Make difference. Different people will bring their different judgment strengths to their workplaces.

Everyone makes a difference. To make a difference we need to be doing something that we love and are passionate about. To make a difference we need to be aware as we journey through our day, looking for opportunities to 'make a difference.'

Our ethnic and cultural identity is a great asset. Amplify it as a competitive advantage. A strong identity reflects an appreciation of your uniqueness and its value.

A strong identity grounds us; a well-defined purpose gives us the self-confidence to know we can choose our own path.

HR leaders are well aware of the importance of employer brand and leadership brand, which defines a company's value proposition for employees.

Employer branding describes how an organization markets what it has to offer to potential and existing employees.

Leadership branding is a method uses by a leader to promote him/herself in order to get influence or positioning him/herself in the organization using his/her power, image, skills, ideas, etc.

A leadership brand extends the concept of employer brand. It defines an organization's leadership philosophy and standards relevant not only to employees but to all stakeholders.

An employer brand shows a set of attributes and qualities that makes an organization distinctive, promises a particular kind of employment experience, and appeals to those people who will thrive and perform best in its culture.

A strong employer brand should connect an organization's values, people strategy and HR policies.

iv.   Diversity: A workplace 'chameleon'; able to work effectively with diverse groups of colleagues.

HR leaders focus on diversity, and are nearly four times more likely than typical companies to make it part of their strategic resource planning.

A HR leader has passion to tolerate an ambiguityshow tolerance to uncertainty and risk. If his/her tolerance for ambiguity is low, he/she will gravitate toward large.

Religious intolerance has become one of the main causes of persecution of minorities around the world.

The London-based Minority Rights Group International calls religious intolerance the 'new racism.' Its impact is felt on religious minorities across the globe.

Discrimination against Muslims is on the rise in the United States and Western Europe, and cites increasing physical violence against religious minorities in Iraq and Pakistan. The report says those attacks include abduction, murder, torture and rape.

Minorities also face increased persecution and reduced freedom stemming from strict government anti-terrorism measures imposed after the September 2001 terror attacks on the United States.

Human Resources can be a unique source of sustained competitive advantage. This is especially true when its parts have high internal and external fit.

HR leaders need to spend more time developing the next generation of leaders within the organizations. They should develop leaders who have the characters, values, wisdom, and depth to lead the organizations in the future.

Only younger generation, the so-called 'Gen Y' place greater emphasis on self-actualization, high expectations of rapid career progression and are willing to change jobs, industries and careers to realize their goals.

Better HR leaders and efforts create great leaders, great leaders create better companies, great companies create great communities in which to live and work.

HR leaders lead with heart. They must engage employees' hearts as well as their minds. Leaders have to involve employees in a purpose greater than any of them.

They build stronger employee-management bonds and boost employee engagement.

9th

TRUST

Trust lies primarily in the realm not of organizational dynamics, but of interpersonal dynamics.

Trust is defined as the extent to which a person is confident in, and willing to act on the basis of, the words, actions, and decisions of another.

Organizations that foster trust are more profitable. Yet, trust is complex and hard to earn. There is only one thing that builds trust—the way people behave.

A study found that trust in Management is the most valued determinant of job satisfaction. They state that a small increase in trust of Management is like getting a 36 percent pay increase.

Conversely, the researchers found that if that same amount of trust is lost, the decline in employee job satisfaction is like taking a 36 percent pay cut.

Mutual trust is the basis of employer and employees relations.

If employees feel they are not getting support then that places them at greater risk for low job satisfaction and higher employee turnover.

Trust in the workplace is the foundation of employee engagement. It would be useful if we could get a better idea of what really constitutes trust between employees and leaders or organizations.

Human Resource leader can play a critical role in building trust with the line leaders and employees which includes:

a. Clear communication: Trust forms the foundation for effective communication, employee retention, and employee motivation and contribution of discretionary energy, the extra effort that people voluntarily invest in work.

    Communication is truly the key to building trust. As a HR leader, if we set specific, measurable expectations, provide both positive and corrective feedback, understand employees' goals and motivations and recognize and reward top performers, we are well on our way to gaining or sustaining the employee's trust.

b. Existence of rules and procedures: The existence of organizational rules will determine the outcomes of organizational decisions.

    The existence of rules will obligate employees to conform their behavior to the rules. They may violate the rules, to create circumstances that they believe a rule exists.

    26% of Cameroonian girls at puberty undergo it, as many mothers believe it protects their daughters from the sexual advances of boys and men who think children are ripe for sex once their breasts begin to grow.

    The practice of 'breast ironing' is on the rise in the African country of Cameroon.

    The procedure—which involves the flattening of a young girl's growing breasts with hot stones, coconut shells and other objects—is considered a way to curb the country's staggering number of teenage pregnancies, particularly high in rural areas, as well as limit the risk of sexual assault.

"What you have to really do is talk about the issue of sexual reproductive health with the child. So that she is aware about what it means growing up and having breasts or having periods," Anthropologist Dr Flavien Ndonko says.

"Massaging the breasts of young girls is very dangerous. This is harmful to health. Do not force them to disappear or appear—allow them to grow naturally."

c. Consistency of organization's business philosophy and goals. HR leaders consistently achieve the highest level of quality in all products and services and to be premier in business. They should aim for greatness.

There is major difference of opinion exists between what HR thinks they are doing, and how the workforce perceives it.

The most striking finding is only 48.9% of executives (Non-HR) trust their own HR Department.

This is echoed by managers (Non-HR) who reported only 48.6% trust their HR department.

Organizations are now seeking for the need of trustworthiness, character, and producing trust in the culture. Trustworthiness has always been a fundamental attribute.

A lack of trust is a problem in many workplaces. If HR leaders never identified their values in workplaces, mistrust is understandable. People don't know what they can expect. If the leaders have identified and shared their values, living the values daily, visibly they will create trust.

Survey shows employees feel they have the least support from HR; increasing number of complaints from employees and customers.

Trust is most real to them when described in terms of integrity, honesty, and competence.

Employees sometimes see the HR leader is unable to provide analytics that are useful in making workforce decisions that build economic value. Companies spend too little effort on attracting and retaining top strategic talent and too much on satisfying the rest of the employee base.

According to them, typical human resources activities have no relevance to organization's success. *"HR people try to perpetuate the idea that job satisfaction is critical,"* Professor Beatty said. *"But there is no evidence that engaging employees impacts financial returns."*

A research has shown that nine of every 10 employees experience some kind of breach of trust in the workplace on a regular basis.

When trust erodes, morale declines, performance plummets and employees become disengaged and leave.

Trust-building behaviors are linked to strategic business results.

Restore trust among stakeholders is the critical competency of HR leader needed today. It is required more than any other competency. Engendering trust is, in fact, a competency that can be learned, applied, and understood.

Human Resource Management has been criticized for being too expensive and providing no added value since no measurable business value could be demonstrated.

We cannot be an effective leader without trust. Trust is divided into two segments includes:

1. Confidence trust: The belief that we can count on the other person to do the right thing or act in positive, ethical ways. This kind of trust is synonymous with one's 'willingness to do the right thing.'

    A person might have great skills and talents and a good track record, but if he or she is not honest, we're not going to trust that person either.

    Confidence trust echoes relationship trust—how to establish and increase the trust accounts we have with others.

2.   Competence trust: Belief in the person's capability to do the job or to complete the task. It's synonymous with one's 'capabilities.'

People's sense of personal worth is often measured by their competence in their jobs. Naturally, people are motivated to develop competence in what they do and how they do it.

People want and need to know they make a difference and contribute to the overall good of the organization.

It's important for HR leaders to be aware of this fundamental need in people and help people apply their abilities in meaningful ways to meet business challenges.

Acting in this way, the leaders do not only honor their relationship with their employees but also contribute to the overall health of the businesses.

We might think a person is sincere, even honest, but we won't trust that person fully if he or she doesn't get results.

Competent trust builds self-trust—the confidence we have in ourselves—in our ability to set and achieve goals, to keep commitments, to walk our talk, and also with our ability to inspire trust in others.

Competent trust involves respecting people's knowledge, skills and abilities, and judgment, involving others and seeking their input, and helping people learn skill.

How we practice the behaviors demonstrates our willingness to trust the capability of ourselves and others. Therefore, we can characterize competence trust as 'trust capability.'

Trust is the foundation of any beneficial and successful relationship between individuals and between organizations. A decision to trust another is a choice, not a moral obligation.

Trustworthiness is an indispensable aspect of good character. As a leader, we should always act so as to be worthy of trust—not simply because it's wise to do so, but because it's the right way to act.

Being worthy of trust entails two distinct qualities: character and competence.

The attribute we first associate with trustworthy behavior is integrity. This crucial aspect of good character must be demonstrated through scrupulous honesty and moral courage.

If we want people to trust us or the organization, they must believe that we will consistently do the right thing, regardless of the circumstances or pressures.

Other aspects of character include accountability and fairness. People trust those who accept responsibility for their choices and don't palm off blame to others. It's also important to be regarded as fundamentally fair.

HR leaders build trust in their competence. The competence trust can be gained through:

a. Define the standard and assessment: We may compare our standard with others. When the standards are clear and agreed, assessment of competence is easy to make.

   Otherwise, when standards for task, job and role being performed are unclear; or people disagree about them. It can easily lead to distrusting our competence.

b. Accept weakness: Cultivating trust in our competence doesn't mean we have to be fully competent from the get-go. It does require being honest with others about what we can and can't do, what we know and what we don't know.

c. Ask for feedback: HR leaders should wait for customers to tell them that they are making mistakes. Often people won't tell us our performance isn't good enough until we've made some big mistakes, and they then distrust our competence.

Trustworthiness comes before trust. There is no leadership without trust, character and a principled life. If a leader loses trust he/she sinks.

To earn and sustain trust, leaders must become aware of the behaviors that build and break trust, and know how to rebuild it again.

A study says that hard-working, unselfish people who are always glad to lend a hand turn out to be hated by their coworkers.

The study found that when given the option to kick one member out of collaborating groups, people often chose to kick out their altruistic partners.

Researchers Craig Parks and Asako Stone speculated that the hatred was due to hardworking members raising expectations for the whole group. "What is objectively good, you see as subjectively bad," Parks explained.

They suggested if we worried about staying on our coworkers' good sides; we should certainly do our job well, but also do it quietly.

Credibility

Leader is to inspire trust. Trust is confidence born of two dimensions: character and competence. Character includes our integrity, motive, and intent with employees. Competence includes our capabilities, skills, results, and track record.

Current competency model of Human Resources (HR) is to serve as a credible leader.

Credibility has to do with the words we speak, employees believe it. When line leaders and employees are evaluating Human Resource Department's credibility, they look well beyond credentials to the person's behavior, demonstrated expertise, and interpersonal demeanor. Credibility fosters an HR leader to:

a.   Keep commitments and meet deadlines: Doing what we say we are going to do and meeting deadlines builds reliability. If something prevents we from doing so, be sure to keep others informed with updates. It emphasizes the HR leader:

1.   Not share confidential and personal information: They should stop themselves before they reveal someone's personal info or discuss delicate information.

        A Chinese executive once touted as the future head of steelmaker Shougang was jailed for leaking commercial secrets.

        Tan Yixin was jailed for three and a half years.

        He and his colleagues had been charged with disclosing commercial secrets including steel production costs and iron ore inventories—information that could benefit Rio Tinto, the world's second-largest miner, during contract price negotiations with Chinese customers.

        The infringement of commercial secrets caused a great loss to the Chinese industry, putting it in a disadvantageous position in iron ore price talks.

2.   Not speculate about information they don't have on hand: If employees asked for our opinion, prepare to back it up with evidence.

        By being reliable, we achieve trust and respect.

3.   Show confidence to take calculated risks that can impress Top Management, such as tasks that directly benefit the bottom line.

        Being good at what we do is not enough. We must be excellent. Achieving excellence takes combining the gifts and passion, i.e. time, effort, and hard work.

b.   Be competent: Being judged as competent leader means doing what we do well enough to satisfy employees. They recognize us as competent leader when we demonstrate skill, knowledge and abilities to act effectively of leading people. HR leaders should have willingness to:

1.   Acquire and share knowledge: Level of knowledge demonstrates our credibility. HR leaders learn how the

business operates. Learning the business is essential in gaining credibility.

Understanding how the activities of the HR Department impact the goals of the organization will help we speak the language of the organization. If we are in a high sales culture, learn what HR activities impact sales revenue and create measures to prove it.

Most people don't know how to think about the organizational consequences of low trust because they don't know how to quantify or measure the costs of such a so-called 'soft' factor as trust.

For many, trust is intangible, ethereal, and un-quantifiable. Employees don't know how to get their arms around it or how to improve it. The costs of low trust are very real, they are quantifiable, and they are staggering. As a trusted leader, we should not act following:

i.   Show a lack of business knowledge: If the financial side isn't our strong suit, take a course so we can discuss balance sheets and budgets.

      Being competent does not mean being perfect. Part of doing something well is to know what we don't know, being willing to learn, and to ask for help when we need it.

ii.   Show a lack of legal knowledge: Top Management will expect HR leaders to know employment laws inside and out. Managing others I s a different skill set from engineering.

      If it has happened to us, the best thing we can do is be clear about what we know we can do, and what we have yet to learn.

2.   Maintain positive emotion: HR leaders make sure they keep emotions in check; show empathy to others; and understand the emotion employees are feeling.

      Not acknowledging this emotion sends the message that you are not listening or do not care.

While positive emotions can fuel our success, negative emotions can destroy our credibility. Emotions and logic do not always work together well. To gain trust from Top Management, line leaders and employees, the HR leaders will:

i.   Avoid favoritism: Align ourselves too closely with one person or group. We should not turn to the same people for input over and over again.

They avoid socializing exclusively with people. If line leaders or employees perceive that we have special relationships with certain people in the organization, they will be much less likely to trust us to be impartial.

ii.   Make decisions based on others' emotions: HR leaders will contemplate their decision if say a line leader is getting angry over an employee's behavior and demanding immediate discipline.

An objective judgment is essential competency in the HR leaders.

iii.   Never overreact: When something upsets us, we should not rush to exclaim negative type words. It will insult others or lead them to doubt our maturity.

However, letting emotion take over for logic in this case increases our risk of saying things that you will later regret.

It is human nature to become defensive when he/she feels attacked.

Find a strategy that works for us in keeping our emotions in check. One way is to count silently for a few seconds before responding.

c.   Awareness: HR leaders play a key role in shaping the future of its employees. When the leaders say they are fully aware of himself, they should be sensitive in:

i.   Recognition: HR leaders give credit where credit is due. Acknowledge the good work of employees especially those who work under them.

Employee feel threatened and lack trust for leaders who try to take credit for their ideas and work.

"Distrust, like a blister, can cause distraction; a distraction can cause a turnover; a turnover in the last seconds of a game can cause you to be outscored," John Wooden, a basket ball coach, says.

HR leaders are person whom able to speak in the forum. They will not remain silent at critical times.

"HR should be active participants," says Dani Johnson of HRCS. "Speak out when we have opinions and don't be a silent note taker at meetings with line leaders or Top Executives."

ii.   Make our role known: Oftentimes, employees misunderstand how HR operates. To combat this phenomenon, advertise our job, including mission, role, and services.

Make it known how we handle confidential information. The more they know, the more they trust and respect us.

The true transformation starts with building credibility at the personal level. The foundation of trust is our own credibility, and it can be a real differentiator for HR leader.

Our reputation is a direct reflection of our credibility, and it precedes us in any interactions we might have. When a leader's credibility and reputation are high, it enables them to establish trust fast—speed goes up, cost goes down.

HR leaders trust employees, as they are capable of greatness.

Competence

Competencies create a competent individual capable of high quality professional performance.

Our reputation depends almost entirely on the opinion of others, i.e. an engineer is judged almost instantly by the quality of work.

In today's world, we should also consider to secure community approval. We are liable to have our reputation tarnished on the whim of others, e.g. webnumber of visits; book—an academic committee or a Sunday supplement book reviewer, etc.

A reputation can be shown by ingenious and innovative solutions to problems we create.

In business, confidence in character is not enough to justify trust. Trust also involves the conviction that employee or organization will successfully do what is expected.

This competency dimension of trust embraces faith in ability, knowledge and judgment as well as a belief that the employee or organization will be reliable and responsive.

Reliability is established through diligence and follow-through while responsiveness involves respectful communication and demonstrated concern.

Since Human Resource Management needs to be a value-added function, the cost and benefits of the Human Resource function should be analyzed in order to maximize the value of any resources directed toward this function.

This analysis requires consideration of specific Human Resource functions (i.e. job analysis, human resource planning, recruitment, selection, compensation system development, benefits administration, performance appraisal, career planning, training, etc.).

Each function is analyzed to determine whether or not services related to this function should continue. If the specific services are considered worth providing, the next decision requires identifying the most cost-effective way to provide these services.

Leaders who demonstrate the right competencies and play the right roles will be more effective than those who do not. Competence that will have an effect on employee trust in HR leaders includes:

1. Technical competence: The ability and knowledge needed to finish a task.

    HR leaders should get clear with themselves. It's tricky to be the liaison between employees and line leaders. If they have unresolved conflicts in their belief systems about the rights, obligations, and ethics of employees versus line leaders, it's important to either resolve them or clarify them.

    People respect the integrity of those they disagree with; but they will never trust those with unclear belief systems.

    The Philippines will hold a thorough investigation into how eight Hong Kong tourists were killed while they were being held hostage on a bus in Manila, President Benigno Aquino says.

    Survivors and experts have criticised the police for being indecisive and slow in their handling of the crisis.

    Frederic Gallois, who once commanded France's elite hostage rescue unit, told that the police operation was 'badly prepared and risky.'

    Gallois said: "The officers involved visibly lacked adequate equipment and tactical competence."

2. Conceptual knowledge. The ability to spot big opportunities by seeing the 'big' picture.'

    Tony Blair describes Gordon Brown, who succeeded him in 10 Downing Street in 2007, as a 'strange guy' and says his time as prime minister was 'never going to work.'

    Blair says: "Brown lacked political instinct 'at the human gut level.' Political calculation, yes. Political feelings, no. Analytical intelligence, absolutely. Emotional intelligence, zero."

Companies are urged to send their people out into the business, but rarely is the business urged to come into HR. Or, many executives continue to regard HR as a purely administrative function, which contributes very little of real business value.

3. Interdependency: Being aware that everything in life is interconnected. A great organization in business is an extended family. Strong bonds exist and positive relationships are developed.

In organization's today, trust is a two-way street. Employees want to work for line leader and the organization they can have trust in, and line leaders want to be able to trust their employees.

HR leaders must find appropriate ways, to show employees in their organizations, that they care about them.

General David Petraeus said the planned torching of Islam's holy book would be a propaganda coup for the Taliban in Afghanistan and stoke anti-US sentiment across the Muslim world.

The Dove World Outreach Center at Gainesville, Florida says it will burn copies of the Koran on ninth anniversary of the September 11 airborne attacks in protest at what it calls 'the evil of Islam.'

Petraeus said of the event: "It could endanger troops and it could endanger the overall effort."

"It is precisely the kind of action the Taliban uses and could cause significant problems. Not just here, but everywhere in the world we are engaged with the Islamic community," he said.

Sincere care and consideration for employees must be expressed. Otherwise, they will ever know they're not considered just a cog in the wheel. They should feel as a critical asset for the company.

Trust is commonly defined as a confident, positive expectation about the actions of another person. When we trust someone, we assume that he/she will meet those expectations by considering our welfare and honoring his/her obligations towards us.

This assumption enables us to coordinate activities in interdependent relationships, that is, relationships in which an individual's outcomes are influenced by another party's actions.

Almost everywhere we turn, trust is on the decline. Trust in employees and in companies significantly decreases.

Research shows that only 49% of employees trust senior management, and only 28% believe CEOs are a credible source of information.

Consider the loss of trust and confidence in the markets today. Indeed, trust makes the world go 'round' and right now we're experiencing a crisis of trust.

There are some strong trends that suggest the HR leader no longer reports to CEO/Top Management. They are not sitting at the top strategy table and the companies are not building the talent discussion into the strategic planning process.

Therefore people propose an argument that Human Resources in organizations may become totally irrelevant and to be totally outsourced.

No one would argue that an HR leader is fully knowledgeable on all that is available today. They are consistently learning.

If employees can do their jobs effectively, they contribute value to the organization. In fact many of the know-it-all HR types are not those inside organizations.

The Human Resource leader faces a crisis of trust and a loss of legitimacy in the eyes of its major stakeholders.

To meet contemporary and future workplace challenges, HR leaders will need to redefine their role and professional identity to advocate and support a better balance between employer and employee interests at work.

Low turnover isn't necessarily a good thing. Think about where we might want to disinvest organization box when it comes to filling the strategic positions that create the bulk of a company's value.

To that end, companies might be better off appointing someone from outside the organization to manage strategic talent.

Integrity

A leader with integrity stands for ethical behaviors that determine clearly what is right and wrong, acting on what one has discerned, even at personal cost, and saying openly that one is acting on what one understands to be right or wrong.

Ethics and integrity are important in all professions but there are some, like management positions and Human Resources that are expected to uphold a higher standard of ethical behavior. They maintained high ethical standards.

HR leaders provide standards of conduct and set forth a common set of values for the organization.

The standards define clearly a holistic balance among employees and organizations, whenever conflicting needs arise.

It clarifies both the general principles and the decision rules that cover most situations encountered by HR leaders.

The findings imply that those involved in today's business must aim to enhance the customer's perception of integrity, and competence, in order to gain trust and engage in meaningful customer relationship programs.

Integrity has also been revealed to enhance company brand or reputation, improve efficiency, attract staff, conserve and sustain resources and mitigate business risk.

A study concludes, that a higher consumer perception of integrity, and competence is positively related to a higher level of customer trust.

Integrity is demonstrated through loyalty to one's rational convictions in action.

A research, for identifying the essential qualities of a leader; found integrity was the number one response, followed by communication, focusing on people, vision, caring, decision making, dedication, model, motivation, expertise and courage.

The important components of maintaining integrity in HR starts with respectful treatment of employees. When employees are not treated with respect HR is no longer trusted.

HR leader integrity behaviors are characterized by:

a. Moral purpose: A value, when articulated, appeals to the innate sense held by some individuals of what is right and what is worthwhile.

    Sam Walton was a tough businessman, but at the company he founded, Wal-Mart, making money was secondary to another moral purpose: giving customers a good deal.

    He made his associates (as he called employees) feel that their work was worthwhile, by tapping into their natural good feelings toward fellow human beings.

    This in turn led them to treat customers in a friendly and helpful way, which (combined with his fierce pursuit of low prices) established the kind of customer loyalty that has been the central competitive advantage of his company.

    Walton could do this because he shared these feelings himself and communicated them at every turn.

b. Lawful and ethical: The purposes of the Code of Conduct and Ethics are to provide evidence of the company's commitment to the lawful and ethical conduct of its business, and to promote lawful and ethical behavior by its employees. The hallmark of the conduct of employees shall be integrity.

c. Consistency: The most successful organizations, over time, are those in which people act consistently. The task of HR leaders is to stimulate these kinds of actions, reliably and continually.

d.   Standing for something: HR leaders give first consideration to objectives of the organization and they recognize that they have the responsibility for meeting the objectives.

They shall carry out their duties with competence and strive to maintain and improve both personal competence and that of others.

In successful companies, there is increasing number of people who are seeing the need to look into their own souls, to sense how they contribute to the organization, and to find exactly what they can do to contribute to the company's objectives.

Integrity and honesty are crucial because employees only act consistently and rationally on the basis of the words and decisions of line leaders if they believe that the words and decisions are those of the leader who can be believed.

When HR leaders give lip service, it can be damaging. When they are committed to follow up on something but they don't or they say one thing and do another or worst of all they flat out lie; they lose integrity.

No professional wants to think about questionable integrity or ethical issues in their profession.

To create trust in employees, HR leaders must know what they are talking about. The leaders must be competent.

Integrity underpins organization's profitability and competitiveness, as well as increasing employees' pride, engagement with their jobs and customer loyalty.

Recognition

Trust and recognition between leaders and employees are critical. Appreciation influences motivation and feelings of accomplishment.

Recognition can help motivate employees to continually improve; to be innovative and manage resources creatively; to set high standards and goals; and to work together in teams. Recognition will attract, retain and engage people.

Trust and recognition is known to have a link with happiness at work.

Recognition increases feelings of pride in the organization; not just about doing things right in workplace—doing the right things, in the right circumstances, for the right people.

Trust is most real to them when described in terms of integrity, honesty, and competence. Creating the kind of environment and providing the kind of support that fosters high competence and integrity fosters trust and thereby benefits the organization as a whole.

It is a great esteem builder and can help create workplace loyalty and build a sense of community. It helps employees see what their co-workers are doing.

Recognition/reward programs can be either peer or management-driven, or both. Such programs can help motivate employees to continually improve; to be innovative and manage resources creatively; to set high standards and goals; and to work together in teams. There are three kinds of recognition, include:

a. Employer recognition: Recognition that acknowledge employers who have developed innovative programs in policy and practice that improve the work and life balance of their employees.

Company, that being family friendly, will help the business to attract the best employees and increase productivity.

It also creates happy, loyal employees, and innovative workplaces. Using this recognition, the companies are able to promote themselves as employers of choice.

Al-Shabab, an Islamic insurgent group in Somalia, had succeeded in killing so many people at Muna Hotel in Mogadishu frequented by security forces and politicians, many of them armed themselves, was a striking symbol of the government's impotence.

After a series of bombings that culminated with the brazen killing of at least 30 people, including six members of parliament, al-Shabab has shown itself to be far more powerful.

"The government does not have enough power to defeat al-Shabab and to secure the safety of Mogadishu," Ali Osman, a senior official. "This is shameful for the TFG [Transitional Federal Government] and I cannot really say there is a government—it is just a name."

Employers that receive recognition for providing a good work environment may receive morale benefits and reductions in employee turnover.

This type of recognition improves the image of employer in the community and also serves as advertising and generates good public relations.

b. Leadership recognition: Good or bad HR leader is depending on organization and employee's perspective. It may come from his/her consciously choosing to give it to another-an act that leads employees to feel the leader's belief whether he/she can add value or not.

There is no leadership without trust, character and a principled life. When a HR leader loses trust, he/she sinks his/her job or organization. He/she will not earn recognition and respect from the employees.

Jan Schill has a message for voters in Oklahoma choosing a district judge in elections—do not vote for my dad.

She has taken out newspaper ads urging voters not to vote for John Mantooth, her dad, who she believes had a lousy record as a judge and does not deserve the job.

"Mantooth did not help matters by running campaign ads showing himself as a family man and a father of three daughters with grandchildren," Schill said. "He has a relationship with none of them."

If the reason company's poor performance is by the HR leader's conduct, it will affect the greatest damage that he/she was doing to himself. He/she was thinking only of his/her own self, disregarding long term outcome.

c.   Employee recognition: Employee recognition is the acknowledgement of an individual or team's behavior, effort and accomplishments that support the organization's goals and values. Every employee has a need for praise and recognition, and the more often they get it the better.

HR leaders are in the best position to give recognition, but few do it often enough. Employee recognition will let employees know that their hard work is valued.

Employees who feel appreciated often go above and beyond what is expected of them; are more productive and motivated; and are more likely to stay with the organization.

Employees can be recognized for both individual and group achievements. Group recognition contributes to team building and informs the group that together, they are valuable to the organization.

One of the most effective ways to express appreciation is saying 'thank you.' Even if most of the duties employees perform are a normal part of the job, hearing 'thank you' in a spontaneous and timely way can mean a lot to them. It should be done often, and can be done privately or in front of co-workers.

Russian Prime Minister Vladimir Putin provided encouragement and sang patriotic songs with 10 agents who were expelled from the United States after they were accused of spying.

The 10 Russian agents pleaded guilty in the United States for failing to register as foreign agents and were ordered out of the country.

None of the 10 had passed classified information and therefore none had been charged with espionage; but they 'were clearly caught in the business of spying.'

A company may receive meaningful recognition for its performance and stand out as a top employer. Its quality represents the great achievements. Qualities of the top employers are judged on, but not limited to:

a.   Pay and benefits: Provide strong competitive advantage and a clear 'return on investment.' Compensation is critical to align what is needed with how people are rewarded.

Competitive compensation means compensation that is competitively benchmarked with the leaders in the industry.

BP chief executive Tony Hayward gets an immediate annual pension worth about £600,000 ($930,000) when he leaves in October 2010.

Hayward is to stand down after sustained criticism of his handling of the Gulf of Mexico oil leak.

BP pension scheme rules say that those who joined before April 2006 can take the pension at any point from age 50. Hayward is 53.

He also receives a year's salary plus benefits worth more than £1m.

Hayward's pension pot is valued at about £11m and he will keep his rights to shares under a long-term performance scheme which could—depending on BP's stock market recovery—eventually be worth several million pounds.

b.   Training and development: Companies may stand to lose their workforces to retirement at a time when there are fewer trained workers to take their places.

       If they value Human Resources as the key asset which contributes to the success of the business, they will hold training and development program for employees consistently.

c.   Career development: Every employee must take control of his/her career; he/she must dare to be in the driver's seat of his/her destiny; and he/she must be in a position to pursue his/her economic prosperity.

       The mindset of passion, creativity, resourcefulness, courage, and resilience is mandatory for success.

       If a high performance culture is the goal, HR function should not carry poor performers within its ranks.

       Employee engagement is the degree to which employees work with passion and feel a profound connection to the company.

       A research says businesses in the top 24% of employee engagement had less turnover and a higher percentage of customer loyalty, profitability and revenue.

       The language of organizations is number. If HR isn't very good at data analytics, it means they do not think like business people. Many of them may enter Human Resources because they wanted to help people. Their existence in the company is for building winning organizations.

d.   Working condition: HR leaders create sense of binding amongst the employees. People will work harder and better if they know they are valued as part of an extended family, a member of an organization that cares about them.

Matt Dubay, a 25-year-old computer programmer in Michigan, was ordered to pay child support after his former girlfriend had a baby.

He says he had made it clear when they were dating that he did not want to have children; she had said she couldn't get pregnant anyway because of a medical condition. When she did get pregnant, he argues, she could have chosen to have an abortion.

Mel Feit, Director of the National Center for Men, argues that within a short window of time after discovering an unplanned pregnancy, a man should have the right to terminate his legal and financial obligations to the child.

Early in pregnancy, if contraception failed, men should have a choice, and women have a right to know what that choice is.

e.   Company culture: Only a company culture that is aligned with employees' goals, that helps them anticipate and adapt to change, will help them achieve superior performance over the long run.

Company culture is the term given to the shared values and practices of the employees.

A clause within the financial reform legislation is offering big cash rewards to whistleblowers who report fraud and other wrongdoing at U.S.-listed companies and Wall Street banks.

Anyone who provides a tip that leads to a successful Securities and Exchange Commission action will be able to collect between 10% and 30% of the amount recovered—as long as the total amount exceeds $1 million.

"We expect the awards will prompt a significantly greater number of insiders to come forward with high-quality evidence of fraud," says SEC spokesman John Nester.

HR leaders understand what is important to their employees. As a leader, developing a strong company culture starts when they take steps to find out what motivates the people who work for the organization.

Leaders inspire. They pull in talented and high performing staffer, and show them the company culture that motivates people to work hard and stay with the business

Promotion

People are promoted for a number of reasons, some fair and reasonable. The most important element of promoting employees is acknowledging and celebrating their achievements within the organization.

Promotion reflects the outstanding contribution and experience demonstrated by the employees.

HR leaders provide effective performance management systems and the value they create for the organization. It depends on how organizations align their strategy, key success factors, and values with a performance management process, talent management practices and rewards and recognition programs.

Compared with men, women were less likely to be promoted for higher grade/level/position. They are reported to have slower career progress.

To be promoted they must show values that are becoming indicators of career success; women were less likely to value leadership than men.

In case of promotion, we should make them happen, not wait for good things to happen. HR leaders don't sit around waiting for that promotion or recognition at work, they go after it.

Promotion evolves significant increase in duties, accompanied by a change in title, grade, and salary. It is a move to a position in a higher grade, whether in the same department (internal promotion)

or another department (promotional transfer). It normally involves a salary increase.

For example:

HR Assistant to HR Generalist; HR Generalist to HR Manager; HR Manager to HR Director; HR Director to HR Vice President (The levels/terms might be different from a company to another).

A promotional increase must place the employee's salary at or above the minimum of the salary range for the new grade.

A promoted employee should be paid equitably compared to an employee with similar skills, experience, and qualifications within the same grade. Promotion results higher level title and higher level job responsibilities. Promotion consists of:

a.   Conditional promotion: A promotion that is given with such conditions, i.e. the conditional offer of new assignment, with exams or not, etc. It includes permanent promotion, temporary promotion

b.   Situational promotion: Promotion based upon the company's own in-house situations, i.e. there are many talented people/ candidates, the positions require such specialties, the pay level of the position to be filled and by other limitations, etc. It includes competitive promotion, non competitive promotion

c.   Categorical promotion: Promotion that is based on a categorical requirement/outcomes, i.e. additional duties/ responsibilities, seniority, or transfer, which includes classified promotion, unclassified promotion, promotional transfer, etc.

Successful employee self-promotion is the key to his/her career success. He/she can't continue to wait for others to decide when he/she should be offered a promotion.

Even if he/she is not ready to make a job or career change today, he/she will benefit from knowing how to put into action a successful self-promotion plan. A proactive promotion plan requires employees to consider the following:

a.   Prepare for courageous conversations with the Management about their career and future contributions to the company, i.e. show what a great job they've been doing and their value to the company, they're ready to take on more responsibilities, be prepared to tackle a larger or more complicated workload and aren't just looking for a bigger office and fatter paycheck.

b.   Possess a winning combination of hard skills and soft skills. Hard skills include savvy technical skills and industry knowledge.

Soft skills include factors such as effective communication, presentation, and social skills. To be successful in promotion, we should go above and beyond the call of duty, and try to come up with solutions to problems that haven't been addressed yet.

c.   Develop strategies to overcome challenges, such as office politics or a poor relationship with a manager or co-worker.

d.   Form relationships with mentors who will offer their support and act as accountability partners throughout the promotion-seeking process. It's a good idea to find somebody in the position we're aiming for who is willing to take we under his or her wing.

Promotion is an advancement of employee to a position with a higher grade level. Therefore, each employee is encouraged to take it proactively.

Proactive promotion plan is applicable if posting positions is policy in the company at least his/her name is on the promotion list first. Without his/her proactive approach to his/her career and potential promotion, his/her superior may decide to promote one of his/her peers.

Human Resource should ensure promotional opportunities be posted and or communicated through internal communication media i.e. notice/bulletin board, e-mail, intranet, telephone, etc.

Conditional Promotion

A promotion describes the appointment of a current to a position in a higher salary range than the one to which the employee is presently assigned. It also depends on conditional on the nature of the promotion. There are two kinds of conditional promotion:

a. Permanent promotion: A promotion to a higher-graded position or to a position with a higher full performance level than previously held on a permanent basis.

    A promotion is usually a move by an employee to a vacant position at a higher grade level either within the current department or in a different department. Changes to a higher grade level obtained through intradepartmental/ interdivisional promotion, job audits or career paths should be covered in company policies.

b. Temporary promotion: When significant changes in duties and responsibilities of a position occur on a temporary basis, an interim promotion or temporary upgrade may be required. Temporary promotion includes:

i. A promotion for more than 120 days or details for more than 120 days to a higher-graded position or to a position with greater promotion potential than previously held on a permanent basis.

ii. When an employee is placed in an 'acting' capacity for a specific period of time, the employee remains in the current position but assumes duties of the higher level position.

    A salary adjustment may be considered with the understanding that the increase will be discontinued when the 'acting' assignment ends.

If an employee is demoted, reallocated, or reassigned to a lower-level with no corresponding salary decrease, and within 12 months is promoted, the salary is not increased unless the promotion is to a higher grade than the grade held prior to the reduction.

iii.   Time-limited Promotion—Promotion made under specific and written conditions with a not to exceed date to meet a need of a short-term nature.

Upon expiration of the need, the employee so promoted normally reverts to the former position. Time-limited promotions include both 'temporary' and 'term' promotions.

When a temporary promotion is made permanent immediately after the temporary promotion ends, the employee is not returned to the lower grade in order to process the permanent promotion. HR leader must convert the employee's temporary promotion to a permanent promotion without a change in pay.

Situational Promotion

Yet many employees botch promotion opportunities. As they begin feeling unappreciated, underpaid and under challenged at work, many search for promising position outside their organization.

"What people fail to realize is that those candidates are often located in their own back yard—with their current employer," says Susan Britton Whitcomb, an author.

A promotion should be relevant to the situation of the organizations; a situation in a context that might be different from on organization and others, i.e. competence required if employees want to keep a job or get a promotion. Situational promotion includes:

i.   Non-competitive promotions: A company may consider positions, with career ladder promotions, are made noncompetitively. Therefore, competitive procedures do not apply. Non-competitive promotion include:

1.	Position upgrade: A review of an existing position that is currently filled. Positions which were appealed should meet the criteria for an upgrade.

	Position upgrade evolves an additional function fulfilled through an existing or incremental headcount in an agency. It is not a readjustment of existing duties, or a current position to which additional responsibilities will be applied.

	Position upgrade may also happen when a job evaluation results in the reclassification of a position to a higher market band due to significant changes. A position upgrade, normally affects a promotional increase, includes:

	a)	Upgrade a position that requires employee to continue to perform the same basic function in the new position that is a clear successor to and absorbs the duties of the old position; in which there are no other employees within the organizational unit to whom the additional duties and responsibilities could have been assigned.

	b)	Upgrading of a position due to application of a new classification standard without a significant change in duties.

	c)	Upgrading of a position resulting from the correction of an initial classification error.

	d)	Selection for training which is part of a promotion program, or required before an employee may be considered for a promotion.

	e)	Promotion by which employees advance from trainee to full performance level.

	f)	Career/Successive promotion: Assignment given to an employee who competed earlier for a position intended to prepare the employee for the position being filled and the intent was made a matter of record and made known to all potential candidates. These are commonly called career ladder promotions.

Career ladder position is a position for which the full performance level is identified and all employees in the same career ladder are given grade-building experience.

Employees may be promoted without further competition (career promotions) as they demonstrate the ability and readiness to perform at the next higher level and when legal requirements, such as time-n-grade, are met.

g) Accretion-of-duties promotion is a noncompetitive promotion of an employee whose position evolves to a higher grade with the old position being absorbed into the new one.

In a career ladder, employee will find a series of positions of increasing responsibility in the same organization and line of work through which the employee may progress from the entry level to the full performance.

The employee is provided developmental goals and may be promoted without competition each time he or she achieves the performance goal at the next higher level.

However, successive promotions (more than one) of an employee in the same job, based on accretion of duties, may violate merit principles.

Merit system principles are principles which insure the requirements for fair and open competition in recruiting and hiring, equal pay for equal work, freedom from arbitrary action and favoritism. Other situations that invite non-competitive promotion, which might be different from one company to another, i.e.:

a) Details to higher-graded positions or temporary promotions not to exceed 120 days.

b) Details made in 120 day increments up to one year to unclassified duties.

c) Details made in 120 day increments to the same grade or lower-graded positions.

    d) Upgrade an employee's salary for the result of the change of the salary band.

A position upgrade occurs when a position is re-evaluated to a higher salary grade. Generally, no salary increase is granted at the time of re-evaluation, except if required to bring to the minimum of the range. However, the incumbent will, of course, have a broader salary range through which to progress.

If the upgrade resulted from a significant increase in duties, it is appropriate to grant an increase that follows the same parameters set forth under promotion. Non-competitive promotion may be approved without posting the job when all the following criteria are met:

a.   There is a clear and direct relationship between the positions.

b.   The employee being considered for promotion meets the minimum educational requirement or equivalent or formal training for the vacant position.

c.   The employee being considered possesses the basic skills required for the vacant position.

d.   There is no more than one employee who meets the above criteria in the same department (i.e. reporting to the same management staff member) as the open position.

e.   The open position must be in the same job category as the employee's current position.

    Non-competitive promotions are open to anyone who meets the qualifications of the job specification. There is no formal examination process.

    Non-competitive promotion is normally the prerogative of management and not a right or entitlement of an employee. An employee may not file a grievance or appeal over the denial of a non-competitive promotion.

ii. Competitive promotion: A promotion may be either competitive or non-competitive. A competitive-based promotion does not require approval by the HR leader of the organization. This promotion is done with job posting, includes:

a.   Employees interested in applying for a posted job are eligible to submit to Human Resources a letter of application, including their qualifications and why they are interested in the position, and an updated resume.

b.   At a minimum, employees must have successfully completed the introductory period before a request for promotion or transfer might be considered.

c.   Current employees who apply for a posted job will be granted a personal interview. Internal and external candidates, when applicable, will be given equal consideration. The candidate who best fits the needs of the company will be selected for the position.

d.   An employee might be promoted out of a classified career service title to an unclassified title, such as seniority within their title and bumping rights.

A position that is announced and filled on a competitive basis with promotion to higher grade levels can also be made on a non-competitive basis; that differs from one to another company.

Categorical Promotion

It's a classification within the promotional line. It starts with downgrading salaries move up to promotions. This promotion applies categorical variables, i.e. outcome, certification, etc. Categorical promotion consists of:

i.   Classified promotions: Promotion that resulting from an employee's position being classified at a higher grade (with no further promotion potential) because of additional duties and responsibilities, commonly known as accretion of duties.

A classified employee who receives an appointment to a higher classified title must take a promotional examination before the appointment. The appointment to the new position is provisional until the exam is offered and the employee passes it.

ii.   Unclassified promotion: When an employee is promoted an unclassified title, as seniority within their title and bumping rights.

iii.   Reinstatement promotion: Reinstatement to a permanent or temporary position at a higher grade or with a higher full performance level than position previously held.

        Reinstatement is the re-employment into a permanent position of a former permanent employee with a break in service with the company, i.e. resignation, dismissal, retirement, reduction-in-force, reorganizations, etc.

iv.   Entrust promotion: Promotions due to the addition of substantive, new and higher-graded duties when the new position is not a clear successor to the old position or there are other employees serving in similar or identical positions within the organizational unit to whom the new duties could have been assigned.

v.   Transfer: A transfer is a move to any other job within the department or in another department. If an employee meets job qualifications and job requirements, he/she can usually transfer from location to location or from organization to organization.

        A transfer within the department may provide an opportunity for an employee to assume different responsibilities and develop new skills.

        Transfers to other departments may also provide career development by enhancing skills and learning about other functions of the corporate.

        A transfer may or may not result in a change in compensation. Transfer consists of:

1. Lateral transfer: A lateral title change is the movement of an employee from his or her title to an equivalent title in a different organization within the company.

   If the natures of the work, education and experience requirements of both titles are substantially similar the employee will be eligible to his or her status.

2. Promotional transfer: Transfers within or outside the employee's department does not always include any salary increase. If, as a result of a transfer, an employee is deemed to be inequitably compensated, adjustments will be made in accordance with the company policies.

   Unlike lateral transfer, an employee who is getting promotional transfer is normally eligible for salary increase.

   a) Intra-departmental promotion: An intradepartmental promotion occurs when an employee in a department/entity is promoted into an open/vacant position in a higher salary range within the same department/entity.

   b) Inter/Cross-departmental promotion: An inter/cross departmental promotion occurs when an employee within the company is promoted into an open/vacant position in a higher salary range in another department within the company.

   In effecting such transfers, the department should attempt to make the most effective use of the employee's skills and abilities and should consider the employee's interest whenever possible.

   c) Demotion: Position/salary change to a lower-graded position because of reassignment, transfer, etc. It may include a promotion to a position with a pay rate equal to or lower than previous position.

   Demotion/downgrade can occur when a position is reclassified to a lower salary grade (band). If the incumbent's current salary is outside the new salary grade (band), the salary may be reduced to the maximum of the new salary grade (band).

d) Reclassification: Positions may, from time to time, be reclassified to a higher or lower salary grade as a result in change of position responsibilities. These changes may have occurred recently or over a period of time.

As the position, not the incumbent, is being reevaluated, the grade change is generally considered neither a promotion nor demotion. It describes the re-evaluation of a current position to a higher or lower salary band.

Reclassification normally occurs whenever the original duties and responsibilities of the position change significantly. Therefore, reclassification may affect demotion or promotion.

Reclassification may also occur when it is deemed that a different salary grade (band) more accurately reflects the value of the position even though the position itself has not changed.

A reclassification involves a change in the functions of a position, which results in the assignment of an employee's current position to a new title with a higher salary range.

A reclassified employee typically retains the majority (50% or more) of the prior functions and assumes additional functions as well. It is usually the case that changes to one aspect of the position do not lead to a reclassification or increase in grade.

Reclassification of a position will not happen unless there is a substantial change to the job.

For example, if new, substantial supervisory requirements are added to a position this may not be considered cause for reclassification.

In general, classification ensures that the employee is paid within the pay range of the assigned pay grade. The classification (grade) of a position is determined by the knowledge, skills, experience; complexity; decision making; contacts; and supervision/management required for the position against those of benchmark positions.

A downgrade occurs when a position is reevaluated to a lower salary grade. Generally, no salary change occurs. If the incumbent's salary is now above the maximum of the new grade, the incumbent's salary is red-circled until the maximum increases enough to allow a pay increase.

However, if the re-evaluation to a lower salary grade occurred when the position had to be redesigned, because the incumbent was unable to perform the duties before the redesign, it may be appropriate to decrease the employee's salary to no more than the maximum of the new grade.

vi.   Reassignment: The movement of a current employee from one position to another, at the same grade level, for which he or she qualifies. It means an employee is changed from one position to another, without promotion or demotion, within or outside the department.

A promotion is also advancement to a position that requires performing accountabilities of significantly increased complexity or responsibility.

Despite the promotional opportunities that abound for employees all across the companies, employees who are in order to generate great rewards, they must exude greater effort in the workplace.

"Getting promoted is not for the faint of heart. It takes a proactive plan, proof of performance, the right perception of you, perseverance, and a positive attitude," Whitcomb says.

Human Resource is responsible for developing and administering the policy on appointment, transfer and promotion.

All employees and applicants for employment should receive fair and equitable treatment in all aspects of Human Resources Management without regard to political or labor organization affiliation or non-affiliation, race, color, religion, national origin, sex, marital status, age, sexual orientation, non-disqualifying disability, and with proper regard for their privacy and constitutional rights.

Courage

It requires a great deal of courage to build a company from the ground up.

A HR leader might have become enemy of the corporation. He/she must be able to organize people and allocate resources for more complicated tasks that are needed.

To be successful, he/she may need to waging war on bureaucracy; earned his/her reputations by attacking entrenched corporate cultures, bypassing corporate hierarchies, undermining corporate structures, and otherwise using the tactics of revolution in a desperate effort to make the system works. Courage leads HR leaders to:

a.　Provide honest input and counsel: Constantly ask for feedback. Conduct annual surveys and customer focus groups to find out what your employee customers think.

　　Pursue continuous improvement as a result of the feedback. Those who are always getting better are always more respected.

b.　Present outside-the-norm ideas.

　　Suraya Ramli and Rafidah Abdul Razak, formerly officials at the government's Islamic judicial department, were named Shariah court judges for Kuala Lumpur and the administrative capital of Putrajaya.

　　Prime Minister Najib Razak said the step was meant to 'enhance justice in cases involving families and women's rights' in Malaysia, where nearly two-thirds of the country's 28 million people are Muslims.

Women have long complained they face discrimination in cases involving divorce, child custody rights, inheritance, polygamy and other disputes in Islamic courts, which handle matters involving family and morality for Malaysian Muslims.

c.   Share an alternative viewpoint: HR leaders should not spend considerable time trying to defend or fix poor performers.

"You'd be better off had you paid these people not to come to work," Richard Beatty, a professor, said. "You'd be a lot better off if you paid them to work for your competitor."

d.   Speak up, rather than being complicit in silence.

Amnesty International accused Iran of harassing the lawyer of a woman sentenced to death by stoning, Sakineh Mohammadi Ashtiani, saying that he has gone missing and two of his relatives have been detained.

A blog maintained by the lawyer, Mohammad Mostafaei, helped generate a wave of international outrage over the stoning sentence.

He wrote on his Facebook account: "It is possible they will arrest me."

He and a number of other lawyers launched a campaign against the execution of juveniles in 2008, demanding that the punishment be abolished.

e.   Not falling prey to the perception that working longer hours equals increased productivity.

Change

HR leaders focus their team on talent acquisition and create a 'people factory,' or even taking the dramatic step of moving 'administrative' activities like benefits, stock plan administration and 401K management to the finance function.

New strategies may undermine important values imbedded in the company. Unless the leader can successfully work at reducing the impact of these issues the force of the old culture can neutralize and emasculate any desired change.

It's the CEO's job to make sure that the work of analyzing and, as necessary, reconstituting the work force gets done by someone qualified to do the job.

If HR leaders are really serious about change, they will inevitably have to wrestle with company's culture.

As change agents, HR leaders deliver capacity for change in employee behavior and organization culture. They should be committed to partnering with line leaders to attract, develop and retain employees. The Human Resources (HR) leaders should consider thoroughly the changing environment of today's world, i.e.:

a.   HR has undergone dramatic transformation: These include downsizing of the HR workforce, structural reorganizations, delegations of HR authority to line managers, and an influx of technology, etc.

b.   The business of HR is in challenging stage: Increased emphasis on the need to improve the efficiency of HR services is leading to innovative approaches to redesigning HR delivery systems.

In addition, organizations are redefining the role of the HR leader to be more consultative than rules-oriented.

c.   The growing concern over how to meet organizational needs with fewer HR professionals: Competencies help organizations to focus on the characteristics their employees must possess in order for them to be successful.

Competencies also provide a way to measure employee performance and to align performance with business strategies.

HR leader perceptions of integrity and trust in HR leaders influence cynicism toward change, i.e. perceptions of integrity, competence, and trust in HR leaders.

Integrity, as an element of trustworthiness, was directly influencing trust in HR leaders as well as cynicism toward change.

Contrary to expectations, employee perceptions of the competence of HR leaders did not to have a direct influence on trust nor on cynicism toward change.

Key factors that will assist HR leaders in managing change effectively include:

1. Good leadership: Influence others and drive changes in attitudes and work practices.

2. Knowledge and utilization of existing drivers of change: Assign high potential employees to change projects represents a good way to develop the organization's change leadership capabilities.

3. Establish processes and committing to them: Demonstrate the commitment of the executives and their willingness to dedicate the best resources to ensure success. It also contributes to building momentum by creating a winning attitude.

4. Accept change: Changes represent excellent opportunities to develop high-potential employees; fundamentally rethink the way they did business; give the folks to react, share their concerns, participate and come up with ideas; balance the short—and long-term benefits

A strategy requires both the thinking and analysis to compare current state to desired state and define the gap, and the execution capabilities to make the requisite changes happen.

Organizational strategy is how the organization needs to changeover time—in order to be able to deliver the strategy of the enterprise and an actionable plan of how to make the transformation.

Organizational strategy enables a company to develop an organization capable of delivering its strategy.

Assigning top performers to lead the implementation of change not only benefits the person but the project and the organization as well.

Convincing people to adopt new habits requires more than intellectual arguments. The change agent has to uncover and understand staff perspectives, motivations and concerns.

Trust is the key to all relationships; it is the glue of organizations. It is the cement that holds the bricks together. Trust is the fruit of the trustworthiness of both people and organizations.

A study estimated that the average American company lost 6% of its annual revenue to some sort of fraudulent activity. The study shows similar effects for the other disguised low-trust taxes as well.

Individuals and organizations that have earned and operate with high trust experience the opposite of a tax—a 'dividend' that is like a performance multiplier, enabling them to succeed in their communications, interactions, and decisions, and to move with incredible speed.

A study showed that high trust companies outperform low trust companies by nearly 300%.

However, while trusting others is essential for maintaining our relationships; trusting also increases our vulnerability. While we assume that others will meet our positive expectations and behave in a trustworthy way, there is no guarantee that this will be so.

HR leaders must maintain a high level of trust with the stakeholders. They must protect the interests of the stakeholders as well as their integrity and should not engage in activities that create actual, apparent, or potential conflicts of interest.

REFERENCE

1. Jennifer Rice, Writing a Brand Manifesto, TypePad, San FranciscoUSA, August 1, 2004

2. Chapel Hill, Human Resource Systems of World Class Companies: Managing for Success, Business Wire, San Francisco, CA—USA, July 22, 2003

3. Matthew Best What's Your Business Manifesto?, ArticlesBase.com, USA, Jan 14, 2009

4. Susan M. Heathfield, Culture: Your Environment for People at Work, About.com, USA, 2010

5. Chris Ferdinandi, Embrace Innovation And Learning, Renegade HR, USA, May 18, 2009

6. Belinda Goldsmith, Attractive Women Overlooked For Certain Jobs, Thomson Reuters, Los Angeles—USA, August 9, 2010

7. Robin Trehan, Core or Competitive Competence in Hospitality Industry?, 4Hoteliers, Hong Kong SAR, 27 June 2007

8. James Manktelow & Associates, Personal Goal Setting, Mind Tools Ltd, London, UK, 2010

9. Kirk L. Rogg, David B. Schmidt, Carla Shull1 and Neal Schmitt, Human Resource Practices, Organizational Climate, And Customer Satisfaction, Journal of Management, USA, 2010

10. Sarah O' Carroll & Associates, Strategic Planning The Key To World-Class HR Practice, Human Resources Magazine, Chatswood—NSW, 25 July 2006

11. The CRF Institute, Top-ranked employers, The Telegraph, UK, 23 Mar 2010

12. Laura Fitzpatrick, Why Do Women Still Earn Less Than Men?, Time Inc, FloridaUSA, April 20, 2010

13. Kate Nelson, Define company's culture to determine effective strategy, Business Courier, Cincinnati, OHUSA, July 17, 2006

14. Daniel Schroeder, Human Resources—Customer Satisfaction Must Be Top Priority, BizTimes, Milwaukee, WIUSA, 2008

15. R. Anthony Inman, World-Class Manufacturer, Advameg, Inc., USA, 2010

16. Edward E. Lawler III & Susan A. Mohrman, Beyond the Vision: What Makes HR Effective?, Human Resource Planning Society, Entrepreneur Media, Inc. Irvine, CAUSA, Dec, 2000

17. Carter McNamara, MBA, PhD, Human Resource Management, Authenticity Consulting, LLC, MinnesotaUSA, 2010

18. Answers.com, Personnel Department, Answers Corporation, New York, USA, 2010

19. BusinessDictionary.com, Top Management, WebFinance Inc., Fairfax, VAUSA, 2010

20. Badre, Leadership in Human Resources Management: The Case of IBM Company, The Third Space, Morocco, December 23, 2009

21. Laura Block-Stewart, Company Roles and Responsibilities, Suite101.com, British ColumbiaCanada, Jan 13, 2009

22. Dale Vile, Are Your Staff Adequately Trained?: Avoiding The False Economy Trap, The Register, UK, 2010

23. Malcolm Tatum,What is Human Resource Management?, Wise Geek, Conjecture Corporation, NVUSA, 08 September 2010

24. Joan Cleaver Citigroup: Not Such A "Best Place to Work" After All, BNET, CBS Interactive, CAUSA, October 21, 2010

25. Chapel Hill, N.C, Human Resource Systems of World Class Companies: Managing for Success, HighBeam Research, Chicago, IllinoisUSA, July 22, 2003

26. Karen Beaman & Associates, Developing Great Talent—Greatness Is In Everyone If You Encourage It, Human Capital Institute, USA, 2010

27. WikipediaThe Free Encyclopedia, Talent Management, Wikimedia Foundation, Inc., San Francisco, CAUSA, 2 November 2010

28. Alan Price, CorpU Study Cites Inadequate Leadership Development As Threat To Business Growth, HRM Guide, Scotland—UK, October 29, 2007

29. Edward Ferris, What Keeps CEOs Up At Night?, LeaderValues, UK, 2007

30. Allan Schweyer, The New Role Of The HR Leader, Human Resources Magazine, Chatswood, NSW—Australia, 28 June 2006

31. Geoffrey James Top 5 Highly-Paid But Useless Corporate Jobs, BNET—CBS Interactive, CAUSA, October 22, 2010

32. Inc., Human Resource Spotlight: Sourcing Candidates, Kennedy Information LLC, May 17, 2001

33. Tony Schwartz The Four Capacities Every Great Leader Needs, Harvard Business School Publishing, Boston, MA—USA, October 13, 2010

34. Tom Crea, Achieve Your Objectives by Communicating Values, All about Leadership, USA, 2010

35. Massimo Calabresi, Obama and Netanyahu: The Limits of Intimacy, Time Inc. All, USA, July 7, 2010

36. Jeff Sacht, HR Customer Satisfaction Survey: Where Do You Stand With Line Management, Workplace Performance Technologies (Pty) Ltd, South Africa, 2010

37. Deborah L. Cohen, Sex Ed Entrepreneur Trades Bananas For Broadband, Thomson Reuters, UK Jul 7, 2010

38. Sabina Castelfranco, Vatican Issues Stronger Sex Abuse Guidelines, VOANews.com, USA, 15 July 2010

39. Karen Dempsey, Getting HR Strategy In Tune With Business Goals, PersonnelToday, UK, 16 May 2006

40. Alan Murray, The End of Management, The Wall Street Journal, USA, August 21, 2010

41. Dr. Paulina Taboada, MD, PhD, The Sources Of Human Dignity, International Association Hospice and Palliative Care, Houston TX—USA, 2010

42. Dan Simon, The Gambling Man Who Co-Founded Apple And Left For $800, CNN—Cable News Network, USA, June 24, 2010

43. Louis La Rocca and John Morrow, Today's HR LeaderIt's All about the Business, HR Management, USA, 2010

44. Janung H., Role of HR in Gaining Competitive Advantage, Bizcovering.com, USA, September 21, 2008

45. Prisca Rollins, What Is an Employee Appraisal?, eHow, Inc., WA—USA, 2010

46. Lisa Johnson Mandell, Debrahlee Lorenzana: Too Sexy for Her Job?, AOL Inc., USA, Jun 3rd 2010

47. Robert W. Jacobs, Barry Johnson, Frank McKeown, How to Add Value in Continuing Strategic Change, About.com, USA, 2010

48. Grace Angel, The Benefits Of Honesty In The Workplace, Helium, Inc., MAUSA, 2010

49. Paul Rogers & Marcia Blenko, Who Has The D? How Clear Decision Roles Enhance Organizational Performance, Bain & Company Inc., MassachusettsUSA, 2010

50. BBC News,Mexico prisoners 'freed for killings' in Durango state, BBC News, UK, 25 July 2010

51. Mary White, A Definition for Business Ethics, LoveToKnow Corp., CAUSA, 2010

52. Jim Seida, Sex In Space? Don't Ask, Don't Tell, msnbc.com, USA, 29 June 2010

53. Barbara Taylor, Traits of "Managers" and "Leaders", itstime.com, WAUSA, June 06, 2009

54. Barry Wolfson, A Culture of Leadership, Center for Simplified Strategic Planning, USA, 2008

55. Jon Ingham, World Class HR, Strategic HHCM Blog, UK, 20 September 2007

56. Norm Smallwood, Four Ways to Create Intangible Value, Harvard Business School Publishing, USA, February 4, 2010

57. Virginia McLaughlin, Leadership Brand Equity: HR Leaders' Role In Driving Economic Value, Emerald Group Publishing Limited, USA, 2010

58. Steffen Walter, Direct Report, ProZ.com, US, 2010

59. Tom Pisello, Measuring The Value Of HR Solutions, TechTarget, USA, 2010

60. William C. Byham, Ph.D & Association, Calculating the Value of a Great Leader, Development Dimensions International, Inc., USA, 2010

61. John A. Byrne, How JACK WELCH Runs GE, BusinessWeek, USA, May 28, 1998

62. Roy Posner, Business: Utilizing Business Values, Growth Online, USA, 2010

63. Ty Bennet, The True Definition of Belief, Success.bz, USA, 2010

64. Debbie McGrath & Associates, As Business Growth Takes Center Court, Many HR Functions Feel Sidelined, HR.com, CAUSA, August 22 2007

65. Peter Rock Consulting Inc., HR Leadership & Greatness, Corporate Leadership Development, NCUSA, 2010

66. Sidhartha Roy, Consumer Behavior And Self Concept: Product Image Congruence, About CiteMan Network, India, July 30, 2010

67. Nandini Biswas, Building Your Self-Esteem, Strategic Human Resources Management India, Pvt. Ltd, India, 20 February 2010

68. Tom Bonnett, Obama Supports Mosque Near September 11 Site, Sky News HD, UK, August 14, 2010

69. Rick Lash, Change From The Inside, Hay Group Holdings, Inc., USA, August 17, 2010

70. Kwasi Dartey-Baah, Human Resource Capacity Building In The Developing World And Mobilising Excess Capacity For Export, Academic Leadership, USA, April 16, 2010

71. Barbra Cooper & Associates, Focus Succession Planning on Business Value, Thomson Reuters, UK, Aug 30, 2010

72. Susan Koval, First, Break All the Rules, EzineArticles.com, WI—USA, 2010

73. N. Nayab and Jean Scheid, Servany Leadership vs. Authentic Leadership: What are the Differences?, Bright Hub Inc., NYUSA, June 8, 2010

74. Kutenk, What Qualities Distinguish Greatness, Business & Life Success Center, June 21, 2009

75. Martha Finney, Why I Love HR, hrjourney.blogspot.com, CAUSA, December 22, 2007

76. Denise Corcoran, Awakening To Greatness: 7 Traits of Greatness for Creating an Extraordinary Business Future, Business know-how, Attard Communications, Inc., NYUSA, 2010

77. Paul Steel, Baldrige Criteria: Human Resource Focus, www.baldrige21.com, USA, 2010

78. John Craven, The Interaction Hierarchy: A Theory of Technical Standards and Regulations, The MIT Entrepreneurship Review, USA, February 28, 2010

79. Arthur Yeung, Wayne Brockbank, Lower Cost, Higher Value: Human Resource Function In Transformation, Questia, USA, 2010

80. Rashmi, Ph.D., Stakeholder Theory, Ethics 209, SlideShare Inc, USA, 2010

81. Helen Peters, M.A. and Robert Kabacoff, Ph.D., Going Global: What U.S. and European Leaders Need to Know About Each Other, Management Research Group, Ireland, 2010

82. Jennnifer Pellet, Moving At The Speed Of Delight: It's Not Enough To Merely "Satisfy" Customers If You Truly Expect To Get Value From Your Technology Investments—Roundtable—Chief Executive Officers, BNET—CBS Interactive, USA, December 22, 2010

83. Judy McLeish, Make Yourself Competitive in This Job Market, The Employee Factor, USA, December 12, 2008

84. Gladys M. Vega, Humor Competence: The Fifth Component, the Education Resources Information Center, CA USA, 1990

85. Frank Roche, On Authenticity, Greatness and Truthfulness in HR, KnowHR, PA-USA, 2010

86. David G. Javitch, Ph.D., Developing Trust and Credibility: The Leader's Challenge, CPCU Society, 2010

87. Arti Bakshi, Responsibility Is The Price Of Greatness, PRLog. Org, USA, Nov 20, 2009

88. Huang Haiying, Honesty is always the best policy, Shanghai Star, China, 2004-03-25

89. Keith Weiss, Employee Recognition As A Competitive Advantage With Generation Y, Conduit, NYUSA, July 19, 2007

90. Dan Fletcher, Facebook Hits 500 Million Users, TIMENewsFeed, USA, 2010

91. John W. Boudreau, Human Resources and Organization Success, Cornell University, School of Industrial and Labor Relations, Center for Advanced Human Resource Studies, NYUSA, February 1996

92. Arinya Talerngsri, HR Struggles With Organizational Growth, Bangkok Post, Thailand, 10 June 2010

93. John Mackey, Creating A High Trust Organization, Industry News, CAUSA, March 14, 2010

94. Randall S. Schuler, Susan E. Jackson and Jacqueline Fendt, Hr Leader, Staff And Department, Rutgers, The State University of New Jersey, USA, 2010

95. Eva Sage-Gavin, Preparing Future HR Leaders, Yahoo! Inc., India, 2010

96. Martha Josephson, Egon and Brian Reinken, The CEO Worked Where?—Putting Human Resources In The Leader's Path To The Top, Egon Zehnder International, 2010

97. Belinda Lucombe, Why E-Mail May Be Hurting Off-Line Relationships, Time Inc., USA,.Jun. 22, 2010

98. Laurie Haughey, Five Standards Of Excellence Practiced By Ethical Leaders, Workforce Management Online, ILUSA, November 2003

99. Eric Cabrow, World-Class Companies Use I.T. More Effectively For HR, InformationWeek, CA —USA, November 15, 2004

100. M. Michele Burns & Associates, How HR Metrics Can Predict Organizational Performance, Mercer LLC, USA, 18 May 2010

101. Patrick M. Wright, HR Strategy: From Execution to Influence, LRP Publications, November 19, 2008

102. Jack J. Phillips, Calculating Return on Investment in Human Resources, QFINANCE, Qatar, 2010

103. Talent Ocean, Staffing Your Business Cost Effectively, ArticlesBase. com, Nov 09, USA, 2010

104. Lowell L. Bryan, The New Metrics of Corporate Performance: Profit Per Employee, USA, 2007

105. Vin D'Amico, How Technology Can Increase Your Revenue Per Employee, Damicon, LLC, USA, 2004

106. Robert Elliott, Human Resources (HR) Measurement Metrics, Balanced Scorecard Designer, US, 2010

107. David Mc. Cann, Memo to CFOs: Don't Trust HR, USA, March 10, 2009

108. Robert H.Rouda & Mitchell E. Kusy, Jr., Career Development, Personal Career Management And Planning, alumnus.alumni. caltech.edu, USA, 1995

109. Stacey Harris, 4 Critical Challenges Facing HR Leaders Today, Bersin & Associates, CAUSA, February 18, 2010

110. Chris, Creating A Business Aligned HR Function Is More Than A Re-Structure, Courageous HR Ltd, UK, 1 November 2010

111. Ben Nash and Kevin Nash, Ph.D., Being An EntrepreneurThe Real Story!, DailyHRTips.com, USA, August 30, 2010

112. DAVID BROOKS, A Case of Mental Courage, The New York Times, USA, August 23, 2010

113. Seth Kahan, Strategic HR: the Time is Now, Fast Company, NYUSA, Jun 11, 2010

114. Nihat Kaya, The Impact Of Human Resource Management Practices And Corporate Entrepreneurship On Firm Performance: Evidence From Turkish Firms, Informa World UK, 2010

115. Michael Crowley, Obama Changes Generals, Time.com, USA, June 23, 2010

116. Allie Townsend, How Much Does It Cost To Make The Worse Film Of The Year? $280 Million, Techland, USA, July 2, 2010

117. Jennifer Maughan, What Is The Legal Definition Of Harassment?, Life123, 2010

118. Congressional Information Service, Preventing Sexual Harassment In The Workplace, Feminism and Women's Studies, USA, 2005-01-20

119. Alastair Lawson, Agencies 'exploit' South Asian workers, BBC News Online, UK, 1 September 2004

120. Prof.M.S.Rao, What Is Sexual Harassment? Learn How To Draw The Line, profmsr.blogspot.com, India, July 30, 2010

121. The Advocates For Human Rights, The Women's Human Rights Program, Sexual Harassment Is Conduct That Is Unwelcome Or Unwanted, The Women's Human Rights Program, MN —USA, 1 April 2007

122. International Labour Organization, World Day Against Child Labour, hrea.org, 12 June 2010

123. Renji Nair, Ways 'Authentic' Leaders Acquire Management Skills, Awesome Inc, USA, December 11, 2007

124. Sean Conrad, Attributes Of An HR Leader, Halogen Software Inc, USA, August 27th, 2009

125. Lori Brewer Collins, Let the Real You Shine: Your Authenticity Breeds Influence, Wisdom a la Carte Blog, USA, 2010

126. Tri Junarso, Comprehensive Approach To Corporate Governance, iUniverse, USA, 2006

127. Tri Junarso, 7th Priciple of Success, Trafford Publishing, Canada, 2007

128. Tri Junarso, Leadership Greatness, iUniverse, USA, 2009

129. Tri Junarso, How To Become A Highly Effective Leader, iUniverse, USA, 2009

130. The Hackett Group, Companies Can Significantly Reduce HR Costs By Cutting Complexity In Key Processes, Programs, Technology, Coskiller.net, France, 2010

131. Douglas P. Shuit, Top Dollar: The 10 Highest Paid Human Resources Leaders, Workforce Management, ILUSA, June 2004

132. Lowell Bryan, The New Metric of Corporate Performance: Profit Per Employee, McKinsey & Co, USA, 2007

133. Vin D'Amico, How Technology Can Increase Your Revenue Per Employee, DAMICON, LLC, New England, 2004

134. Rick Brenner, Express Your Appreciation And Trust, Point Lookout, USA, January 16, 2002

135. Jo Romano, 8 Steps To Foster Employee Happiness, Evan Carmichael, USA, 2009

136. Dean Royles & Associates, Quality standards and approaches, CIPD, UK, May 2009

137. Prof. Tan Wee Liang & Associates, Study Meeting On Creative Entrepreneurship: Value Creation, APO, China, 2005

138. Aileen Wang and Alan Wheatley U.S. Slips in WEF's Competitiveness Rankings, ABC News, September 9, 2010

139. Boudreau, J.W., HR Information Systems: Exploiting The Full Potential, IDEAS, USA, 2010

140. Maggi Coil, The Work Environment And Employee Productivity, HR Village, USA, 2008

141. Henry Goldman, Ground Zero Mosque Plans Move Forward After Key Vote, Bloomberg, USA, Aug 4, 2010

142. Dave Crisp, Rant: Outsourcing Core Business Factors Is Dubious, Crips Leadership Strategies, Toronto—Canada, 29 March 2010

143. Paul R. Lawrence, Moral Leadership As Shaped By Human Evolution, Harvard Business School Publishing, USA, May 31, 2010

144. J. Hum Ergol, Long Working Hours And Occupational Stress-Related Cardiovascular Attacks Among Middle-Aged Workers In Japan, National Center for Biotechnology Information, USA, 1991

145. Karin Landgren, Child Protection From Violence, Exploitation And Abuse, Unicef, 19 October 2010

146. Cynthia D. McCauley & Associates, Interdependent Leadership In Organizations, Center for Creative Leadership, CAUSA, 2008

147. Anand, TeamworkThe Key To Effective Entrepreneurship, Google, USA, 2009

148. David G. Javitch, Ph.D., How to Foster Effective Teamwork, Entrepreneur Media, Inc., CAUSA, May 5, 2003

149. Maia Szalavitz, Who's High? A School Suspends A Student For Bloodshot Eyes, HealthlandTIME, USA, September 14, 2010

150. Frank Kern, What Chief Executives Really Want, Bloomberg Businessweek, USA, May 18, 2010

151. Martha Lasley, Difficult Conversations: Authentic Communication Leads To Greater Understanding And Teamwork, Group Facilitation: A Research and Applications Journal, USA, 2005

152. Leo Hollander, Authenticity As Key Succes Factor, Hollander HR, Holland, 2010

153. Ryan McCarthy, Walmart Reportedly Spending Millions To Fight $ 7000 Fine Trampling Death Of Employee, The Huffington Post, USA, 07—7-10

154. David Lee, What Managers and HR Leaders Can Learn From Sales Superstars, TLNT.com, NYUSA, Oct 4, 2010

155. N. Nayab, Servant Leadership vs. Authentic Leadership: What are the Differences?, Bright Hub, NYUSA, Jun 8, 2010

156. Malcolm Levene, How To Build Authenticity, People Management, UK, 14 October 2010

157. Alison Bond, Three Key Qualities Of Exceptional Leaders, Customer Think, CAUSA, Aug 03, 2010

158. Mary Cook, M.A., R.A.S., The Virtue Of Humility, SelfGrowth. com, NJ—USA, 2010

159. David Hakala, The Top 10 Leadership Qualities, HR World, CAUSA, March 19, 2008

160. Steve Denning, Putting The H In HR: The Opportunity For HR In Radical Management, The Leader's Guide To Radical Management, USA, July 24, 2010

161. Charles Feltman, Trust, The Thin Book Publishing, USA, 2008

162. Stephen M. R. Covey, How The Best Leaders Build Trust, LeadershipNow, USA, 2009

163. Don Jacobson, Making Creative Use of Employee Recognition Programs, GovLeaders.org, USA, 2008

164. John Meredith, Trust and CompetenceLosing and Regaining Trust, The Learning Center, UK, 2010

165. Martha Josephson and Brian Reinken, The CEO Worked Where?—Putting Human Resources in the Leader's Path to the Top, Egon Zehnder International, Germany, 2010

166. Michael Josephson, Trust Involves Character & Competence, Apple Seeds, USA, 2010

167. Sheri Mazurek, Seven Ways To Build Credibility, Free Management Library Blog, USA, April 5, 2010

168. F. John Reh, Company Culture: What It Is And How To Change It, About.com, USA, 2010

169. Buckley, Lenore M. MD, MPH and Associates, Obstacles to Promotion? Values of Women Faculty about Career Success and Recognition, Association of American Medical Colleges, March 2000

170. Debbie McGrath and Associates, Opportunities Abound for Promotion Seekers, JIST Publishing, USA, August 30, 2007